THE COMPLETE
JEWISH
PILGRIM

To Kim e Paul -
Happy travels.

THE COMPLETE
JEWISH
PILGRIM

Guide to 200 of the world's most sacred, historic,
tragic and triumphant places of Jewish interest

HOWARD KRAMER

Published by **The Complete Pilgrim, LLC**
Marietta, GA

Copyright © 2021 by Howard Kramer

Front Cover Photo: East Wall of the Temple Mount, Jerusalem, Israel
Back Cover Photos: Ruins of the Masada Fortress and
Dead Sea, Masada, Israel
Main Street of the Old Jewish Ghetto, Prague, Czech Republic

Cover Design and Typesetting: JD Smith Design

ISBN 978-1-7325081-6-3 (paperback)

978-1-7325081-7-0 (mobi)

For my Grandmothers

Ida Kramer & Anne Horowitz

TABLE OF
CONTENTS

WESTERN EUROPE

INTRODUCTION

Judaism as a faith is very old. It is the oldest continually practiced religion in the world outside of the Indian Subcontinent and the Far East. It was the first of the Abrahamic faiths, which include Christianity and Islam. As of the time of this writing there were approximately fifteen million Jews in the world, roughly one-fifth of one percent of the global population. Despite this relatively small size Judaism is still counted among the world's great religions.

But Judaism is not just a religious distinction. The Jewish people have always been just that: a people, with an epic history, fascinating culture and rich traditions. While most modern Jews live in Israel, Europe and the United States, there are Jewish communities all over the world. Their legacy can be found within the walls of thousands of synagogues, schools, museums and historic sites.

Because of this *The Complete Jewish Pilgrim* is somewhat different from my previous books on religious travel. For example, while *The Complete Christian Pilgrim* focuses almost entirely on historic churches, this work embraces a greater variety of sites that more comprehensively explores the Jewish experience. There are synagogues and yeshivas; museums of archaeology and art; inspiring monuments and poignant memorials.

Over the last twenty-five years I have had the pleasure and privilege of visiting some of the world's most sacred Jewish places. I experienced many of these in 2017, when I went on pilgrimage first to Germany and then to the Holy Land. Of the two hundred sites in this book, I have personally visited about one-third at the time of this writing.

Religious pilgrimage and history related travel is my life's passion. It began a few years ago with the travel blog *The Complete Pilgrim* (www.thecompletepilgrim.com). In 2018 *The Complete Pilgrim* was expanded to written form with the release of my first book, *The Complete American Pilgrim*. *The Complete Jewish Pilgrim* is the fourth book of the series.

It is my hope that *The Complete Jewish Pilgrim* will engender a sense of cultural identity among Jewish readers, intercultural understanding among non-Jewish readers, spiritual inspiration among the religious, and an interest in Jewish history and culture among those who are not.

Most importantly, I hope that it will inspire its readers with a desire to travel.

Methodology

The process of selecting two hundred sites of Jewish interest, while not quite as daunting a task as some of my earlier projects, was still difficult. Judaism is more than just a religion. It is a truly ancient community, with its own history, culture and traditions. It consists of far more than just synagogues. The Holy Land is full of locations tied to the Hebrew Bible. Archaeological sites of Jewish interest can be found throughout the Eastern Mediterranean region. Europe is home to many historic Jewish neighborhoods and ghettos, as well as numerous sad reminders of the Holocaust. Jewish museums can be found all over the globe.

As can be imagined, this book could easily have been much longer. As it is I tried to make it as inclusive and diverse as possible. During my initial review I identified a list of about four hundred places that could have been included. The list was then narrowed down keeping the following factors in mind:

1) Is the site already a widely recognized Jewish pilgrimage destination, with a substantial number of annual visitors; 2) Is the site directly associated with Hebrew Biblical history, or was it important in the early days of Judaism; 3) Was the site critical as a religious center or a major point from which Judaism expanded into new areas; 4) Is anybody buried at the site who played a critical or famous role in Jewish history; 5) Is there an artifact or document of great religious importance associated with or located at the site; and 6) Was the site the location of an important or tragic event in Jewish history.

Obviously, this was a highly subjective process. I truly hope that I did not underemphasize any particularly worthy location, or worse, overlook one altogether. Whether or not I succeeded in getting it right I leave up to the reader. Like the previous books in *The Complete Pilgrim* series, all sites have been organized geographically.

Traveler Cautions

This book references places of Jewish interest all over the world. The majority of these sites are to be found in major cities in modern countries. In the cases of more recently constructed buildings accessibility is generally not a problem. However there are a lot of very old locations, mostly in the Middle East and parts of Europe, where accessibility may be difficult, both in terms of getting to a site and in terms of ramps and other facilities for visitors with physical handicaps. *The Complete Pilgrim* strongly urges its readers who have physical limitations to thoroughly research their visit to any of these sites well in advance.

Similarly places of Jewish interest are not infrequently the targets of anti-Semitic vandalism and hooliganism, even in generally safe neighborhoods. Anti-Semitic sentiment has been on the rise again in recent years. *The Complete Pilgrim* strongly urges its readers to review safety warnings in advance, such as on the United States Secretary of State website, and avoid areas that may pose a threat to tourists and pilgrims. Even in very safe cities travelers should always take basic safety precautions when sightseeing.

When this book was in production, every effort was made to insure that all visitor information was as accurate and up-to-date as possible, and all information contained herein was deemed reliable as of the completion of writing in 2021. However, information such as opening hours, worship times and admission fees change so frequently that it is impractical to update this in the editing process.

Instead, addresses and website information have been included whenever possible. The latter, which were generally up to date and operational at the time of this writing, typically have all necessary visitor and contact information (author's note – websites change frequently, and some are not neccesarily secure; readers may wish or need to verify website information independently). It is therefore up to the reader to investigate relevant visitor information. In any event, *The Complete Pilgrim* and its writers are not responsible for visitor information. Visitors to all sites in this book are strongly advised to verify any and all visitor information prior to travel.

The Complete Pilgrim would like to remind all of its readers that Judaism is a very ancient faith, with very strong traditions and practices among its members. Orthodox communities in particular are extremely devout, and may be wary of casual sightseers with cameras in their neighborhoods. This is especially true at major Jewish shrines in the Holy Land, particularly on the Sabbath as well as on major holidays. Please note that the Jewish Sabbath runs from sundown on Friday until sundown on Saturday, and this is very strictly observed by some Jewish groups. Be respectful of the religious practices of others, and double check hours of worship before you go.

Finally, many active synagogues, even historic ones, frown on visitors taking pictures and videos inside. I have personally been told at many synagogues to put my camera away. Even explaining that I was a religious travel writer typically got me nowhere in these instances. Before taking photographs or video footage inside an active synagogue, check with a staff member to verify that this is permitted.

Accuracy of Contents

Every effort was made to ensure the accuracy of information about each and every location herein. As of the time of this writing the author had personally visited approximately sixty-five of these destinations and wrote based on first hand observations supplemented by research. For those places not personally visited, writing was based on thorough research from sources deemed reliable both online and in print.

If any part of this book is found to be in error, or some information of significance has been omitted, *The Complete Pilgrim* encourages its readers to reach out to us at our website (www.thecompletepilgrim.com) with any suggestions. Upon confirmation, changes may be made accordingly at the discretion of the author.

Dates and the Hebrew Calendar

All dating in *The Complete Jewish Pilgrim* is based on the Western (Gregorian) calendar rather than on the Hebrew (Jewish) calendar. This was done for several reasons. First and foremost was for research purposes. The vast majority of available information resources work primarily in the Western calendar, so the author used this dating convention.

Second was to accommodate the target audience. It is anticipated that most readers of this work will be westerners who, while understanding that Hebrew dating is different, are almost certainly going to be more familiar with the Gregorian calendar. For reference, this book was first published in 2021, or 5781 of the Hebrew calendar, representing a difference of 3760 years.

Finally, CE = "Common Era" is used rather than AD; and BCE = "Before Common Era" is used rather than BC.

A Note about the Jewish Holy Scriptures

A number of places discussed in this book have references to the "Hebrew Bible". The Hebrew word for the Holy Scriptures collectively is the "Tanakh". The Tanakh in turn is made up the "Torah", or the Law, which encompasses the five books of Moses; the "Nevi'im", or books of the Prophets; and the "Ketuvim", or general writings.

For the convenience of western readers, including those who might not be Jewish, the term "Hebrew Bible" is used to reference scripture, or occasionally "Torah" when that is applicable. For Christian readers, the Hebrew Bible is effectively the same text as the Christian Old Testament, though with a slightly different collection and ordering of the books.

A Note about Ancient Sacred Sites

The story of the Jewish people is a truly ancient one. Histories and traditions recorded in such documents as the Torah, the Tanakh, the Mishnah and the Talmud date back thousands of years. While *The Complete Pilgrim* will not comment on the historicity of these or other documents, they do form the basis for what we know about the history and geography of ancient Israel, Judah and Judea.

Modern day Israel and its neighbors are home to many places that were sacred to the ancient Israelites and later the Jews, and which remain sacred to many Jews in the modern day. Knowledge about such sites is heavily dependent on ancient texts and local traditions, and in many cases do not meet modern day standards of academic and archaeological scrutiny. This is particularly true of shrines and tombs that predate the Roman era.

The purpose of this comment is not to dissuade pilgrims from visiting these ancient sites. It is just a reminder that such places should be taken with a grain of salt. This is particularly true in regards to traditional burial sites of figures of the Hebrew Bible. While a few of the more important Biblical burial sites have entries in this book, such as that of King David, most do not. However a comprehensive list of these traditional sites is included in the appendices.

A Note about Holocaust Sites

The defining event of the Jewish people in the modern era was the Holocaust. Also known in Hebrew as the Shoah, or "catastrophe", the Holocaust resulted in the deaths of roughly six million European Jews, almost forty percent of the world's Jewish population at the time. The ability to carry out murder on such a massive scale required an immense infrastructure of ghettos, rail transportation and concentration camps, not to mention a complete disregard and contempt for human life.

After the war Europe was littered with the remains of places used to carry out the Nazi's Final Solution. From France to Russia, hundreds of concentration camps were discovered, ranging in size from small transit camps to sprawling extermination camps. Many of these have been preserved as a reminder to future generations that they should never forget what happened. In the decades since then monuments and memorials to the victims have been erected all over Europe. Museums and documentation centers related to the Holocaust can now be found throughout the world.

In researching this book the author identified well over a hundred Holocaust sites that were considered for inclusion, enough to merit its own written work. Due to space constraints, only about twenty were included. This represents a diverse albeit limited sampling of preserved camps, ghettos, monuments and museums around the world. A more comprehensive list of Holocaust related sites has been included in the appendices.

TIMELINE OF JEWISH HISTORY

Note – Years reflected use the Western calendar, rather than the Hebrew calendar. This includes the use of the terms BCE ("Before the Common Era") and CE ("Common Era"). At the time of this writing the Gregorian year was 2021 CE and the Hebrew year was 5781.

Early History, the First Temple and the Kingdoms of Israel and Judah (all dates BCE)

c. 1800-1500 – Age of the Patriarchs Abraham, Isaac and Jacob

c. 14th-13th century – Events of the life of Moses; the Exodus; Israelites receive the Ten Commandments

c. 1279 - Beginning of the reign of Rameses II in Egypt, believed to be the pharaoh of the Exodus

c. Mid-13th century – Joshua leads the Israelites in the conquest of Canaan; beginning of the period of the Judges

c. Early 12th century – Bronze Age collapse; Phillistines invade Canaan around this time

c. 1030 – Saul anointed first king of Israel

c. 1010 – David becomes king of Israel

c. 1004 – Israelites conquer Canaanite city of Jebus; it is renamed Jerusalem and becomes the capital of Israel

c. 984 – Rebellion of Absalom

c. 970 – Death of David; his son Solomon becomes the King of Israel

c. 960 – First Temple is completed in Jerusalem; the Ark of the Covenant is placed inside

c. 947 – Solomon's Palace completed

c. 945 – Queen of Sheba visits Solomon in Jerusalem

931 – Death of King Solomon; his son Rehoboam becomes king

930 – Northern tribal lands under Jeroboam secede; Rehoboam remains king in the South; beginning of the divided kingdoms of Israel and Judah

874 – Ahab becomes King of Israel

870 – Jehosaphat becomes King of Judah

c. 869 – Elijah prophecizes during the reign of Ahab

c. 852 – Death of Elijah

c. 840 – Moabite Stone mentions war between the Israelites and Moabites

767 – Uzziah becomes king of Judah

c. 740 – Isaiah becomes active as a prophet around this time

732 – Hoshea becomes the last King of Israel

726 – Assyrians invade Northern Kingdom of Israel

725-723 – Assyrians besiege and destroy the city of Samaria; end of the Northern Kingdom

716 – Hezekiah becomes King of Judah

701 – Assyrians besiege Jerusalem but fail to take it; they withdraw without capturing the city

c. 700 – Death of Isaiah

641 – Josiah becomes King of Judah

612 – Babylonians conquer Assyrian capital at Nineveh

605 – Babylonians defeat Egyptian army in Syria; Kingdom of Judah exposed to Babylonian invasion

598-597 – Babylonians briefly occupy Jerusalem

597 – Zedekiah becomes the last King of Judah

c. 593 – Ezekiel begins to prophesize around this time

589-587 – Babylonians besiege Jerusalem; fall of Jerusalem and destruction of the First Temple; end of the Southern Kingdom

Late Biblical Period, the Second Temple and the Kingdom of Judea (all dates BCE)

c. 575 – Hebrew Temple on Elephantine Isle is built around this time

539 – Persians conquer the Babylonian Empire

538 – Exiles in Babylon are permitted to return to Jerusalem; beginning of the Jewish people, as distinct from Israelites and Judeans

516 – Construction of the Second Temple is completed

c. 500 – Death of Esther

c. 444 – Ezra returns to Jerusalem from Babylon with five thousand Jewish settlers; it is believed that he prepared an early version of the Hebrew Bible around this time

c. 428 – Samaritans build a new Temple on Mount Gerezim

333-332 – Alexander the Great defeats the Persian Empire; Judea is occupied by the Macedonian Greeks

320 – Empire of Alexander the Great is partitioned; Judea becomes a territory of the Ptolemaic Empire

c. 247 – The Septuagint, the Hebrew Bible written in Greek, is completed

167 – Seleucids place a statue of Zeus in the Temple of Jerusalem; beginning of the Maccabean Revolt

165 – Jerusalem is liberated; Jews establish the first independent state in Judea in over four centuries

161 – End of the Maccabean Revolt against the Seleucids; most of Judea is liberated

142 – Simon Maccabee becomes the first king of the Jewish Hasmonean dynasty in Judea

c. 110 – Birth of Hillel the Elder

63 – Romans under Pompey invade Judea; it is made a protectorate of the Roman Empire

c. 50 – Birth of Shammai

40 – Herod the Great appointed king of Judea by Roman Senate; beginning of the Herodian dynasty

(beginning here all dates CE)

6 – Romans declare Judea a province of the empire

c. 34 – Christianity begins as a splinter sect of Judaism

c. 50 – Birth of Akiva ben Yosef

66 – Beginning of the Great Jewish Revolt under the Zealots

70 – Romans conquer Jerusalem; the Second Temple is destroyed; the surviving members of the council of Jewish elders known as the Sanhedrin relocate to the Galilee region

73-74 – Siege and fall of the fortress of Masada; end of the Great Jewish Revolt

115-117 – Kitos Revolt; many Jews killed in Libya and on the island of Cyprus

132 – Beginning of the Bar Khokba Revolt

135 – End of the Bar Kokhba Revolt; last vestiges of the ancient Jewish kingdom destroyed; Judea renamed Palestine

Roman Era and Early Middle Ages (all dates CE)

c. 2nd century – Galilee region becomes new religious center of Judaism

c. 200 – Mishnah is completed around this time

313 – Edict of Milan legalizes Christianity in the Roman Empire; restrictions against Jews begin emerging over the next century

358 – Creation of the Hebrew calendar; ancient council of the Sanhedrin is finally dissolved

c. 450 – Talmud of Jerusalem is completed around this time

476 – End of the Roman Empire in the west; Roman Empire in the east becomes known as the Byzantine Empire

484 – First Samaritan Revolt against the Byzantine Empire

529-531 – Second Samaritan Revolt

c. 550 – Talmud of Babylon is completed around this time

556 – Joint Samaritan and Jewish Revolt against Byzantine Empire

572 – Final Samaritan Revolt

613-628 – Jews briefly reoccupy Jerusalem during the Byzantine-Sassanian War

628 – Battle of Khaybar; Jewish tribes in Arabia defeated by rising power of Islam; over the next few years Jews who don't convert to Islam are driven out of the Arabian Peninsula

629 – Last attempt at restoration of a Jewish state in ancient times ends with slaughter of Jews in Palestine

711 – Muslims conquer Spain; restrictions on Jews there are eased

740 – Royal family of the Khazar Empire, in what is now Ukraine, converts to Judaism; the Khazar Empire, a quasi-Jewish state, survives for two centuries

760 – Schism between Rabbinical and Karaite Judaism

Middle Ages (all dates CE)

800 – Charlemagne crowned first emperor of the Holy Roman Empire; Jews are invited to his realm to serve in professional capacities

846 – First Jewish prayer book written in Iraq

912 – Beginning of the Jewish Golden Age in Spain

1013 – Pogrom against Jews in the Spanish city of Cordoba

1040 – Birth of Rashi

1066 – Muslim mob massacres an estimated four thousand Jews in the city of Granada in Spain

1090 – Pogroms in Spain force many Jews to flee to Christian territory in the north

1096 – After the declaration of the First Crusade, Christian mobs attack Jewish communities throughout Central Europe, especially in Germany

1099 – Jerusalem captured by Christian armies of the First Crusade; thousands of Jews and Muslims are slaughtered

1107 – Jews expelled from Morocco

1135 – Birth of Moses Maimonides

1187 – Saladin conquers Jerusalem; small numbers of Jews are allowed to resettle in the city

1190 – Jews of York in England commit mass suicide rather than be taken alive by anti-Semitic mob

1204 – Death of Moses Maimonides

1267 – Ramban Synagogue built in Jerusalem

c. Late 13th century – Modern practice of Kabbalah emerges around this time

1290 – Jews expelled from England

1343 – Casimir the Great invites Jews to settle in Poland

1346-1353 – Black Plague; persecutions against Jews become widespread across Europe

1453 – Ottoman Turks conquer Constantinople; end of the Byzantine Empire

Renaissance & Enlightenment (all dates CE)

1478 – Beginning of the Spanish Inquisition leads to widespread persecution of Jews in Spain and Portugal

1486 – First Jewish prayer book printed using a printing press

1492 – Mass expulsion of Jews from Spain; hundreds of thousands of Jews are forced to leave; most relocate to the Netherlands and the Ottoman Empire

1493 – Jews expelled from Sicily

1496 – Jews expelled from Portugal

1500 – First Jews arrive in the Americas around this time

1516 – First Jewish Ghetto established in Venice, Italy

1550 – Academy for the teaching of Kabbalah established in Tzfat

1567 – Jewish Yeshiva established in Lublin, Poland

1676 – Death of Sabbatai Zevi, who was believed for a while to be the Jewish Messiah

1648-1655 – Pogroms by Cossacks in Poland kill tens of thousands of Jews

1655 – Jews allowed to settle in England

1658 – First Jewish community in America established at Newport, Rhode Island

c. 1740 – Hasidic Judaism founded by Baal Shem Tov

1740 – Great Britain allows Jews to become citizens in the American colonies; Ottoman sultan invites Jews to rebuild the city of Tiberias

1781 – American Revolution; Jews granted full freedom of religion in the United States

1789 – French Revolution; Jews granted freedom of religion and citizenship in France

1790 – Letter written by George Washington encourages good relations between American Jews and Christians

Modern Era (all dates CE)

1791 – Russia organizes conquered Polish lands into Pale of Settlement, which becomes home to the world's largest Jewish population

1830 – Jews allowed to become citizens of Greece

1837 – Earthquake decimates Jewish communities in Tiberias and Tzfat

1841 – First Jewish congressman elected in the United States

1858 – Jews achieve full equality in England

1861 – Zion Society founded in Germany

1867 – Jews achieve full equality in Hungary

1868 – Benjamin Disraeli becomes Prime Minister of England

1870 – Jews achieve full equality in Italy

1881 – Zionist Congress held in Romania to discuss possible formation of a Jewish state in Palestine

1881-1884 – Widespread pogroms against Jews begin in Russia; millions of Jews leave Eastern Europe over the next four decades

1894-1899 – Dreyfus Affair; a Jewish military officer is framed and court-marshalled for treason in France; he is later exonerated

1897 – Theodor Herzl calls for the establishment of an independent Jewish homeland; World Zionist Organization formed

1916 – Louis Brandeis becomes first Jewish justice on the United States Supreme Court

1917 – Balfour Declaration; British Empire supports the establishment of a Jewish homeland in Palestine

1917-1923 – Russian Civil War leaves tens of thousands of Jews dead

1929 – Hundreds of Jews are killed in riots in Palestine

1933 – National Socialists come to power in Germany

1935 – Nuremberg Laws enacted severely restricting Jewish life in Germany

1938 – Kristalnacht; anti-Jewish pogroms unleashed across Nazi Germany

1940 – Auschwitz-Birkenau Concentration Camp opened in Poland

1942 – Wannsee Conference; details of the Final Solution against the Jews and others are discussed

1943 – Danish Jews evacuated to Sweden; virtually all survive the war; Warsaw Ghetto Uprising

1945 – Defeat of Nazi Germany; end of the Holocaust, which took the lives of approximately six million Jews

Restoration of Israel

1947 – United Nations recognizes the establishment of independent Jewish and Arab states in Palestine

1948 – Zionists declare homeland in Israel; beginning of Israeli War of Independence

1949 – Israeli War of Independence ends in armistice; hundreds of thousands of Jews, mostly refugees from Europe and Yemen, relocate to Israel

1956 – Suez War; England and France fight alongside Israel to protect shipping rights in the Suez Canal

1967 – Six Day War; Israeli forces drive Jordanians out of Jerusalem

1972 – Olympic massacre; Jewish athletes taken hostages and murdered at the Olympic Games in Munich

1973 – Yom Kippur War

1976 – Entebbe Raid; Jewish hostages being held in Uganda are rescued by Israeli commandoes

1977 – Simon Wiesenthal Center founded in Los Angeles

1978 – Camp David Accords; peace treaty between Israel and Egypt

1979-1983 – Ethiopian Jews evacuated to Israel

1982 – Lebanon War

1987 – First Intifada; Palestinians rise up against Israel

1990 – Soviet Union allows Jews to leave; hundreds of thousands relocate to Israel

1993 – Oslo Accords; peace nominally agreed to between Jews and Palestinians

1994 – Jordan normalizes relations with Israel

2000 – Beginning of Second Intifada; Great Synagogue of Jerusalem is completed

2017 – United States recognizes Jerusalem as capital of Israel

2020 – Four Muslim countries normalize relations with Israel

JERUSALEM

1. WESTERN WALL

Jewish Quarter, Old City, Jerusalem, Israel

Site Type: Ancient Structure, Synagogue
Dates: Completed c. 20 BCE
Designations: UNESCO World Heritage Site
Web: https://thekotel.org (Western Wall Heritage Foundation website)

The Western Wall, also known as the Wailing Wall, is the most sacred place on Earth for the Jewish people. An enormous retaining wall constructed by Herod the Great in the 1st century BCE, it is believed that this is the closest point to the former location of the Second Temple without actually ascending the Temple Mount. Although it is possible to get closer to the suspected location, particularly religious Jews will generally avoid walking on the Temple Mount for fear of accidentally stepping on the section that once contained the Holy of Holies.

According to Biblical tradition, the hill known as Mount Moriah was the site of an ancient threshing floor acquired by King David around 1000 BCE. The First Temple constructed by his son Solomon stood on this site for nearly four centuries before being destroyed by the Babylonians. A new temple was built here after the Jews were allowed to return from the Babylonian Exile.

This Second Temple was rededicated by the Maccabees, and later greatly expanded in the days of Herod the Great. Herod endeavored to turn the Temple Mount into one of the wonders of the world, and enclosed Mount Moriah with an absolutely gargantuan retaining wall. The Second Temple was refurbished and the rest of the hill was covered in a massive complex of colonnaded courts and worship areas.

Unfortunately the Second Temple was laid waste by the Romans in 70 CE and Jewish worship there ceased. However portions of Herod's massive retaining walls have survived. In the two thousand years since then the Western Wall has been revered by the Jewish people. Today it is the most popular destination of Jewish pilgrims visiting the Holy Land. The Western Wall is part of the Old City of Jerusalem UNESCO World Heritage Site.

Of Interest: The Western Wall is not the only surviving part of Herod's retaining wall, but it is the most famous. Jews and other pilgrims come here from all over the world to pray and weep tears of ecstacy. Every crevice of the public section of the wall is crammed full of pieces of paper upon which have been written prayers. The plaza in front of the wall is designated as a synagogue, and there are separate worship areas for males and females. Those who do choose to ascend and visit the Temple Mount will not find a temple but rather a pair of medieval mosques. For those who are interested there is also a tunnel system that runs beneath the Temple Mount which can be visited by tour.

---

2. TOWER OF DAVID MUSEUM

Jaffa Gate, Old City, Jerusalem, Israel

Site Type: Fortress, Museum
Dates: Fortress originally built in 2nd century BCE; Museum opened in 1989
Designations: UNESCO World Heritage Site, Israeli National Park
Web: www.tod.org.il (official website)

The Tower of David is a fortress that anchored the defenses on the west side of Jerusalem's Old City for many centuries. For over thirty years it has housed a museum that tells the history of Jerusalem. Despite its name, the current fortress was largely built during the late Middle Ages and has nothing to do with Israel's ancient king. The Tower of David stands just inside the Jaffa Gate, and is the first major landmark that most pilgrims see upon entering the Old City.

The current site of the Tower of David has been occupied by

fortifications since at least the 2nd century BCE. The original fortress was built by the Hasmoneans, and later expanded during the reign of Herod the Great. It survived, at least in part, through many wars and sieges, including that of the Romans in 70 CE and the Crusaders in 1099 CE. The name "Tower of David" was probably adopted during the Byzantine era, possibly because it was thought that it stood on the former site of David's palace. The structure was finally destroyed in the 13th century.

Following the Muslim reoccupation of Jerusalem, a massive new fortress was constructed around 1310. It was later expanded by the Ottoman Turks who used the tower as a garrison for over five centuries. After the collapse of the Ottoman Empire the fortress came under the control of the British, and was later occupied by the Israelis during the War of Independence. It has been home to a museum since 1989. The Tower of David is part of the Old City of Jerusalem UNESCO World Heritage Site, as well as the Jerusalem Walls-City of David National Park.

Of Interest: The Tower of David Museum is one of the most popular and fascinating museums in a city full of amazing museums. It houses a series of galleries meant to be seen consecutively that trace the history of Jerusalem's Old City through eleven different periods of history. In addition to the excellent exhibits, visitors get to tour one of the finest fortresses in Israel, including a tower which offers superb views of the city.

---

3. ANCIENT RUINS OF THE JEWISH QUARTER

Jewish Quarter, Old City, Jerusalem, Israel

Site Type: Archaeological Sites
Dates: Jerusalem Archaeological Park opened in 2001
Designations: UNESCO World Heritage Site
Web: www.rova-yehudi.org.il (Company for the Reconstruction and Development of the Jewish Quarter website)

The Jewish Quarter is the oldest area, aside from the Temple Mount, contained within the current walls of the Old City of Jerusalem. This area was settled during the First Temple period and is home to some of Jerusalem's oldest ruins. Remnants of the city from both the First and Second Temple periods can be found scattered around the Jewish Quarter, and are important to understanding the history of Jerusalem's development.

The Biblical city of Jerusalem began in the area now known as the City of David around 1000 BCE. It later expanded to the north where Solomon likely built the First Temple on Mount Moriah. Over the next few centuries the city continued to grow towards the northwest into the area now known as the Jewish quarter. By the beginning of the 6th century BCE that part of Jerusalem was enclosed by a wall and was probably home to a large portion of the city's population at the time.

When the Jews returned to Jerusalem following the Babylonian Captivity, this was possibly the first area that was resettled. Jerusalem reached its height in the 1st century CE when the ancient city had its largest population and the walls were expanded to encompass a much greater area than they do today. What is now the Jewish Quarter was more or less at the city center, with excellent access to the Temple Mount. Much of this area was destroyed along with the rest of the city in 70 CE. Some of these ruins are now part of the Old City of Jerusalem UNESCO World Heritage Site.

Of Interest: Bits and pieces of ancient Jerusalem can be found all over the Jewish Quarter, but there are a few places of particular interest. Two remnants of the city's defensive system from the First Temple period are here: portions of what are known as the Israelite Tower and the Broad Wall. The latter is easy to find, and almost anyone wandering the Jewish Quarter is likely to stumble upon it. Several sections of the city's residential areas from the Second Temple period can be found at two locations: the Wohl Museum of Archaeology and the Burnt House Museum. The Jerusalem Archaeological Park, run by the Davidson Center, can be found at the base of the southern retaining wall of the Temple Mount. It preserves some of ancient Jerusalem's most impressive ruins from both the First and Second Temple periods.

4. HISTORIC SYNAGOGUES OF THE JEWISH QUARTER

Ha-Yehudim Street, Jewish Quarter, Old City, Jerusalem, Israel
(Hurva Synagogue)

Amatsya Street 4, Jewish Quarter, Old City, Jerusalem
(Ramban Synagogue)

8 Karaite Street, Jewish Quarter, Old City, Jerusalem
(Karaite Synagogue)

Site Type: Synagogues
Dates: Karaite Synagogue originally built c. 9th century CE;
Ramban Synagogue completed 2005; Hurva Synagogue completed
2010
Web: www.rova-yehudi.org.il (Company for the Reconstruction and
Development of the Jewish Quarter website); www.heritage-center.
org.il (Karaite Synagogue website)

The Jewish Quarter of Jerusalem is home to numerous synagogues,
some historic, some very new. While there are also a sprinkling of synagogues in the Armenian and Muslim Quarters, the major synagogues
in the Old City of Jerusalem are here. Almost every synagogue in
the Old City serves an Orthodox congregation, with some exceptions.
While it is easy to overlook these houses of worship in a rush to see the
city's more famous sites, its worth at least a short visit to one or two.

The Old City of Jerusalem has been home to synagogues throughout much of its history. Unfortunately these have been destroyed on
a regular basis thanks to centuries of warfare. Despite this several
ancient synagogue sites have been preserved, as newer synagogues
were constantly being rebuilt on the site of older ones. Perhaps the
best example is that of the Karaite Synagogue, the first incarnation of
which was completed in the same spot in the 9th century CE.

The Old City became adorned with many synagogues during the

centuries of stability that came under the Ottomans. Unfortunately almost all of the city's synagogues were completely destroyed during the Israeli War of Independence. Only part of one, the Karaite Synagogue, survived and is still in use. That said the community here has been busy rebuilding the city's synagogues for over fifty years. More than a dozen historic and new synagogues are once again active in this part of the Old City.

Of Interest: Of the numerous synagogues of the Old City, there are several that really stand out. The architectural centerpiece of the Jewish Quarter is the magnificent domed Hurva Synagogue. Completed in 2010, this structure stands on a site occupied by synagogues at least as far back as the 15th century CE, and possibly much older. The Ramban Synagogue, named in honor of the Rabbi Nachmanides, was originally completed in the 13th century. It managed to survive many of the city's tribulations until finally being destroyed in 1948. The current building was completed in 2005. Arguably the most historic synagogue in the city is the Karaite Synagogue. Founded in the 9th century CE and rebuilt in the late 12th century, this synagogue, which is so old it has elements below the current street level, partially survived the Arab-Israeli Wars. It remains in use by the Karaite Jews, a tiny sect of Judaism that dates from the Middle Ages.

---

5. MUSEUMS OF THE JEWISH QUARTER

Or HaHaim Street 6, Armenian Quarter, Old City, Jerusalem, Israel
(Old Yishuv Court Museum)

The Kardo, Jewish Quarter, Old City, Jerusalem, Israel
(Last Battle for the Old City Museum)

Ha-Pisga Street 5, Jewish Quarter, Old City, Jerusalem, Israel
(Ariel Center for Jerusalem)

Misgav Ladach Street 40, Jewish Quarter, Old City, Jerusalem, Israel (Temple Institute)

Site Type: Museums
Dates: Museums opened post-1967; Temple Institute Opened in 1987
Web: www.oyc.co.il (Old Yishuv Court Museum website); https://templeinstitute.org (Temple Institute website)

The Jewish Quarter of Jerusalem, while ancient, is the most recently developed neighborhood of the Old City. Taking up about one-fifth of the area within the city walls, this part of Jerusalem was almost completely destroyed by the Jordanian military during the Israeli War of Independence. The Jewish Quarter was completely rebuilt following the Six Day War, and is now home to an excellent collection of small museums that focus on various aspects of the city's history.

During the late Ottoman and British Mandate periods, the Old City of Jerusalem was home to a sizeable Jewish community, most of whom were crowded into the area west of the Temple Mount. This part of the city was the site of intense fighting during the War of Independence, and it actually fell to the army of Jordan in 1948. In order to dissuade Jews from returning to the city, the Jordanians leveled the entire quarter. Few buildings were left standing, and Jordan remained in control of the area for the next two decades.

In 1967 the Israeli army drove the Jordanians out of the Old City and retook the Jewish Quarter. Over the next few decades the entire quarter was rebuilt, with modern buildings but in a style and layout that still evoked the charm of the rest of the Old City. With this redevelopment came several small museums that together tell the story of the Jewish Quarter.

Of Interest: There are number of museums packed into the Jewish Quarter. The Old Yishuv Court Museum mainly focuses on the history of the neighborhood. It documents the lives and culture of the Jews who lived here in the centuries prior to Israeli Independence. The Last Battle for the Old City Museum has exhibits on the fall of the Jewish Quarter to the army of Jordan in 1948. The Ariel Center for Jerusalem in the First Temple Period has exhibits on Jerusalem in the 6th century BCE and earlier. There is also a model of what the city might have looked like in the days of Hezekiah. Finally there is the Temple Institute, which runs the Third Temple Museum. This museum documents what will be needed to rebuild the Third Temple, a highly controversial subject.

---

6. TOMB OF KING DAVID

Mount Zion, Old City, Jerusalem, Israel

Site Type: Biblical Site, Burial Site
Dates: Original completion date unknown (possibly c. 2nd century CE)
Web: www.keverdavid.co.il (official website)

The Tomb of King David is one of Jerusalem's most famous and unusual sites. Located towards the top of Mount Zion, the tomb can be found in a building that was probably constructed, at least in part, during the Roman era. What makes the site unusual is that the room directly above the tomb has been associated with the Last Supper of Christian tradition. Despite skepticism about its authenticity, this shrine has been regarded as a sacred site by Jews, Christians and Muslims for at least a thousand years.

Mount Zion is a hill just south of the Old City of Jerusalem's wall and just west of the area known as the City of David. The hill was probably not part of the original Jebusite settlement when David conquered it, but it became part of the city of Jerusalem during the kingdoms period. Zion was enclosed within the city wall during the Roman era. There is even speculation that the Temple of Solomon stood on Zion rather than on the Temple Mount, though archaeological evidence of this is inconclusive.

While Mount Zion would have been a prime location for a royal tomb, the tradition that David was buried there does not appear to have emerged until the early Middle Ages. This belief probably began with the Muslims and was later adopted by the Christian Crusaders.

For over a thousand years the site of the tomb has changed hands many times. It came under Jewish control during the Israeli War of Independence.

For several decades the Tomb of King David was one of the city's most important Jewish sites; not just for the tomb, but also because the roof offered an excellent view of the Western Wall, which was under Jordanian control and off limits to Jews until the 1960s. The room with David's Tomb, formerly a mosque, is now a Jewish shrine. Despite the fact that the authenticity of the tomb is questionable, it nevertheless remains an important sacred and historic site.

Of Interest: The building that the Tomb of King David is located in, also known as the Cenacle, is very old, with construction details from many periods. There are two floors, with David's tomb located on the lower floor. This chamber is a sacred space with a focus on the great stone sarcophagus which according to tradition contains the body of David. The upper floor, accessible by an external staircase, is known by Christians as the "Upper Room", and is believed by some to be the room where the Last Supper took place.

7. CITY OF DAVID ARCHAEOLOGICAL PARK & HEZEKIAH'S TUNNEL

City of David, Old City, Jerusalem, Israel

Site Type: Biblical Site, Archaeological Site
Dates: Hezekiah's Tunnel completed c. 700 BCE
Designations: Israeli National Park
Web: www.cityofdavid.org.il (official website)

The City of David Archaeological Park, which includes Hezekiah's Tunnel, is the oldest part of the city of Jerusalem. This was the location of the original Jebusite settlement which David conquered in the 11th century BCE, and almost everything that has been discovered here dates from the kingdoms period or earlier. The archaeological site is fairly extensive and research here is ongoing.

The hill where the City of David is located has been inhabited since ancient times. The main advantage of the site for early settlers was the presence of the Gihon Spring, a plentiful fresh water source which supported the local population for thousands of years. The ancient Jebusites maintained a fortified settlement here prior to the arrival of the Israelites and throughout the rule of the Judges. Around the year 1003 BCE an Israelite army under King David conquered the fortress, possibly by entering the city through a tunnel that provided water to the city from the Gihon Spring.

David subsequently chose it to be the site of the capital of his new kingdom and renamed it Jerusalem. Although Jerusalem expanded significantly in later years, the City of David probably remained the city's royal enclave for several centuries. During this period the City of David became heavily fortified. The Gihon Spring was concealed and a tunnel, built during the reign of King Hezekiah, rerouted the water to what is known as the Pool of Siloam.

After the Babylonians sacked Jerusalem in the 6th century BCE, the City of David never really recovered its preeminent position in the city. It was included inside the city wall during the Hasmonean and Roman periods, thanks to the presence of the Gihon Spring. However after the fall of Jerusalem and destruction of the Second Temple in 70 CE the City of David was largely abandoned. The area was excluded from the city's later walls, and remains outside of them to the present day. The City of David is part of the Jerusalem Walls-City of David National Park.

Of Interest: The City of David archaological site stretches southward from the walls of the Old City just outside of the Dung Gate. A number of the area's ancient buildings have been excavated and can be viewed from a surrounding walkway. A visually impressive section of the ancient city wall, which was actually built by the Jebusites, dominates the site. Towards the center of the park is the entrance to Hezekiah's Tunnel, which can be accessed through Warren's Shaft. There are actually two tunnels, one wet and one dry, that visitors can walk through to get to the Pool of Siloam.

8. KIDRON VALLEY & SILWAN NECROPOLIS

Kidron Valley, Old City, Jerusalem, Israel

Site Type: Biblical Site, Cemetery
Dates: Necropolis established c. 10th century BCE
Web: www.itraveljerusalem.com/evt/a-tour-kidron-valley (municipal tourism website)

The Kidron Valley is an historic geological feature that has played a role in Jewish history since Biblical times. It has gone by several names, including the Valley of Fire, the Valley of the Kings and the Valley of Jehosaphat. It is famous primarily for the many magnificent ancient tombs that can be found in the Silwan Necropolis, including some that date back over twenty-six centuries.

When most visitors to Jerusalem think of the Kidron Valley, they are usually thinking of that portion that separates the Mount of Olives on the east from the Temple Mount and the City of David on the west. In actuality it starts outside the walls of the Old City of Jerusalem and runs approximately seventeen miles southeast towards the Dead Sea. Because the Kidron is directly adjacent to the oldest parts of Jerusalem, it probably witnessed several Biblical events, including David's assault on the original Canaanite settlement.

Because of its nickname, the Valley of the Kings, and because of its proximity to the City of David, it is possible that the valley was the personal property of the ruling dynasty during the First Temple Period. It was about this time that the part of the valley below the Mount of Olives began to be built out with burial monuments and rock-cut tombs. This necropolis is now one of the world's most famous ancient cemeteries, and home to a number of tombs from the Biblical era.

Of Interest: The major tombs of the Silwan Necropolis can be roughly divided into two sections. The northern section is closer to the Temple Mount at the head of the valley. Among the major tombs here are those of several priests of the First Temple period. There are also a number of possible Biblical tombs here, including those of Jehosaphat, the fourth king of Judah, and Absolom, the son of David. The latter is marked by the Pillar of Absolom. Three Biblical prophets, Haggai, Zechariah and Malachi, are also believed to be buried here. The southern section near Silwan has some of the more spectacular tombs, including the Tomb of the Royal Steward and the Tomb of the Pharoah's Daughter, the latter of which may be the burial site of one of Solomon's wives.

9. MOUNT OF OLIVES CEMETERY

Mount of Olives, East Jerusalem, Israel

Site Type: Biblical Site, Cemetery
Dates: Modern Cemetery established c. 19th century CE
Web: https://mountofolives.co.il (official website)

The Mount of Olives Cemetery is, along with the neighboring Silwan Necropolis, the oldest and most historic Jewish cemetery in the world. Covering a large portion of the mountain just east of the Old City of Jerusalem, there are probably more than one hundred thousand people buried here, with some burials dating back thousands of years. However most of the graves date from the last two centuries.

The Mount of Olives, or Mount Olivet, is one of the great landmarks of Jewish tradition. Named for the groves of olive trees that grow on its slope, it is mentioned in the Bible almost as early as David's reign. Solomon may have constructed shrines to pagan deities for his wives here. The Romans and other conquering armies used the Mount of Olives as an observation post during sieges of the city. Throughout the Diaspora, Mount Olivet was a place of mourning due to its proximity to and view of the Temple Mount.

According to Jewish tradition, when the Messiah finally comes, he will arrive on the peak of the Mount of Olives, and from there enter the city of Jerusalem through the Golden Gate. It is for this reason that many Jews have desired to be buried on the mountainside. The cemetery now sprawls over a large area of Mount Olivet.

Of Interest: The Mount of Olives Cemetery started near the Silwan Necropolis nearly three thousand years ago and has spread out from there (the Silwan Necropolis is addressed in its own section). Most of the known gravesites date from the 19th and 20th centuries. Many prominent religious leaders, politicians and others from modern Israel's early years are interred here. Arguably the most famous modern grave is that of Menachem Begin, the sixth prime minister of Israel, who was instrumental in achieving peace with Egypt in 1978.

---

10. ZEDEKIAH'S CAVE

Muslim Quarter, Old City, Jerusalem, Israel

Site Type: Biblical Site, Ancient Structure
Dates: Quarry established c. 7th century BCE
Web: www.goisrael.com/en/zedekiahs-cave-65451 (Israel national tourism website)

Zedekiah's Cave is one of Jerusalem's lesser known sites, but an historical treasure nevertheless. An ancient stone quarry that was in use at least as far back as the 7th century BCE, the cave has been tied to the life and reign of Zedekiah, the last ruler of the Kingdom of Judah. The quarry was probably used during the Herodian era, and it is possible that stones from here may have been used in the construction of Solomon's Temple.

According to archaeological research, Zedekiah's Cave was almost certainly prospected for stone during the Kingdoms period. However there is no way to tell for certain if the quarry was used during the reign of Solomon. Tradition indicates the cave might have been tied to a system of tunnels through which Zedekiah attempted to escape during the Babylonian siege of Jerusalem.

The quarry was used periodically during the Roman, Byzantine and Ottoman eras, with large quantities of stone removed for various projects. The most recent documented use of the quarry was in the early 20th century. During the British occupation of the city following World War I, knowledge of the cave spread, and it became a popular tourist attraction. Today it is open to the public, and archaeological research in the quarry is ongoing.

Of Interest: Zedekiah's Cave is basically a natural cave entrance that opens into a massive man made system of underground tunnels and galleries. In recent decades the quarry has been outfitted with permanent paths and lighting that allow parts of the tunnel system to be explored. The walls are covered with marks made from chisels dating back many centuries, along with ancient graffiti. Markers throughout the quarry note points of interest.

---

11. ROCKEFELLER MUSEUM

27 Sultan Suleiman Street, Jerusalem, Israel

Site Type: Museum
Dates: Opened in 1938
Web: www.imj.org.il/en/wings/archaeology/rockefeller-archaeological-museum (official website)

The Rockefeller Museum was formerly the primary archaeology museum of the Holy Land. Established during the British Mandate period, it was a major repository for artifacts recovered in the region during the early 20th century. Due to the vast number of pieces accumulated over the years, much of the collection was relocated to the Israel Museum in the 1960s. The Rockefeller Museum is now run as an annex of the Israel Museum.

It has been suggested that it is impossible to dig up a shovel full of dirt in the Holy Land without uncovering some ancient artifact or bit of ruin. Although that might be an exaggeration, there is no denying the literally hundreds of thousands of pieces of history that have been discovered in the region over the course of the last two centuries. During that period archaeological expeditions sponsored by governments and universities from around the world have descended on the Holy Land intent on recovering the region's sacred and historic treasures.

In 1925 James Breasted, an archaeologist and professor at the University of Chicago, was visiting Palestine where he discovered that there was no proper institution for the preservation, study, display and storage of the region's antiquities. Using funds provided by John D. Rockefeller Jr, an archaeology museum was established in Jerusalem. In 1938 the Palestine Archaeological Museum, also known as the Rockefeller Museum, was opened. It became the official repository for many of the Holy Land's greatest finds. Since 1948 it has also been home to the Israel Department of Antiquities and Museums, now known as the Israel Antiquities Authority.

Of Interest: The Rockefeller Museum is home to a number of collections of artifacts discovered in the Holy Land. While most of the major Judaica pieces and the Dead Sea Scrolls are now on display at the Israel Museum, there is still a wealth of items spanning thousands of years of the region's history, including antiquities of Jewish interest. There is also an exhibit of rare photographs of archaeological expeditions that were taken at the height of the colonial era.

12. GREAT SYNAGOGUE OF JERUSALEM & JEWISH HERITAGE CENTER

King George Street 56 & 58, Jerusalem, Israel

Site Type: Synagogue, Museum
Dates: Synagogue completed in 1982; Jewish Heritage Center opened in1958
Web: www.jerusalemgreatsynagogue.com & http://eng. hechalshlomo.org.il (official websites)

The Great Synagogue of Jerusalem, not to be confused with the Great Belz Synagogue, and the neighboring Heichal Shlomo Jewish Heritage Center are both historical buildings which have played a role in the development of religious Judaism in modern Israel. The former is the current seat of the chief rabbis of Israel, while the latter served as home to the rabbinate from 1958 until 1982. The heritage center is now home to the Jewish Museum of Art.

The idea of religious leadership in Jerusalem dates back to the construction of the First Temple around three thousand years ago. However the institution of the Chief Rabbinate is relatively new. The position of chief rabbi of Jerusalem was created under the Ottomans. It took place at a time when many Sephardic Jews fleeing from the Inquisition in Spain were resettling in Ottoman territory, and thus the chief rabbis of the period came from the Sephardic tradition.

The rabbinate was continued under the British Mandate, and later expanded to two chief rabbis, one Sephardic and one Ashkenazi, along with a council of advisors. After the War of Independence the rabbinate was maintained in order to oversee religious law in Israel. They worked out of the Heichal Shlomo building for several decades. In 1982 the construction of the Great Synagogue of Jerusalem was completed. It is now the religious seat of the Chief Rabbinate of Israel.

Of Interest: The Great Synagogue of Jerusalem is an enormous structure that towers above King George Street. Its exterior design, with its memorable façade, is evocative of what the Second Temple might have once looked like. The interior sanctuary is huge and can accommodate well over a thousand worshippers at a time. The entry hall is home to an interesting collection of mezuzahs. Right next door to the synagogue is the Heichal Shlomo Jewish Heritage Center. The center is an important historic building which is home to, among other things, an early modern synagogue, an observation deck and the Wolfson Museum. The latter houses a large collection of Judaica as well as important works of art.

---

13. KNESSET BUILDING

Kiryat Ben-Gurion, Jerusalem, Israel

Site Type: Government Building
Dates: Opened in 1966
Web: www.knesset.gov.il (official website)

The Knesset Building is the home of the Israeli Parliament, the legislative branch of the government of Israel. Located in the Givat Ram district of West Jerusalem, the building was originally designed by Joseph Klarwein and financed by the Rothschild family. The Knesset Building is a highly secure facility, especially when the government is in session.

The Israeli government has its origins with the Provisional State Council which was formed in 1948 following Israel's declaration of independence. The council oversaw Israel's first election in January of 1949, and the Knesset formally took office on February 14th of that year. In honor of the ancient Great Assembly, which nominally ruled over the Jewish people for a time during the Second Temple period, the Knesset numbers one hundred and twenty members.

For seventeen years the Knesset met in a series of buildings in Jerusalem, most notably the Frumin House. The Frumin House, which still exists, is slated to become home to a Knesset museum at some point in the future. After a design competition, construction on the current Knesset Building began in 1958. This building was completed and dedicated in 1966. The Israeli parliament has met here ever since.

Of Interest: The Knesset Building is an elegant but strictly modern structure. The parliament meets in the Plenum Hall in the original part of the building. Later additions and wings were added as space needs increased. A number of prominent architects and artists worked on the building, including Marc Chagall, who designed some of the tapestries and mosaics now on display in the State Hall. Tours of the Knesset are available on select days, and access to the building may be limited as security requires.

14. ISRAEL MUSEUM & SHRINE OF THE BOOK

Derech Ruppin 11, Jerusalem, Israel

Site Type: Museum
Dates: Opened in 1965
Web: www.imj.org.il (official website)

The Israel Museum is one of the world's greatest museums of Jewish history and culture. A sprawling modern complex designed to capture the epic history of this ancient land and its people, it is home to an immense assortment of Judaica and more. Among its many exhibits is the Shrine of the Book, which houses a magnificent collection of ancient Bible-related documents, including a selection of the Dead Sea scrolls. No trip to Jerusalem is complete without a stop at this unparalleled institution.

The Israel Museum collection originated with its antiquities department. Beginning in 1925, many of Israel's most important antiquities were housed at the Rockefeller Museum near Jerusalem's Old City. By the early 1960s the collection had grown so huge that a new facility was required. Moreover, the Rockefeller Museum's location near the city's disputed areas prompted concerns for the collection's safety, and the government sought to move it to a more secure location.

The first buildings of the massive new complex opened in West Jerusalem in 1965. Among these was the Shrine of the Book, a domed structure designed to house and display ancient sacred writings. Many of the Rockefeller's most important antiquities were moved and re-displayed here. The new museum also expanded on the Rockefeller Museum's mandate, housing exhibits on art and culture as well as archaeology and history. The Israel Museum continues to expand every year as its collection grows ever larger. At the time of this writing it was one of the largest and most comprehensive museum complexes in the Middle East.

Of Interest: The Israel Museum is a sprawling masterpiece of modern architecture. Both the exterior and interior areas are adorned with works of modern art. The main museum building consists of two major permanent exhibit halls: Israeli archaeology and Jewish art; several smaller permanent exhibit halls, and a number of temporary exhibit halls. The museum's archaeology collection includes pieces from all periods of Israel's history as well as Judaica from around the world. One of the most popular exhibits of the main museum is neither art nor artifact, but rather a breathtaking scale model of what Jerusalem probably looked like during the Second Temple Period. The highlight of the Israel Museum is the Shrine of the Book. Some of the greatest historical Jewish documents ever found are kept and displayed here, including the Dead Sea Scrolls. Another of the Shrine's great treasures is the Aleppo Codex, the oldest, though somewhat incomplete, copy of the Hebrew Bible.

---

15. BIBLE LANDS MUSEUM

Shmuel Stephan Weiz Street 21, Jerusalem, Israel

Site Type: Museum
Dates: Opened in 1992
Web: www.blmj.org (official website)

The Bible Lands Museum is another of Jerusalem's major archaeology museums. This one focuses on telling the story of the various peoples that appear in the Bible, most notably those who had significant interactions with the ancient Israelites. In a series of exhibits that progress from prehistoric times to the Roman era, this museum helps to put the history of the ancient Jewish people into a greater geographical context.

In the seventeen centuries or so between the time of Abraham and the Great Revolt against Rome, the ancient Israelites, and later the Jews, came into contact with dozens of major civilizations from the Middle East, Europe and North Africa. These included Egypt, the Hittites, the Phoenicians, the Sea Peoples, Assyria, Babylon, Persia, the Greeks and finally the Roman Empire, just to name a few. While all of these great civilizations have faded from history, they live on in memory thanks in part to their association with the Bible.

The Bible Lands Museum was opened in 1992 to house and display the private collection of artifacts of Elie Borowski. This magnificent and comprehensive collection was accumulated over the course of a long career, and has been expanded since the museum's opening. The Bible Lands Museum is located just across the street from the Israel Museum making it is easy to visit both institutions in a day.

Of Interest: The Bible Lands Museum has a wide array of exhibits covering many peoples and cultures of the ancient world. The primary exhibit hall has over a dozen galleries, each of which covers a different civilization that appears in the Bible: Egypt, Babylon, Rome and many others are represented here. There are also other temporary galleries which, at the time of this writing, included exhibits on the Yeminite Jews and the Babylonian Captivity.

---

16. BELZ GREAT SYNAGOGUE

Binat Yisas'har Street 7, Jerusalem, Israel

Site Type: Synagogue
Dates: Completed in 2000
Web: www.worldofbelz.org/see-the-shul (official website)

The Belz Great Synagogue in west Jerusalem currently enjoys the distinction of being the world's largest synagogue. Dedicated in the year 2000, this absolutely gargantuan house of worship can accommodate between seven and ten thousand worshippers at a time. It was built and named in honor of the synagogue of the city of Belz in what is now the Ukraine, and which was destroyed by the Nazis during World War II.

The Jewish community of Belz dated back to the late Middle Ages. It was founded sometime around the 1300s, and by the 1800s was home to a thriving Hasidic Jewish community. A number of distinguished rabbis of the 19th and early 20th centuries came from Belz.

The city's great synagogue, at the time one of the largest in Europe, was completed in 1843.

Like many other Jewish communities in Nazi occupied territory, that of Belz was laid waste during World War II. The synagogue was largely destroyed, and most of the city's Jews were killed. However the rabbi of the community managed to escape and make his way to Israel. There he helped to rebuild the Hasidic community in the Holy Land. The Belz Great Synagogue is now one of Jerusalem's most important religious centers.

Of Interest: The Belz Great Synagogue is an absolutely immense structure that towers over the surrounding neighborhood. Loosely modeled after the former synagogue of Belz, it reflects a modern style blended with traditional design elements. The main sanctuary is enormous and magnificently decorated. The ark of the synagogue is massive in size, and may be the largest such structure in the world. According to some counts, it is able to accomadate over fifty full sized Torah scrolls.

---

17. MOUNT HERZL & HERZL MUSEUM

Herzl Boulevard, Jerusalem, Israel

Site Type: Cemetery, Museum
Dates: Cemetery established in 1952; museum opened in 2004
Web: www.herzl.org (Herzl Museum website)

Mount Herzl, also known as the Mount of Remembrance, is the location of Jerusalem's memorial district. Named for Theodor Herzl, the founder of the Zionist movement, it is home to Israel's national and military cemeteries, as well as to Yad Vashem, the national Holocaust museum and memorial. Many of modern Israel's leaders and heroes are buried here, as well as those who suffered during the Holocaust. Mount Herzl and its immediate environs are home to several related museums, including the Herzl Museum, with exhibits on Herzl's life and the early days of the Zionist movement.

Theodor Herzl was a Jewish journalist and writer who is credited with starting the movement for the establishment of a Jewish homeland in Palestine. He was born and raised in Budapest but later moved to Vienna with his family. It was there where he first conceived of the idea of a Jewish homeland. During the events of the Dreyfus affair in France, Herzl became convinced that anti-Semitism would never go away, and that ultimately no country would be a safe for the Jews.

Herzl spent the rest of his life pursuing the idea of a Jewish homeland, and though he died before this dream came to fruition, the creation of Israel was the legacy of his efforts. Theodor Herzl died in 1904. Forty-four years later the nation of Israel became a reality. In 1949 his body was moved from Vienna to Jerusalem and reinterred on top of the hill that now bears his name. A few years later Mount Herzl was designated as the site of Israel's national cemetery. Many of Israel's leaders, as well as other important political figures and members of the early Zionist movement, are buried here.

Over the years the burials and memorials on Mount Herzl have grown in number. The Israeli Military Cemetery dominates the area to the north, while Yad Vashem, Israel's national Holocaust memorial, is to the west (Yad Vashem is covered in its own section). Many state events are held on Mount Herzl. If the Western Wall is the religious heart of Israel, Mount Herzl is its national heart.

Of Interest: The once small Mount Herzl National Cemetery is now quite extensive. A short list of famous Israelis buried here includes Theodor Herzl and members of his family, Israeli president Chaim Herzog, Israeli prime ministers Levi Eshkol, Golda Meir and Yitzhak Rabin, and military hero Jonathan Netanyahu. The Herzl Museum was dedicated in 2004 on the 100th anniversary of Theodore Herzl's death. While fairly small, it houses a number of interesting exhibits on his life and the beginning of Zionism. Some of his writings are also on display here.

18. YAD VASHEM & GARDEN OF THE RIGH-TEOUS AMONG THE NATIONS

Yad Va-Shem Street, Jerusalem, Israel

Site Type: Museum, Holocaust Memorial
Dates: Opened in 1957
Web: www.yadvashem.org (official website)

Yad Vashem, which translates as "a monument and a name", is Israel's national shrine to the victims of the Holocaust, or Shoah. The catastrophic events of the Holocaust are so closely tied to the creation of modern Israel that the murder of six million European Jews will always be an integral part of the national story. It was the Holocaust that at last convinced the surviving Jews that there would never be safe for them among the other peoples of the world. It was the memory of the Holocaust that drove many Jews to establish their own homeland in Palestine. Because of this the Holocaust is vividly remembered at Yad Vashem.

The idea of a memorial to commemorate the victims of the Holocaust existed before Israel was formally established as a nation, and even before World War II was over in Europe. Funding was underway within months of Germany's surrender. The establishment of Yad Vashem was formally authorized by the Israeli Parliament in 1953, and the first sections of the memorial were open to the public four years later.

Yad Vashem is the largest Holocaust memorial site in the world. It became the prototype which inspired the construction of many other Holocaust museums and monuments in cities throughout the world. In the last few years Yad Vashem was completely rebuilt and vastly expanded. The new building is not only a moving museum, but an architectural masterpiece. Yad Vashem is arguably the most poignant Jewish pilgrimage destination of Israel's modern age.

Of Interest: Yad Vashem is a sprawling complex of exhibits and memorials that covers a large area of the Mount of Remembrance. The main building consists of a series of exhibition halls that begin underground and progress upwards, symbolically representing the rebirth of the Jewish people. Perhaps the most memorable gallery is the Hall of Names which individually commemorates as many of the six million Jewish Holocaust victims as are known. Also at Yad Vashem is the Valley of the Communities, which commemorates the thousands of Jewish villages and neighborhoods that the Nazis destroyed in Europe. Nearby is the Garden, or Avenue, of the Righteous among the Nations. This memorial honors those non-Jews who risked everything to rescue their Jewish neighbors from Nazi atrocities. To date more than twenty-two thousand heroes from over forty nations have been honored here.

CENTRAL AND SOUTHERN ISRAEL

19. GREAT SYNAGOGUE OF TEL AVIV

Allenby Street 110, Tel Aviv-Yafo, Israel

Site Type: Synagogue
Dates: Completed in 1926
Designations: UNESCO World Heritage Site
Web: www.tlvgreatsynagogue.or (official website)

The Great Synagogue of Tel Aviv is one of the most historic synagogues of modern Israel. Constructed in the 1920s, it was for more than half a century one of the busiest synagogues in the Holy Land. Although it has since been eclipsed by newer and larger synagogues in Jerusalem, it remains an indelible landmark of the Tel Aviv skyline.

Tel Aviv began in the early 20th century as a new Jewish neighborhood extending north from Jaffa. By the time the Ottoman Empire collapsed at the end of World War I it was one of the largest Jewish communities in Palestine. In the 1910s it was decided that a major new synagogue was required to serve the community, and in 1926 the Great Synagogue of Tel Aviv was completed.

The Great Synagogue was the heart of early Tel Aviv, and remained so after Israel became an independent nation. Over time Tel Aviv grew into a major metropolis, and the residential neighborhoods moved outward as the city center was swallowed up by commercial development. Despite this the Great Synagogue remains a place of active worship, and is one of Tel Aviv's most important religious and architectural treasures. The Great Synagogue of Tel Aviv is part of the White City of Tel Aviv UNESCO World Heritage Site.

Of Interest: The Great Synagogue of Tel Aviv was, in some ways, the first major building of modern Israel. It is a huge, stately structure crowned by an impressive dome. A major renovation in the 1960s gave the synagogue a modern facelift. The building's stained glass windows were updated during a renovation. The new ones are replicas of windows of synagogues destroyed by the Nazis during their reign of terror in Europe during World War II.

---

20. INDEPENDENCE HALL MUSEUM

16 Rothschild Boulevard, Tel Aviv-Yafo, Israel

Site Type: Government Building, Museum
Dates: Completed in 1932; Museum opened in 1978
Designations: UNESCO World Heritage Site
Web: http://eng.ihi.org.il (official website)

The Independence Hall Museum is the building where David Ben-Gurion proclaimed the new state of Israel in 1948. One of the oldest buildings in Tel Aviv, this former home of Meir Dizengoff has previously served as the mayor's residence and later as the city's art museum. Now known as Independence Hall, the building has been home to the national independence museum since 1978.

Israel's Independence Hall was originally built as a residence by the first mayor of Tel Aviv in the early 20th century. He bequeathed the building to the city for use as a museum after his death. The Tel Aviv Art Museum was housed here from the 1930s until the 1970s when it was moved to a new facility.

On May 14, 1948 Israeli leaders met here to declare independence for the Jewish state of Israel. The room where the declaration was signed later went on to become known as Independence Hall. In 1978, on the 30th anniversary of the signing, the hall was restored and became home to an exhibit on the Israeli Declaration of Independence. The room and building are both preserved as one of modern Israel's most historic sites. The Independence Hall Museum is part of the White City of Tel Aviv UNESCO World Heritage Site.

Of Interest: Independence Hall Museum is located in one of Tel Aviv's original neighborhoods. The main point of interest of the museum is Independence Hall, which houses exhibits on the Israeli declaration of independence as well as the early history of Tel Aviv. In addition, the upper floor of the building houses the Bible Museum, a small gallery of artifacts and art pertaining to the Hebrew Bible. NOTE – At the time of this writing in 2021 the museum was closed for renovations and exhibits were moved for temporary display to the Shalom Mayor Tower.

---

21. ERETZ ISRAEL MUSEUM

Chaim Levanon Street 2, Tel Aviv-Yafo, Israel

Site Type: Museum
Dates: Opened in 1953
Web: www.eretzmuseum.org.il (official website)

The Eretz Israel Museum is a large museum complex in Tel Aviv and one of the most popular tourist destinations in the city. Like many of Israel's museums, there is an extensive archaeology collection at Eretz Israel. However, while exhibits do cover the history of the region, there is also a focus on the culture and day-to-day life of the Holy Land, especially in ancient times.

Eretz Israel was founded in 1958 as the Haaretz Museum. It originally housed the private antiquities and glass collections of Walter Moses, a wealthy philanthropist from Germany who settled in the British Mandate of Palestine in the 1920s. It was the first major museum to be founded in Israel after achieving independence.

Over time the museum was greatly expanded as more items were acquired, until it became a sprawling complex. The collection is now incredibly diverse, and features items from ancient times to the modern day. In terms of the historical and cultural importance of its collections Eretz Israel is one of the most comprehensive museums in Tel Aviv.

Of Interest: The Eretz Israel Museum is home to an extensive and unusual assortment of artifacts, from glass and pottery exhibits to coin and stamp collections. Among the more popular galleries in the museum is the Nechustan Pavillion, which houses exhibits on the mining and production of copper and other metals in ancient Israel. It includes a reconstructed copper mine from Solomon's day, as well as a recreation of a Midianite Temple. The Eretz Israel Museum is also home to Israel's largest planetarium.

---

22. ANU - MUSEUM OF THE JEWISH PEOPLE

Tel Aviv University, Klausner Street 15, Tel Aviv-Yafo, Israel

Site Type: Museum
Dates: Opened in 1959
Web: www.anumuseum.org.il (official website)

The ANU-Museum of the Jewish People at Beit Hatfutsot, formerly known as the Nahum Goldmann Museum of the Jewish Diaspora, is a major educational institution located on the campus of Tel Aviv University. A museum of Jewish history of sorts, it primarily focuses on showcasing Jewish roots and culture from communities around the world. The institute has recently been rebranded with the word ANU, which means "we" in Hebrew.

The Jewish people constitute a very ancient society, and one of only a handful of ethnic groups on Earth that has remained more or less religiously intact from antiquity. A major reason for this was the Diaspora, which saw Jewish communities in exile spring up all over the world after the Romans destroyed the Second Temple. While the modern world's fifteen million or so Jews are united by faith and tradition, the global Jewish cultural experience is incredibly diverse.

By the 1950s, as the number of returning Jews swelled the population of Israel, the true extent of this diversity became evident. A Museum of the Diaspora was founded at Tel Aviv University to celebrate the vast and rich cultural heritage of the world's Jews. In 2005

Beit Hatfutsot was named by the Israeli parliament as the National Center for Jewish Communities in Israel and Around the World. In 2018 it was redesignated as the Museum of the Jewish People.

Of Interest: The ANU-Museum of the Jewish People at Beit Hatfutsot is an expansive and comprehensive facility. The main exhibit, which was being overhauled at the time of this writing, will offer an in depth look at the many Jewish communities that have evolved all around the world over the course of the last three thousand years. Also here are exhibits on Jewish heroes and a fascinating showcase of synagogues from around the world.

---

23. OLD JAFFA

Yafo, Tel Aviv-Yafo, Israel

Site Type: Historic Neighborhood
Dates: City founded c. 1800 BCE; modern community founded in 1820
Web: https://visit.tel-aviv.gov.il/see-do/jaffa-(old-city) (municiple tourism website)

The Old City of Jaffa, now a neighborhood of Tel Aviv, is one of modern Israel's oldest communities. In ancient times it was the major port city of the Israelites and an important regional trading center. Unlike many other cities of the Holy Land which were destroyed or abandoned over the centuries, Jaffa has remained inhabited more or less uninterrupted for thousands of years. Nevertheless most of "old" Jaffa actually dates from the 19th and early 20th centuries.

Jaffa has been around for a very long time. A settlement may have existed on the site as early as the 19th century BCE. It was already an important commercial center when the Israelites showed up. Although Jaffa was part of the territory assigned to the tribe of Dan, the port spent many years, possibly several centuries, caught in the tug-of-war between the Israelites and the Philistines. Jaffa probably did not come solidly under the control of Israel until the time of David.

From the reign of Solomon to Herod nearly a thousand years later Jaffa remained the region's most important port. Materials for the construction of both the First and Second Temples arrived here before being transported to Jerusalem. Jaffa's importance as a port waned in the 1st century CE following the establishment of the city of Caesarea Maritima by Herod the Great.

Much of Jaffa was rebuilt in the 19th century, and the old city largely dates from this time. Jaffa witnessed regular fighting between the British and the local Jewish and Arab populations in the early 20th century. The city came under Jewish control during the Israeli War of Independence. Tel Aviv, the capital of Israel, began as an extension of Jaffa in the late 19th century. Old Jaffa is now just a neighborhood of Tel Aviv, but one rich in history and popular with strolling tourists.

Of Interest: Old Jaffa is a beautiful old neighborhood that offers a glimpse into Jewish life prior to the creation of the modern state of Israel. It is also known as a place where there is a lot of interaction with Muslims and Christians, which also both have historic communities here. Visiting Old Jaffa is mostly about exploring the neighborhood. The small port where modern pleasure boats and fishing vessels are now berthed witnessed a booming international trade in ancient times. The district's central site is the Clock Tower, which was constructed in the early 20th century in a joint effort of the city's Jews and Arabs. Also of interest is the Arab-Hebrew Theater, which is home to both Jewish and Muslim theater companies.

---

24. BABYLONIAN JEWRY HERITAGE CENTER

83 Mordechai, Ben Porat Avenue, Or Yehuda, Israel

Site Type: Museum
Dates: Opened in 1973
Web: www.bjhcenglish.com (official website)

The Babylonian Jewry Heritage Center is a museum dedicated to the history and culture of the Jews of Iraq. For over twenty-five centuries the Jewish community in Iraq was almost continuously uninterrupted. It largely disappeared in the early 1950s when most of the community emmigrated enmasse to the newly formed state of Israel.

In 587 BCE the Babylonian Empire laid siege to the city of Jerusalem. The city fell and was largely destroyed, putting an end to the ancient Kingdom of Judah. Many Jews were killed during the war, while some fled to Egypt or into the wilderness. But a large segment of the surviving population was sent into exile in what is now Iraq and Iran. While some Jews were repatriated back to Israel during the Persian era, many remained in their new homes. Those communities continued to exist for well over two thousand years.

The Jewish community of Iraq became incredibly important after the Romans destroyed the Second Temple in the 1st century CE. Many Jews fled to Mesopotamia, which became a major center of Jewish religious life. The Babylonian Talmud was produced in Iraq in the centuries after the destruction of the Second Temple. However the community's size and importance began to wane after the Middle Ages, and faced outright hostility after the collapse of the Ottoman Empire in 1918.

Following Israel's declaration of independence in 1948, the persecution of Iraqi Jews increased dramatically. Israel helped well over a hundred thousand Jews escape from Iraq during Operation Ezra and Nehemiah. The few thousand who remained behind were largely allowed to leave in the 1970s. Today most former Iraqi Jews live in Israel, with some communities in the United States, Europe and Iran. Their story is preserved at the Babylonian Jewry Heritage Center.

Of Interest: The Babylonian Jewry Heritage Center is home to a wealth of exhibits on Jewish life in Iraq as well as an extensive collection of records. There are exhibits on the Diaspora in Babylon and the return to Israel, the Great Synagogue of Baghdad, medicine, music and more. Parts of the collections are displayed in recreations of rooms from Jewish residences as they might have existed in Iraq a century ago.

---

25. FOREST OF THE MARTYRS

Beit Meir, Israel

Site Type: Holocaust Memorial, Nature Reserve
Dates: Established in 1951
Web: www.kkl-jnf.org/tourism-and-recreation/forests-and-parks/
martyrs-forest.aspx (Jewish National Fund website)

The Forest of the Martyrs is, along with Yad Vashem, Israel's major monument commemorating the victims of the Holocaust. Located west of Jerusalem, this woodland consists almost entirely of trees planted in the last seven decades. Each of the roughly six million trees here stands in memory of the Jewish victims, both known and unknown, who died during the Nazi regime's reign of terror.

The founding of the forest predates almost all other Holocaust memorial sites, even Yad Vashem. In fact it was one of the first major projects undertaken in the newly independent nation of Israel. The project was organized and financed under the auspices of the Jewish National Fund and B'nai B'rith, and the first trees were planted in 1951.

The Jewish tradition of planting trees on special occasions is a very old one. Trees are planted upon the birth of a newborn, and to commemorate those who have died. Jews the world over have contributed to the planting of trees throughout Israel, sometimes even traveling to the Holy Land to do it in person. Israel is now dotted with young, green forests, the most famous of which is the Forest of the Martyrs.

Of Interest: The Forest of the Martyrs is now full of millions of fully mature trees. Species present include cypress, oak, pine and eucalyptus, and more. There are also a number of monuments in the forest, most notably the immense bronze Scroll of Fire which depicts the destruction and rebirth of the Jewish people. Added more recently is the Anne Frank Memorial, designed to recall the attic where the author and her family hid out for two years before being discovered and killed by the Nazis.

26. VALLEY OF ELAH & KHIRBET QEIYAFA

Bet Shemesh, Israel

Site Type: Biblical Site, Archaeological Site, Fortress, Nature Reserve
Dates: Fortress originally constructed c. 1000 BCE
Web: http://quiyafa.huji.ac.il (official website)

The Valley of Elah was the location of one of the best known battles in ancient history: the showdown between the Israelites and the Philistines, in which a young shepherd named David defeated a giant named Goliath in single combat. This event made David a national hero and set the stage for his eventual rise to the kingship. A fortress, the Khirbet Qeiyafa, was later constructed near the site of the battle. The ruins and the stream from which David probably retrieved his five famous stones are still there to this day

Sometime around the 12th century BCE the people known as the Philistines were expanding their coastal empire in Canaan. Eventually the Phillistines and Israelites met, and what ensued was a very long and bloody conflict. The Israelites appear to have had the advantage of numbers, geography and religious fervor, while the Philistines seemingly enjoyed superior weaponry and military organization. Neither side managed to maintain the upper hand for very long, and the conflict dragged on for at least a century.

The greatest period of fighting took place in the 11th century BCE. The Israelites, divided and poorly led, suffered a series of crushing defeats that left the southern and central tribal territories vulnerable. The Philistines were briefly halted by Samuel's victory at the Battle of Mizpah, and then routed by an army led by King Saul at the Battle of Michmash. Both sides then raised fresh forces and met at the Valley of Elah. Strangely, no fighting occurred for some days, possibly weeks, while the two armies encamped across the valley from one another.

In order to break the stalemate, the Philistine champion Goliath offered to settle the battle in single combat. Young David took up the challenge, and the rest is Biblical history. David defeated and killed Goliath in what is considered to be history's definitive upset.

The Philistines, demoralized, were driven from the field, and David was rewarded with an appointment to Saul's court. At the time of this writing the site of the battle and the fortress were slated to be designated as a national park.

Of Interest: The Valley of Elah is relatively undeveloped and looks pretty much today as it did in David's time: a sparsely vegetated valley with a dry streambed running through the middle. During heavier rain periods, the stream reappears and the valley blooms. The camp of the Israelites probably stood to the north, while that of the Philistines was probably to the south. Virtually no archaeological evidence of the battle or the encampments has survived. However the ruins of the fortress of Elah, the Khirbet Qeiyafa, which date from the 10th century BCE, are preserved here in an archaeological park.

---

27. ABRAHAM'S WELL

Derekh Hebron 2, Be'er Sheva, Israel

Site Type: Biblical Site, Ancient Structure
Dates: Current well originally constructed c. 12th century CE
Designations: UNESCO World Heritage Site, Israeli National Park
Web: www.beer-sheva.muni.il/eng/tourism/pages/abrahamswell.aspx (municipal tourism website)

Abraham's Well is an ancient water source in the old city center of Be'er Sheva. According to tradition it is the same well dug by the Patriarch Abraham more than three and a half thousand years ago as recounted in the Biblical book of Genesis. While it is highly unlikely that a well would remain in use for such a long period, especially in a location abandoned for over a thousand years, the current well is likely close to the original location and probably uses the same water source.

At some point between his sojourn in Shechem and his burial in Hebron, the patriarch Abraham resided in the Canaanite settlement of Be'er Sheva. This seems to have been his primary residence in Canaan.

Around the time of his arrival Abraham concluded a peace treaty with a neighboring king named Abimelech. The pact included the right of ownership to the local well in exchange for seven lambs.

Biblical accounts indicate that the patriarchal family probably stayed in the area of Be'er Sheva even after Abraham's death. The city periodically appeared in other Biblical accounts of the Israelites, though little is known about Be'er Sheva for many centuries afterwards. It was probably abandoned, except by Bedouin nomads, during the early Islamic era. A new settlement was established here by the Ottomans in the late 19th century.

The structure known as Abraham's Well has been around since at least the mid-19th century. Some of the stonework indicates that it has existed since the 12th century. While there is no way to determine if this is the same location as Abraham's original well, the tradition is certainly very strong, and the site is considered to be of historic and religious importance. Abraham's Well is part of the Biblical Tels UNESCO World Heritage Site, as well as Tel Be'er Sheva National Park.

Of Interest: Abraham's Well is located on the edge of Be'er Sheva's old city center. While it still has access to water, the mouth of the well is protected by a grate. A visitor's center, recently completed at the time of this writing, is near the well. It has exhibits which talk about the life of Abraham and ancient Be'er Sheva. About three miles east of the old city is the primary location of Tel Be'er Sheva National Park, with ruins that date back to the 11th century BCE.

28. ISRAELI AIR FORCE MUSEUM

Hatzerim Airbase, Hatzerim, Israel

Site Type: Military Base, Museum
Dates: Opened in 1991
Web: www.iaf.org.il/46-en/iaf.aspx (official website)

The Israeli Air Force Museum is the largest military museum in Israel. Located on the grounds of Hatzerim Air Force Base, it is home to approximately a hundred aircraft that span the history of modern Israel. The extensive collection of military planes on display is comparable to some of the larger air force museums around the world.

The Israeli Air Force was founded in 1948, just after Israel's declaration of independence. In its early years it consisted of a hodge podge of aircraft hobbled together from a variety of sources. The Israeli Air Force saw its first actions during the War of Independence, which while limited in scope were nevertheless important in contributing to the outcome of the conflict.

Over the last seventy years the Israeli Air Force has grown significantly, playing a vital role in all of the wars of the Arab-Israeli conflict. Its darkest days came during the Yom Kippur War, when Arab strategic planning briefly hobbled Israeli air power. However the situation was soon reversed, and Israel inflicted serious losses on the air forces of Egypt and Syria. Today Israel fields the most modern air force in the Middle East.

Of Interest: The Israeli Air Force Museum is located at the Hatzerim Air Force Base. The collection was started in the 1970s as a boneyard and became a public museum in 1991. The hundred or so planes here are displayed out in the open. They represent virtually every type of plane ever used by the IAF. There are also a number of enemy planes on display that were either captured or shot down in Israel's various wars.

29. EIN GEDI NATURE RESERVE

Ein Gedi, Israel

Site Type: Biblical Site, Nature Reserve
Dates: Established in 1971
Designations: Israeli National Park
Web: www.parks.org.il/en/reserve-park/en-gedi-nature-reserve
(Israel national park website)

The Ein Gedi Nature Reserve is one of the most beautiful places in the Holy Land. Close to the Dead Sea and surrounded by the desert, Ein Gedi is an island of life in the wilderness. The oasis was well known to the Israelites in ancient times, and is famously associated with King David, who took refuge in a cave here when he was in hiding from Saul. Sparsely inhabited except for a relatively modern kibbutz, the Ein Gedi oasis and surrounding area is now part of the popular Ein Gedi Nature Reserve.

The area of the Ein Gedi oasis has been known to the people living in the area since prehistoric times. Ein Gedi is first mentioned in the Book of Joshua as the site of a town assigned to the territory of the tribe of Judah. Other Biblical accounts mention that Ein Gedi was a fishing village, and was probably a stopover point for caravans and travelers coming to the Judean heartlands from the southeast.

Ein Gedi is perhaps most famous for its role in the story of David. In the years following the Battle of Elah, David became a national hero. Unfortunately he became a little too popular, and King Saul, consumed with jealousy, decided to have him killed. David fled into the Judean wilderness with a small band of followers, hiding out in or near what is believed to be the Ein Gedi Oasis.

Ein Gedi is mentioned several other times in the Bible. Solomon wrote of it in the Song of Solomon, mentioning the oasis' palm trees and vineyards. It was also the gathering place for the armies of Moab and Ammon when they invaded Judah in the 9th century BCE. For a time Ein Gedi seemed to have escaped the worst of the carnage brought upon Israel by successive waves of conquerors, but its luck ran out in the 6th century CE when the Jewish settlement was destroyed by a punitive expedition of the Byzantine Empire. Afterwards it remained only periodically inhabited until the restoration of Israel in the 20th century.

Of Interest: The Ein Gedi Nature Reserve is a large park that includes both the oasis and some of the surrounding desert. The scenery boasts a rugged, rocky landscape, caves, freshwater pools and waterfalls. The entire park is criss-crossed with hiking trails. The oasis is fed by four springs and supports an array of vegetation and wildlife. There are a number of caves in the Ein Gedi area, including some which may have sheltered David and his men. Also in the reserve is the Ein Gedi National Antiquities Park, which is home to the ruins of the ancient Jewish settlement and synagogue.

---

30. MASADA NATIONAL PARK

Arad, Israel

Site Type: Archaeological Site, Fortress
Dates: Originally completed c. 30 BCE; national park opened in 2001
Designations: UNESCO World Heritage Site, Israeli National Park
Web: www.parks.org.il/en/reserve-park/masada-national-park (Israel national park website)

Masada National Park is home to one of Israel's most tragic and beloved historic sites: the Masada Fortress, a sprawling mountaintop palace built by Herod the Great in the 1st century BCE. The location of one of the saddest chapters in the history of ancient Israel, it was here that Zealots of the Great Revolt made their final stand against the Roman Empire. After a ferocious and literally suicidal defense, the fortress finally fell to the Romans. Afterwards the site was largely abandoned. The Masada Fortress has become one of modern Israel's most popular pilgrimage destinations.

The mountain where the Masada ruins can be found was probably not inhabited or built upon until Jonathan the Maccabee established a small military outpost there in the 2nd century BCE. During the prolific building period of Herod the Great, the fortifications of Masada were expanded on a massive scale as a defense for the remote palace he constructed here.

The fortress was probably of little military importance until the Roman destruction of Jerusalem in 70 CE. During the Great Revolt the Zealots seized Masada. After the Romans had conquered all of Judea, the last free Jews still in rebellion fled here. In 73 CE the Romans surrounded the mountain and began a siege of the fortress. Masada was fanatically defended by fewer than a thousand Jews, many of whom were women and children. Nevertheless the siege lasted for months, a situation which favored the well-supplied defenders.

In order to break the stalemate the Romans constructed an immense ramp with which to reach the top with their siege weapons. Despite the desperate and valiant efforts of the defenders the Romans eventually breached the wall. Rather than be taken alive, almost every one of the rebels committed suicide. There are no further records of military operations at the site, though archaeological expeditions to Masada have uncovered evidence of occupation by Byzantines, Muslims, Crusaders, and others. After Israel reoccupied the area, the fortress became an important pilgrimage destination. Masada National Park is a UNESCO World Heritage Site.

Of Interest: Masada National Park consists of the massive plateau where the fortress is located and some of the surrounding area. Steep slopes on every side rise almost vertically at the summit. There are several ways to reach the top: a winding road known as the Snake Path, the Roman siege ramp which still stands to this day, and a cable car. Most tourists arrive via the cable car. The ruins at the top of Masada are extensive. The perimeter of the plateau is still partially fortified with Herod's massive wall. Most of the more interesting sites are located at the north end where Herod built his main palace and scenic terrace. A small synagogue stands just to the west. The ruins of a second palace are located near the center of the western wall. Other ruins scattered about the place include residences, baths, storehouses and the like. The southern tip of the plateau is occupied by the ruins of a small citadel.

31. BEN-GURION DESERT HOME

Kibbutz Sde Boker, Sde Boker, Israel

Site Type: Historic Residence, Kibbutz, Museum
Dates: Kibbutz founded in 1952; Museum opened in 1977
Web: www.bgh.org.il/web/en/bengurionhut (official website)

The Ben-Gurion Desert Home, also known as Ben-Gurion's Hut, was the home of David Ben-Gurion for the last twenty years of his life. Located at the Sde Boker Kibbutz in southern Israel, the hut was symbolic of the simple life Ben-Gurion wished to lead after serving as the Prime Minister of Israel. After his death the hut was preserved the way he left it and repurposed as a museum honoring his life and work.

David Ben-Gurion is one of the great heroes of the Jewish people in the 20th century. The first prime minister of modern Israel, he is regarded as the nation's founding father. Born in Poland in 1886, he spent his early years in the Pale of Settlement and his twenties traveling and living in the Middle East. In 1915 he settled for a time in New York City.

After the issuance of the Balfour Declaration, Ben-Gurion became a leading figure in the Zionist movement. It was Ben-Gurion who read Israel's declaration of independence to the world in 1948. He was elected the country's first prime minister in 1949, serving in that post until 1963 with a two-year hiatus in the mid-1950s. By the time of is death in 1973 David Ben-Gurion had become firmly established as a national hero and as one of the leading world figures of the postwar era. The house where he lived in the desert is now a popular tourist site.

Of Interest: The Ben-Gurion Desert Home is the preserved residence of David Ben-Gurion at the Sde Boker Kibbutz. The hut itself was left exactly as it was in 1973. A visitor's center on site serves as a museum with exhibits on the life and work of Israel's first prime minister. There is also an exhibit on the settlement of the Negev. David Ben-Gurion and his wife Paula are buried near Sde Boker at the Midreshet Ben-Gurion.

32. TIMNA PARK

Timna Park, Eilat, Israel

Site Type: Archaeological Site, Nature Reserve
Dates: Established in 1981
Web: www.parktimna.co.il (official website)

Timna Park at the southern end of Israel is both a natural wonder and one of the country's oldest inhabited areas. The region is home to some of the world's earliest copper mines, an incredibly valuable commodity during the Bronze Age. It is possible that these mines were a major source of King Solomon's wealth. Timna Park is home to several archaeological sites as well as spectacular scenery.

Copper mining in the area of Timna was first carried out either by the Egyptians, Midianites or Edomites, or possibly all three. The ancient Israelites were certainly aware of the abundance of this precious metal, and they may have worked mines in the region even before the kingdoms were established. It is also possible that Israelite merchants were actively involved in the copper trade as early as the period of the Judges.

The ancient Kingdom of Israel reached the peak of its political and military might during the reign of Solomon. At this time the southern border reached to the Brook of Egypt, a line of control that probably extended from the Mediterranean Sea to the Gulf of Aqaba. This gave the Israelites access to the lucrative sea trade with the Arabian Peninsula as well as the copper mines of the Sinai.

The Israelite control over the region probably ended soon after Solomon's reign. Nevertheless copper mining continued at Timna by other nations and empires who passed through the region. This went on at least until the early Muslim era, and it was mostly finished by the Late Middle Ages. Timna Park became part of the modern state of Israel at the time of its independence. It is now a popular destination for both archaeologists and nature lovers.

Of Interest: Timna Park, located near the southern edge of the Negev Desert, is an incredibly beautiful area reminiscent of the American southwest. There are spectacular natural features, including rock monoliths and caves. Archaeological ruins include the remains of ancient settlements, mines, copper smelting facilities and even an Egyptian temple. Of particular interest is the Timna mine, thought to be the oldest known copper mine in the world. Much of the history of the site is recounted at the Mines of Time exhibit in the park's visitor's center, where artifacts from the area are also on display.

NORTHERN ISRAEL

33. ELIJAH'S CAVE

Allenby Road, Mount Carmel, Haifa, Israel

Site Type: Biblical Site
Dates: Possibly inhabited c. 9th century BCE
Web: www.kkl-jnf.org/tourism-and-recreation/tours/elijah-mount-carmel-prophet (Jewish National Fund website)

Elijah's Cave on Mount Carmel is a site that has been revered by Jews and others for millennia. The prophet Elijah spent several years residing on Mount Carmel, possibly in this cave. Evidence suggests that Elijah's Cave has been recognized as a sacred site at least as far back as the Byzantine period, though Jewish tradition placing Elijah here may be far older. A second site located beneath the Stella Maris monastery further up the slope also has a shrine identified as Elijah's Cave. This article is about the Jewish shrine.

Elijah was one of the most important figures in the later history of the Hebrew Bible. Little is known of his early life. According to tradition he lived on Mount Carmel. Most of his career revolved around his confrontations with Ahab, the king of Israel, and Jezebel, his Phoenician wife, both of whom endeavored to introduce the religion of Baal into the Northern Kingdom. Almost all of these confrontations involved miraculous activites and disasters brought down upon Israel.

Elijah is regarded as one of the most important prophets of the Hebrew Bible. Some of the greatest miracles of the Old Testament were enacted by Elijah. Like Moses he spoke to God upon Mount Horeb, and later ascended directly to Heaven from an undisclosed location on the far side of the Jordan River. Both Elijah and Moses are closely connected to Jewish messianic teachings, and both are commemorated during the festival of Passover.

Much of Elijah's life took place in and around Mount Carmel. When he wasn't in hiding elsewhere or confronting Israel's rulers, he seems to have spent most of his time here. He prayed in a cave on the mountain before his famous confrontation with the priests of Baal. In his later years he instructed his disciples here, including his successor Elisha. Many hermits have lived in the cave, and it has been recognized as a sacred place for at least fifteen centuries.

Of Interest: The Cave of Elijah, specifically the Jewish shrine on Mount Carmel's lower slopes, is an actual cave with some stone masonry work. It can be accessed by a ramp and bridge from the bottom of the mountain or a steep staircase from the top. The cave is an active place of Jewish worship, and is divided down the middle by a screen to separate male and female visitors. An alcove at the back, covered by a curtain, is believed by tradition to be where Elijah slept.

---

34. NATIONAL MARITIME & CLANDESTINE IMMIGRATION AND NAVAL MUSEUMS

Allenby Road 198 & 204, Haifa, Israel

Site Type: Museums
Dates: National Maritime Museum opened in 1953; Clandestine I&N Museum opened in 1969
Web: www.nmm.org.il & https://museums.mod.gov.il/sites/haapala (official websites)

The National Maritime Museum and Clandestine Immigration and Naval Museum are neighboring instutitions in Haifa that tell the story of Israel at sea. The first museum covers the history of seagoing vessels in the region, from ancient times through the Ottoman era. The second museum covers the history of the navy of modern Israel, as well as the maritime operations which smuggled thousands of Jews into the Holy Land during the British Mandate period.

The National Maritime Museum was founded in the 1950s as an exhibit for the collection of Aryeh ben Ali. It was conceived as an institution that would tell the maritime history of the Eastern Mediterranean Sea, from the early Egyptians to the Phoenicians and

Greeks and so forth to the early modern era. The museum moved to its current site in the 1970s.

The Clandestine Immigration and Naval Museum tells the story of the Jewish people at sea for the last century. Most of the focus is on the epic struggle to rescue Jews from Europe and relocate them to the Holy Land during the years of the British Mandate. These efforts took on great importance, especially in the wake of the devastation of the Holocaust and the rise of anti-Semitism in the post-war Middle East.

Of Interest: The National Maritime Museum covers maritime history and marine archaeology. Its collection ranges from ancient artifacts like anchors and pottery to artwork. The main exhibit tells the story of the seagoing vessels that have plied the waters of the Eastern Mediterannean for thousands of years. The Clandestine Immigration and Naval Museum has exhibits on Jewish smuggling operations and on the Israeli navy. Of particular interest are the naval craft on display on the grounds of the museum, including an Israeli submarine and an immigration ship that was used in the 1940s. Of related interest is a recently dedicated memorial to the ship Exodus, featured in the film of the same name, which brought Jewish immigrants to Israel from Europe. The monument is located nearby at the Port of Haifa.

35. UNDERGROUND PRISONERS MUSEUM

Ha-Hagana Street 10, Akko, Israel

Site Type: Prison, Museum
Dates: Museum opened in 1991
Designations: UNESCO World Heritage Site
Web: https://museums.mod.gov.il/sites/aco (official website)

The Underground Prisoners Museum commemorates those fighters who defied the authority of the British Mandate in Palestine in order to protect Jews and Jewish communities. During this period there were two prisons for insurrectionists in the Holy Land. One was in

Jerusalem and the other one in Akko. Both prisons are now home to underground prisoner museums. This chapter is about the one located in Akko.

From 1920 until 1948 the former Ottoman territory of Palestine came under the jurisdiction of the British Empire through a mandate from the League of Nations. This was a period of great unrest in the Holy Land, with regular infighting between the Jews, Arabs and the British. In order to protect the Jews living in Palestine several paramilitary organizations were formed, notably Haganah, a forerunner of the Israeli Defense Forces.

Although such groups were mainly organized to resist Arab raids, they grew strong enough to cause problems for the British. Following several particular violent clashes, some of these fighters were arrested and imprisoned in the old Ottoman garrison of Akko. Among the more famous prisoners incarcerated here was Moshe Dayan, who later served as chief of staff of the Israeli Defense Forces. A mostly successful prison break took place at Akko in 1947. The prison was converted into a museum in 1991. The Underground Prisoners Museum is part of the Old City of Acre UNESCO World Heritage Site.

Of Interest: The Underground Prisoners Museum, located in the former Akko Prison, houses exhibits related to the Jewish resistance fighters of the British Mandate period. In particular it focuses on the time they spent incarcerated here prior to Israel's declaration of independence. There is also an exhibit on the prison break of 1947. A monument commemorating the breakout is located nearby along the old city waterfront.

36. GHETTO FIGHTERS' HOUSE

Ghetto Fighters, Lohamei HaGeta'ot, Israel

Site Type: Kibbutz, Museum, Holocaust Memorial
Dates: Established in 1949
Web: www.gfh.org.il (official website)

The Ghetto Fighters' House is considered by some to be the world's first Holocaust museum. Known in full as the Itzhak Katzenelson Holocaust and Jewish Resistance Heritage Museum, the Ghetto Fighters' House commemorates the victims of the Holocaust with a focus on the activities of Jewish resistance fighters. The house now serves as a major Shoah memorial in Northern Israel.

At the end of World War II a number of survivors of the Warsaw Ghetto Uprising, along with other Jewish partisans who fought against the Nazis, relocated to Israel. In 1949 they established the kibbutz known as Lohmei HaGeta'ot, or Ghetto Fighters' Kibbutz. This became one the new nation's most famous communities, and numerous Holocaust survivors settled here after the war.

Over time the Ghetto Fighters' Kibbutz became a popular location in Northern Israel for Holocaust observances. It was one of the first places in the world to commemorate Holocaust and Heroism Remembrance Day. A number of monuments and museums have been erected here, and the kibbutz has become a popular tourist destination.

Of Interest: The Ghetto Fighters' House is a large complex that dominates the Lohmei HaGeta'ot Kibbutz. The main museum houses exhibits on Jewish Warsaw and the Warsaw Ghetto Uprising. There is also a documentation exhibit with first hand accounts of those who survived the Holocaust and founded the Ghetto Fighters' Kibbutz. A newer addition to the complex, the Yad Layeled Children's Memorial Museum, has exhibits on Jewish children who lived in the ghettos and concentration camps during the Nazi reign of terror.

---

37. ATLIT DETAINEE CAMP MUSEUM

Highway 7110, Atlit, Israel

Site Type: Detention Camp, Museum
Dates: Camp opened in 1940
Designations: Israeli National Heritage Site
Web: https://Shimur.org/sites/atlit-detention-camp (Council for Conservation of Heritage Sites in Israel website)

The Atlit Detainee Camp Museum is a former detention center dating from the time of the British Mandate. Originally established as a prison camp, Atlit is most famous for the thousands of Jewish refugees that were detained here after fleeing from Nazi occupied Europe. It continued to be used to incarcerate Jews who illegally arrived in the Holy Land after the war. The camp is now maintained as a museum.

Jews from Europe began immigrating to the Holy Land as early as the 1880s. In general immigration was fairly well organized and controlled by first the Ottoman Empire and later the British Empire. However, with the Nazi rise to power in Germany in 1933, Jewish immigration to the Holy Land increased from a trickle to a flood. With the implementation of the Final Solution, the flood became a torrent.

Large numbers of Jews desperately tried to reach the safety of Palestine. However, due to political pressure, the British only allowed a small number of refugees in. Others tried to get there by any means possible. Many of these were caught and interred at Atlit. This continued even after the war, ending only with the establishment of the modern nation of Israel. The Atlit Detainee Camp is now run as a museum and was declared an Israel National Heritage Site in 1987.

Of Interest: The Atlit Detainee Camp Museum is located at the original site of the camp. Many of the buildings and structures have been preserved and restored, including barracks where immigrants were incarcerated, common ares, watchtowers and fences, some of the latter still crowned with barbed wire. There are also exhibits on the journey of Jewish immigrants to the Holy Land in the years leading up to Israeli independence.

---

38. TEL MEGIDDO NATIONAL PARK & JEZREEL VALLEY

Road 66, Megiddo Junction, Israel

Site Type: Biblical Site, Archaeological Site, Nature Reserve
Dates: Originally settled by Israelites c. 12th century BCE
Designations: UNESCO World Heritage Site, Israeli National Park
Web: www.parks.org.il/en/reserve-park/tel-megiddo-armageddon-national-park (Israel national park website)

Tel Megiddo National Park is an archaeological site located in Israel's Jezreel Valley. This valley, also known as the Plain of Megiddo, is Israel's most famous battlefield. Countless armies have raged across this vast open and highly strategic valley, from the Egyptians and Canaanites in ancient times to the British and Ottomans during World War I. The best known Biblical conflict that has occurred at Megiddo was the conflict between the Canaanites and the Israelites that occurred during the days of the prophetess Deborah.

The Jezreel Valley stretches out from the eastern slopes of the Carmel Mountains towards the Jordan River Valley. One of the first documented battles in history was fought here around 1480 BCE, when an expeditionary force from Egypt crushed a coalition of Canaanite kingdoms. The Egyptians passed through the area again a few centuries later on their way to fight the Hittites at the Battle of Kadesh.

The most famous battle that took place at Jezreel in Biblical times occurred sometime around the 12th century BCE. During the days of the Judges, Deborah was called upon to defend the northern tribal territories from an army of Canaanites. Assisted by Barak, a general from the tribe of Naphtali, she assembled an army of ten thousand warriors at Mount Tabor on the western side of Megiddo. From there she led the Israelites to victory, routing the Canaanites and securing the northern frontier of Israel.

Egyptian armies returned in the 10th century BCE, and again in the 9th century BCE. The second time they were merely passing through when the Judean King Josiah unwisely decided to deny them passage. He paid for the decision with his own life and the lives of many of his soldiers. Over the course of centuries virtually every army that conquered the region passed through the Jezreel Valley at some point. The last major battle at Megiddo took place between the British and the Ottomans during one of the final campaigns of World War I. Tel Megiddo National Park is part of the Biblical Tels UNESCO World Heritage Site.

Of Interest: The Valley of Jezeel stretches between Mount Tabor in the east and Mount Carmel in the west. A great pass runs through it from north to south. Megiddo technically refers to Tel Megiddo, a long-inhabited hill that commands a wide view of the valley. Tel Megiddo and part of the surrounding area have been incorporated into the Tel Megiddo National Park. This park includes a number of archaeological sites, including excavations of at least twenty layers of civilization dating back well over three thousand years. The park also has a museum with exhibits on the history of the area.

---

39. MUSEUM OF PIONEER SETTLEMENT

Kibbutz Yifat, Yifat, Israel

Site Type: Kibbutz, Museum
Dates: Opened in 1972
Web: www.pioneers.co.il (official website)

The Museum of Pioneer Settlement, located at Kibbutz Yifat, tells the story of Jewish settlers who came to Palestine in the late 19th and early 20th centuries. This period in Israel's history, when the modern

Aliyahs began, was critical in the eventual establishment of a Jewish homeland in the Holy Land. Those who immigrated to Israel at this time were for all intents and purposes pioneers, paving the way for large numbers of Jews who relocated here after World War II.

The decades leading up to the First World War were not easy for the Jews of Eastern Europe. Pogroms were rampant and growing increasingly brutal in Russia and its territories. In 1882 the Aliyahs began, Aliyah being a reference to the Jewish return to Zion. In the following three decades approximately seventy-five thousand Jews fled Russia and went to the Ottoman province of Syria. From there they continued to Palestine where they settled in Tel Aviv as well as smaller communities around the country.

The new settlements were a real challenge for the immigrants. Most of the early work was agricultural in nature, and farming had largely been denied to the Jews of Europe for centuries as they were not allowed to own land. There was also the threat of hostile neighbors, and for the first time in many centuries the Jewish people had to learn to take up arms in self defense. The Museum of Pioneer Settlement commemorates the efforts of these early immigrants.

Of Interest: The Museum of Pioneer Settlement is appropriately located on the grounds of a kibbutz. It is home to exhibits on Jewish settler life in the late 19th and early 20th centuries. The main point of interest is an early settler dwelling, including furnishings and possessions typical of the era. There is also a turn of the century wagon as well as an exhibit of farming tools.

---

40. DEGANIA ALEF KIBBUTZ

Degania Alef Kibbutz, Degania Alef, Israel

Site Type: Kibbutz
Dates: Established in 1910
Web: https://degania.org.il (official website)

Degania Alef near the southern shore of the Sea of Galilee was one of the first of modern Israel's great institutions: the kibbutz. Founded in the early 20th century by Jewish settlers who wished to work the land as farmers, it became famous as a successful commune which was soon emulated by many other similar communities around Israel. For much of the 20th century the idea of Jewish life in Israel was often associated with life on a kibbutz. Today the settlement of Degania Alef is a cultural treasure of Israel and a model of the idea of communal living.

The late 19th and early 20th centuries saw the first large waves of Jewish immigration back to Israel in modern times. Many of these early settlers were idealists who desired to get back to the land and work the soil as farmers, an activity that had long been denied to them in Europe. In 1909 some unsettled land was acquired near the Sea of Galilee, and within two years a worker's commune had been established on the site. Thus was born Israel's first kibbutz: Degania Alef.

The formation of Degania Alef was a milestone in modern Israeli history. Throughout the rest of the 20th century many similar settlements sprang up all over Israel. Degania Alef served as a training base for workers at newly formed kibbutzes. Moshe Dayan, one of Israel's most important early leaders, was born here in 1915. Modern Israel also achieved its first major military victory here when the residents of Degania Alef held off invading soldiers from Syria in 1948. While the Degania Alef Kibbutz remains in operation, its decision to partially privatize in 2007 signaled the end of an era.

Of Interest: Degania Alef has long been one of Israel's best examples of kibbutz life, from the farms to the homes to the communal facilities. It is also something of a showpiece, with a number of sites of interest to visitors. One of the highlights is the Pioneer's Yard, a restoration of the original turn-of-the-century settlement. The Pioneer's Yard includes a small museum which details the history of Degania Alef. Also of note is the Defender's Garden, which commemorates those from the kibbutz who died in Israel's various wars. A Syrian tank, left in the spot where it was disabled in 1948, recalls the settlement's 1948 victory.

41. TOMB OF AKIVA BEN YOSEF

Karkom Street, Tiberias, Israel

Site Type: Burial Site
Dates: Akiva ben Yosef buried c. 134 CE
Web: https://info.goisrael.com/en/tiberias-4-286141 (Israel national tourism website)

The Tomb of Akiva ben Yosef, an important rabbi of the post-Temple period, is one of the reasons that Tiberias is one of the four sacred cities of Judaism. Akiva, who lived through several Jewish revolts against the Romans, was a champion of Rabbinic Judaism after the destruction of Jerusalem. He had many followers and helped to reestablish Jewish religious and political leadership in the 2nd century CE. For these reasons Akiva ben Yosef is considered among the most influential rabbis of all time.

It is generally believed that the destruction of the Temple in Jerusalem, the crushing of the various Jewish revolts and the Diaspora that followed left the Holy Land devoid of Jews. This is actually far from the case, and a large community continued to thrive in the north, especially around the Sea of Galilee. The council of the Sanhedrin, now dominated by rabbis, retreated to the north and began to assert its religious authority over Jewish life.

Akiva ben Joseph played a critical role at this juncture in Jewish history. In addition to helping to keep religious life intact after the fall of Jerusalem, he was one of the authors of the Mishnah, a central text of the Talmud. Many Jewish leaders of the era studied under Akiva, including Shimon bar Yochai. According to tradition Akiva had thousands of students and followers at the time of his death.

Rabbi Akiva backed Simon bar Khokhba in his revolt, and may have even fought alongside the rebels. He was eventually captured by the Romans, tortured and killed sometime around 134 CE. Nevertheless the roots of Jewish leadership that he helped to establish in the north survived. His efforts made him one of the first great leaders of the Jewish Diaspora.

Of Interest: The Tomb of Akiva ben Yosef is something of an architectural oddity, consisting of a mix of ancient and modern elements. It is located in a small courtyard partially enclosed by very old walls as well as newer walls and fencing. The tomb itself is embedded in the wall, flanked by stones engraved with some of the rabbi's writings.

---

42. TOMB OF MOSES MAIMONIDES

Ben Zakkai Street, Tiberias, Israel

Site Type: Burial Site
Dates: Moses Maimonides buried c. 1204 CE
Web: https://info.goisrael.com/en/tiberias-4-286141 (Israel national tourism website)

The Tomb of Moses Maimonides is one of the great Jewish pilgrimage sites of the Galilee. Maimonides, also known as Rambam, was among the most important rabbis of all time, and arguably the most influential Jewish leader of the Middle Ages. An outstanding philosopher and physician, he walked with the giants of his day, Jewish, Christian and Muslim alike. His writings are among the most studied Jewish theological works ever composed. His gravesite is one of the most visited places in Tiberias.

Moses Maimonides was born in 1135 CE in Cordoba in Spain. Most of his early life was spent in the cities of Andalusia in southern Spain where he mastered medicine and Jewish law. When he turned thirteen the Almohads conquered Cordoba, and all Jews in the city were forced to choose between exile, conversion or death. His family chose the former. Maimonides relocated to Morocco where he studied at the prestigious Al Karouine University.

Sometime around the year 1169 he moved east to spend time in Palestine and Egypt and where he developed a great reputation as a physician. His fame grew so great that he was invited to personally attend the Muslim king Saladin. His influence was such that when he gave his blessing to the Biblical codex produced by Aaron ben Moses ben Asher, it was accepted as authoritative by the Jewish community at large. Maimonides was also acting physician to King Richard the Lionheart during the Third Crusade, and also probably studied under Ibn Rushd, the renowned Muslim scholar.

Maimonides died in Fustat in Egypt in 1204, although his body was later moved and buried in the city of Tiberias. By the time of his death he was universally known and respected by Jews, Muslims and Christians alike. He is renowned both for his adventures and his fourteen volume commentary on the Torah. His ideas continue to be a major cornerstone of Jewish scholarship. In addition to Tiberias, Maimonides is honored as a favorite son of Cordoba in Spain.

Of Interest: The Tomb of Moses Maimonides is one of the major Jewish pilgrimage sites of Tiberias. The tomb has seen a major renovation in recent years. Reopened in 2018, it is now located in a large built-out plaza and covered by a canopy. The entire site is topped with a modernesque superstructure resembling a crown, beneath which is the burial site of Maimonides.

---

43. TOMB OF THE MATRIARCHS

Tiberias, Israel

Site Type: Biblical Site, Burial Site
Dates: N/A
Web: https://info.goisrael.com/en/tiberias-4-286141 (Israel national tourism website)

The Tomb of the Matriarchs in Tiberias is, according to tradition, the location of the burials of several very prominent women of the Hebrew Bible. It is in some ways a companion to the Tombs of the Patriarchs in Hebron. While there are considerable questions about the authenticity of the site among both theologians and academics, the tomb is generally recognized as a monument to these historic women.

The six women represented at the Tomb of the Matriarchs come from three different periods in the history of ancient Israel. The first two, Zilpah and Bilhah, were the handmaidens of Leah and Rachel respectively, and each bore two children to Jacob. While the burial of Rachel in Bethlehem was documented in the Bible, and the burial of Leah in Hebron makes sense, there was no indication of where Zilpah and Bilhah were buried.

The next three women are Jochebed and Zipporah, the mother and wife of Moses, respectively; and Elisheba, the wife of Aaron. There is no indication of the fate of any of these women in the Biblical narrative, although it is likely that Jochebed died in Egypt and the others died in the wilderness. The final woman, Abigail, was the third wife of King David. She almost certainly lived in the tribal territory of Judah, and her death is undocumented. Based on the above, the presence of the graves of these six women in Tiberias at the Tomb of the Matriarchs should be taken with a large grain of salt.

Of Interest: The Tomb of the Matriarchs is, unlike most other Biblical tombs scattered around the Holy Land, a fairly modern structure. The graves of the six Matriarchs are located inside. However, most of these women likely died outside of the Holy Land, in some cases centuries before the area around the Galilee was even settled by the Israelites. The sixth, Abigail, had no known connection to the region. Most visitors accept the Tomb of the Matriarchs as more of a memorial than a true mausoleum.

---

44. ANCIENT SYNAGOGUE RUINS OF THE GALILEE REGION

Migdal, Capernaum & Nabratin, Galilee Region, Israel

Site Type: Synagogue Ruins
Dates: Magdala Synagogue originally built c. 1st century BCE, Capernaum Synagogue originally built c. 4th century CE, Nabratein Synagogue originally built c. 6th century CE
Web: None Available

The northeastern corner of modern Israel is home to some of the oldest synagogue ruins to be found anywhere. This is especially true in the area along the northern shore of the Sea of Galilee, which was the heart of the Jewish community in the Holy Land after the destruction of Jerusalem. Dating from the Roman and Byzantine periods, some of the best of these synagogue ruins are to be found at Migdal, Capernaum and Nabratein.

The first Israelite settlers in the Galilee region were probably members of the tribe of Naphtali in the time of the Judges. Despite being a major source of fresh water, the Galilee appears to have been only sparsely settled throughout much of ancient Jewish history. This changed dramatically after the revolts of the 1st and 2nd centuries CE, when many Jews relocated to the relative safety of the north. Eventually Jewish relations with the Roman Empire normalized, and the Galilee region became dotted with Jewish communities and synagogues.

Over time most of these ancient settlements and their synagogues succumbed to foreign invaders and natural disasters. However archaeological research around Galilee in recent years has led to the rediscovery of a number of these synagogues, including those of ancient Magdala, Capernaum and Nabratein. These are now counted among northern Israel's most important archaeological treasures.

Of Interest: The ruins of the ancient Synagogue of Magdala can be found in modern day Migdal. Built sometime around the mid-1st century BCE it is uncertain exactly when the synagogue was destroyed. Almost the entire foundation is intact, including some floor sections with surviving mosaics. Also here is a replica of the Magdala Stone, which has a rare ancient depiction of the great Menorah of Jerusalem. A little further north along the shore are the ruins of the Synagogue of Capernaum. These date to the Byzantine era, but stand on the ruins of another synagogue completed in the 1st century. The Nabratein Synagogue, built in the 6th century, is about ten miles north of the Sea of Galilee. While smaller than the other ruins, it survived longer, and was still in use during the early Muslim era.

45. SYNAGOGUE QUARTER OF TZFAT

Synagogue Quarter, Tzfat, Israel

Site Type: Historic Neighborhood, Synagogues
Dates: Abuhav Synagogue originally built c. 15th century CE; Caro Synagogue built c. 16th century; Ari Ashkenazi Synagogue built c. 16th century
Web: www.safed-home.com/touristinformationsafed.html (municipal tourism website)

The Synagogue Quarter of Tzfat is at the center of one of Judaism's four sacred cities. This is due in large part to the fact that the area around Tzfat was the focal point of Jewish religious leadership in the Holy Land following the Bar Kokhba Revolt. It was also an important center for Jewish scholars during the Ottoman era. For these reasons the city is packed with synagogues.

Tzfat, also known as Safed, is an ancient Jewish city that has existed at least as far back as the Roman era. The area around Tzfat and the neighboring town of Meron became an important center of Jewish learning after the final collapse of the Kingdom of Judea in the 2nd century CE. Unfortunately there is very little information available about the Jewish community here prior to the later Middle Ages.

Large numbers of Jews began to settle in Tzfat during the Ottoman period. Many of these were Sephardic Jews who had fled from Spain in the 15th and 16th centuries. Kabbalah, which had been developed in the area by Shimon bar Yochai centuries earlier, enjoyed a revival here around the same time. During the later years of the Ottoman Empire tensions between the Jews and local Arab Muslims led to periodic violence in Tzfat.

Things came to a head under the British Mandate. During the Israeli War of Independence Tzfat saw some of the most vicious fighting in the north. An Arab siege of the city's Jewish quarter nearly succeeded, but was ultimately defeated by Israeli forces. Since 1948 Tzfat has been a Jewish city. Its old quarter is packed with an impressive collection of synagogues.

Of Interest: The Synagogue Quarter earned its name from the fact that at its height this neighborhood had over thirty synagogues. Some of these are still standing. Among the most popular is the Abuhav Synagogue. Originally built in the 15th century, the current building dates from a reconstruction following an earthquake in the 19th century. Among its treasures is a Torah scroll written in the 1300s, one of the oldest in the world still in regular use. Other historic synagogues in the neighborhood include the Caro Synagogue, the Ari Ashkenazi Synagogue and the Ari Sephardic Synagogue. The latter two are both named in honor of the same rabbi. The Chernobyl Synagogue is more recent. Opened by Jews who left the ill-fated city during the Soviet era, it commemorates those who died in the disaster in 1986.

---

46. TOMBS OF HILLEL AND SHAMMAI

Mount Meron, Tzfat, Israel

Site Type: Burial Sites
Dates: Buried c. 1st century CE
Web: www.safed-home.com/touristinformationsafed.html
(municipal tourism website)

The Tombs of Hillel and Shammai are the traditional burial sites of two of ancient Judea's most influential rabbis. These theologians, who preceded Shimon bar Yochai, Akiva ben Joseph and Gamaliel, founded important schools of Jewish religious and legal thought that laid the groundwork for both the Talmud and rabbinic Judaism. Together these two schools became the foundation of Jewish ideas and practices that are still studied in the present day.

Hillel the Elder is considered by many to have been the greatest Jewish theologian during the Roman occupation of Judea. Born in Babylon, Hillel relocated to Judea sometime in the 1st century BCE. There he distinguished himself as a scholar, becoming active with the religious party known as the Pharisees. By the late-1st century BCE Hillel had become the head of the order of the Pharisees and had established the rabbinical school which later came to be known as the House of Hillel. He also wrote some of the earliest passages that were later incorporated into the Mishnah, the core text of the Talmud.

Shammai, the other great Jewish philosopher of the Roman era, was born about a half century after Hillel. He also established an important school and contributed important writings to the Mishnah. The schools of Hillel and Shammai were rival institutions. Shammai espoused a more orthodox philosophy which was predominant among the Sanhedrin, while Hillel was more progressive and dominant among the Pharisees. The rivalry was reflected in Jewish politics during the 1st century CE.

Debates between the two factions were apparently lively and productive. Nevertheless when Shammai's faction came to dominate the Council of the Sanhedrin, they made it clear who was in charge by dictating a number of ordinances deliberately confounding to the followers of Hillel. However the Hillel school ultimately won out, and it was that school which came to dominate after the fall of Jerusalem. Both Hillel and Shammai were pivotal figures in the establishment of rabbinical Judaism, and are among the most honored Jewish leaders of the Herodian era.

Of Interest: The Tomb of Hillel the Elder is located not too far away from that of Shimon bar Yohai. It occupies a humble sepulcher in a rocky cave on the hillside. Only the fact that the entrance has been hewn into a square shape gives any indication of anything noteworthy about it. A small pool of water near the tomb is reputed to have miraculous properties. The Tomb of Shammai is located at the bottom of the hill and close to the banks of the Meron River.

47. TOMB OF SHIMON BAR YOCHAI

Mount Meron, Tzfat, Israel

Site Type: Burial Site
Dates: Shimon bar Yochai buried c. 160 CE
Web: www.safed-home.com/touristinformationsafed.html
(municipal tourism website)

The Tomb of Shimon bar Yochai is one of the most important gravesites in Israel, especially to those interested in the practice known as Kabbalah. Bar Yochai was a student of Akiva ben Yosef and arguably the first great rabbi to emerge following the end of the Bar Kokhba revolt. Thousands of pilgrims travel to Tzfat every year to study Kabbalah and visit his tomb.

Shimon bar Yochai was born around the year 80 CE when the Jewish people were probably still in collective shock over the fall of Jerusalem and the destruction of the Second Temple. He lived in Northern Israel where he studied under some of the most prominent teachers of the day, including Akiva. In the years following the Bar Kokhba Revolt many of the leading rabbis of the day were killed. Bar Yochai survived but was forced to go into hiding. However he continued to study and write in secret.

Bar Yochai became famous among the Jews of Galilee for cleansing the city of Tiberias of the taint of the Herodians. He was the primary author of the Zohar, an early text associated with Jewish mysticism. Although an extra-Talmudic discipline, some of the Kabbalah's teachings were later incorporated into Talmudic study. The city of Tzfat was the unofficial center of the study of Kabbalah throughout the Jewish Diaspora and remains so today.

By the time Shimon bar Yochai died around 160 CE Northern Israel had become one one of the major centers of Jewish religious life. This was especially true after the Sanhedrin were permanently disbanded in the 5th century. For nearly two thousand years the community in Tzfat managed to survive the turbulence of over a dozen major wars. Scholars and pilgrims still make their way here to study Kabbalah and see the tomb of bar Yochai.

Visiting: The Tomb of Shimon bar Yochai is actually located in the Safed suburb of Meron, which in turn is located on the lower slopes of Mount Meron. The tomb is a large stone building crowned with a dome. The interior of the shrine is segregated to accommodate male and female visitors separately. The site where bar Yochai is buried is marked by a fenced-in stone memorial. Other Diaspora era rabbis who spent their lives trying to follow in bar Yochai's footsteps are also buried nearby.

---

48. TEL DAN NATURE RESERVE

Israel National Trail, Dan, Israel

Site Type: Biblical Site, Archaeological Site, Nature Reserve
Dates: Reserve established in 1974
Designations: Israeli National Park
Web: www.parks.org.il/en/reserve-park/tel-dan-nature-reserve
(Israel national park website)

Tel Dan is the site of the Biblical city of Dan, marking the north-ernmost end of Israel in both ancient and modern times. Some truly exceptional ruins can be found at the archaeological sites here, some of which predate the arrival of the Israelites in Canaan. In addition, Tel Dan and the surrounding area are part of a nature reserve, a lightly forested park filled with springs, streams and small lakes.

Dan is among the oldest settlements in the Holy Land, with evidence indicating the area's earliest residents arrived here more than six thousand years ago. Archaeological research has discovered ruins that date from the Canaanite period. The name of the city at this time was Laysha, and it was likely inhabited by Canaanites, Phoenicians or both.

According to the Bible the Dannites, one of the Twelve Tribes of

Israel, were displaced from their territory near the central coast of the country by invading Philistines some time around the 11th century BCE. Relocating north they conquered Laysha and took it as their new capital. Dan became part of the Northern Kingdom and was home to one of Israel's two famous calf statues. Dan was destroyed during the Assyrian invasion in the 8th century BCE. The Tel Dan Nature Reserve is an Israel National Park site.

Of Interest: Tel Dan is home to one of the most extensive archaeological sites in Northern Israel. A canopy protects portions of the archaeological dig site. Ruins span both the Bronze and Iron Ages and include the remains of some of the fortifications and several city gates. There are also remains of a site possibly used for religious purposes as well as an ancient flour mill. The nature reserve is home to the Dan Spring and the stream it feeds, as well as several other tranquil water features.

WEST BANK

49. CAVE OF THE PATRIARCHS

Simtat Erez, Hebron, West Bank

Site Type: Biblical Site, Burial Site, Synagogue
Dates: Originally constructed c. 4 BCE
Designations: UNESCO World Heritage Site, Israeli National Heritage Site
Web: www.hebronfund.org/cave-machpelah-overview (The Hebron Fund website)

The Cave of the Patriarchs was among the earliest places of pilgrimage for the ancient Israelites, and possibly the oldest major shrine of the Abrahamic faiths. According to tradition that dates back thousands of years, it is the place where Abraham, Isaac and Jacob are buried along with some of their wives. For many Jews it is the second most sacred site after the Western Wall in Jerusalem. While the shrine above the cave was built at a much later period, it still dates back to the days of Herod the Great, making it the Holy Land's most enduring shrine.

According to the Torah, Abraham purchased the Cave of Machpelah from Ephron the Hittite for four hundred silver shekels. It was originally intended for the burial of his wife Sarah, but over the next century it became a family tomb. The body of Jacob, brought back from Egypt by his sons, was probably the last to be interred here. Following the return of the Israelites to Canaan, Hebron became an important center of religious life. It was assigned to the territory of the tribe of Judah, and briefly served as capital of the united kingdom of Israel during the reign of David.

After the Bar Khokba Revolt in the 2nd century CE Hebron and the Cave of Machpelah changed hands numerous times. Each subsequent conquerer apparently treated the site with reverence, and unlike virtually all other shrines in the Holy Land, the structure has remained mostly intact for the better part of two thousand years. Under the various Islamic dynasties Hebron became a major pilgrimage destination for Muslims, and though Jews continued to venerate the shrine, by the end of the 13th century they were barred from entering.

In the ensuing years the fortunes of the Jews of Hebron slowly ebbed, until the 20th century when significant numbers began to return to the area. Religious tensions between Hebron's Jews and Muslims broke out in open hostility in 1929 when many settlers in the area were killed and the rest forced to flee. Over the next thirty-eight years Jews were kept out of Hebron and all signs of Jewish habitation were destroyed. This state of affairs continued until 1967 when Israel annexed the city, and Jews visited the shrine for the first time in centuries. The Cave of the Patriarchs is part of the Hebron/Al-Khalid Old Town UNESCO World Heritage Site has been designated an Israel National Heritage Site.

Of Interest: The Cave of the Patriarchs consists of the Roman era shrine above and two caves below. The construction style is similar to major projects of the Herodian period, and the exterior appears much the same today as it did two thousand years ago. The interior of the shrine is divided into two halves, a mosque and a synagogue. A cenotaph honoring Isaac and Rebecca is in the mosque, and a cenotaph honoring Jacob and Leah is in the synagogue. The cenotaph of Abraham and Sarah is incorporated into the divider and can be seen from either side. According to tradition the actual bodies are buried beneath the shrine in the caves.

---

50. RUINS OF THE BETAR FORTRESS

Battir, West Bank

Site Type: Archaeological Site, Fortress
Dates: Originally completed c. 1st century CE
Designations: UNESCO World Heritage Site
Web: None Available

The Betar Fortress Ruins are the remains of an ancient walled city located near modern day Battir in the West Bank. This fortification has a history very similar to the much more famous Masada. It was here that Jewish rebels made their last stand against the Roman Empire at the end of the Bar Kokhba Revolt more than sixty years after Masada fell. The siege of Betar was much greater and more destructive than at Masada, and little remained standing when the Romans were through with it. The surviving ruins can still be seen nearly nineteen centuries later.

When the Great Revolt ended at Masada in 73 CE, many of the people of Judea lived to fight another day. The loss of their ancient capital was a situation that the surviving Jews could not bear. Within a few decades rebellion was again in the air. In 115 CE many conquered peoples in the eastern provinces rose up in open revolt while the Roman army was preoccupied fighting a major war against Persia. Around this time a new Jewish leader, Simon bar Kokhba, arose in Judea. A charismatic man and astute military leader, bar Kokhba was hailed by many of his Jewish contemporaries as the Messiah.

Simon bar Kokhba took his time carefully planning the the uprising, and when fighting broke out in 132 CE the Jews caught the Romans completely unprepared. The size and scope of the rebellion was much larger than before, and the Romans suffered enormous losses. It is believed that the entire 22nd Legion was annihilated by Jewish freedom fighters. But then the Romans countered by assembling one of the largest armies in the history of the empire.

The Bar Kokhba Revolt ended in much the same way as the Great Revolt did. Jerusalem was retaken, and the surviving rebels retreated to a hilltop refuge in the south, this time the Betar Fortress. Unlike at Masada, however, the rebels maintained a strong army which fought to the very end. According to legend, the Romans were so vengeful after Betar that the Jewish dead were not buried for nearly two decades. The fall of Betar marked the final end of the ancient Kingdom of Judea. The Ruins of the Betar Fortress are part of the Land of Olives and Vines UNESCO World Heritage Site.

Of Interest: The ruins of the Betar Fortress offer only a glimpse of the size and strength of the city as it might have stood in ancient Roman times. The original fortress and the surrounding Judean settlements were almost completely destroyed by the Romans in the 2nd century CE. Most of the best surviving remnants of the ancient city can be found on or close to the hill-top.

---

51. TOMB OF RACHEL

Hebron Road, Bethlehem, West Bank

Site Type: Biblical Site, Burial Site
Dates: Buried c. 16th century BCE
Designations: Israeli National Historic Site
Web: http://visitpalestine.ps/where-to-go/listing/bethlehem/
sites-attractions-bethlehem/christian-sites-bethlehem/rachels-tomb
(Palestine national tourism website)

The Tomb of Rachel is one of the oldest sacred sites in Israel. According to Biblical accounts, Rachel, the second wife of Jacob and the mother of Joseph and Benjamin, was buried here after dying in childbirth. Because of the tomb's documentation in the Hebrew Bible dating back thousands of years, it is one of the more reliable Biblical burial sites. The Tomb of Rachel is contemporary to the Tombs of the Patriarchs in Hebron.

Bethlehem was originally a fortified Canaanite town dating as far back as 3000 BCE. It made its first appearance in the Hebrew Bible long before the the time of David. Jacob, the grandson of Abraham, was passing through Bethlehem when his second wife Rachel gave birth to his twelfth and last son, Benjamin. She died while in labor, and Jacob acquired a small parcel of land and buried her beside the road here.

Pilgrims probably began visiting the tomb in very ancient times. Bethlehem continued to play a role in the Biblical narrative. It was home to Ruth, and later her great-grandson David, who went on to become King of Israel. More than a thousand years later Bethlehem became a sacred place to many non-Jews as the location of the Nativity in the Christian narrative. The Tomb of Rachel is an Israeli National Heritage Site.

Of Interest: The Tomb of Rachel is truly ancient, possibly dating back as far as the days of the Patriarchs. The shrine above the tomb is much more recent. It consists of two rooms, an antechamber and a small rotunda. The latter is crowned by a dome, which suggests either Islamic or Byzantine construction, but the building was actually financed and built by a Jewish businessman in the 19th century. A large stone marks the gravesite, while eleven smaller stones rest upon it. According to an unlikely tradition, these stones were put in place by Jacob's eleven sons, Benjamin being a newborn infant at the time.

---

52. QUMRAN NATIONAL PARK

Qumran, West Bank

Site Type: Archaeological Site, Nature Reserve
Dates: Dead Sea Scrolls discovered in 1947
Designations: Israeli National Park
Web: www.parks.org.il/en/reserve-park/qumran-park (Israel national park website)

Qumran National Park is a breathtaking place that combines ancient ruins with magnificent scenery. But it is not for either of these that the park is best known, but rather for one of the greatest archaeological finds in history: The Dead Sea Scrolls. Discovered by accident in 1947, these writings are among the most important surviving documents of ancient Judaism, and have become immensely valuable to religious scholars. Qumran, where the Dead Sea Scrolls archaeological site is located, has drawn hordes of historians, scientists and the curious ever since.

The history of Qumran and the Dead Sea Scrolls is closely bound to the Jewish sect known as the Essenes. The seclusive Essenes espoused communal living and kindness as being more important than strict obediance to the laws and customs enforced by the Sanhedrin. They rejected such practices as slave ownership and animal sacrifice, which put them at odds with Temple authorities.

The Essenes were apparently most active during the 1st century

BCE and the 1st century CE. The sect seems to have died out in the 2nd century CE, possibly because its members were absorbed by other groups. It is also possible that they were simply driven out or broken up by the Roman authorities after the Jewish revolts.

Despite being mentioned by writers of the day such as Josephus, the Essenes were largely forgotten by the end of the Byzantine period. They might have remained forgotten if not for the discovery of a vast cache of scrolls in the area around Qumran. Academic investigations have led to the conclusion that the Dead Sea Scrolls were left here by the Essenes. These writings have since proved immensely helpful for scholars in understanding the development of the Hebrew Bible.

Of Interest: Qumran National Park is home to a number of archaeological sites, including the ruins of an Essene settlement and the caves where the Dead Sea Scrolls were found. Excavations of the ruins have uncovered the remains of homes, a library, and buildings where pottery was manufactured. There are also a number of cisterns and baths used for ritual cleansings. The cliffs around the settlement are riddled with caves. To date scrolls and other ancient artifacts have been found in eleven different locations. The most important location is cave four, which was found to have well over a hundred Old Testament scrolls among other writings. Cave six is the most accessible and the most visited.

---

53. RUINS OF ANCIENT JERICHO

Jericho, West Bank

Site Type: Biblical Site, Archaeological Site
Dates: Original settlement established c. 10th millennium BCE
Web: http://visitpalestine.ps/jericho-intro (Palestine national tourism website)

The area around modern Jericho is home to some of the Holy Land's oldest archaeological sites. First settled over ten thousand years ago,

Jericho has a serious claim to the title of the world's oldest city. Jericho is also a place of Biblical fame thanks to its association with Joshua. Because of the Battle of Jericho that was fought there sometime around the 13th century BCE, it is arguably the best known of the Canaanite cities of the pre-Israelite era.

The city of Jericho is ancient even by Biblical standards. The earliest evidence of civilized habitation at the site is estimated to date back to around 9000 BCE. Ancient Jericho was probably rebuilt several times even before age of the Patriarchs, and was one of the region's leading cities by the middle of the 2nd millennium BCE.

Jericho's most famous moment on the world stage occurred when the Israelites arrived around 1300 BCE. This great walled city near the Jordan River guarded the eastern approaches into the Promised Land and was the Israelites' first military objective. Under the leadership of Joshua, warriors from the Twelve Tribes surrounded the city, and a weeklong siege ensued. On the seventh day of the battle Jericho's wall was breached. The city was subsequently destroyed and its inhabitants put to the sword.

The fall of Jericho sent shockwaves throughout the region, kicking off decades of warfare between the Israelites and the Canaanites. While Jericho has continued to be inhabited on and off ever since, it never quite returned to the status it had during the age of the Canaanites. Since the restoration of Israel, Jericho has once again grown into a sizeable city with a large Palestinian population. It was the first Palestinian city to be granted automony in the 1990s.

Of Interest: The area around the modern city of Jericho has many places of historical interest, with most of these located on or near the Tel Jericho archaeological site. Unfortunately almost nothing remains of the settlement of Joshua's time. However ruins of the ancient city walls from other periods are scattered around. Also here is the Spring of Elisha, the remains of a palace from the Hasmonean and Roman periods, and the ruins of a synagogue dating from the 1st century BCE. Not too far away is the site of what may have been ancient Gilgal, along with ruins that are believed to be the remains of an ancient Israelite encampment.

54. NABI SAMUEL NATIONAL PARK
& TOMB OF SAMUEL

Nabi Samwil, West Bank

Site Type: Biblical Site, Burial Site, Synagogue, Archaeological Site
Dates: Established in 1955
Designations: Israeli National Park
Web: www.parks.org.il/en/reserve-park/nebi-samuel-park (Israel national park website)

Nabi Samuel National Park is an archaeological site just north of Jerusalem that is home to an important Biblical treasure: the Tomb of the Prophet Samuel. Actually located in a shrine at the heart of the park, the tomb is counted among the more reliable locations for a Biblical burial site. The tomb is located beneath a former church which now houses both a mosque and a synagogue.

Samuel, the great prophet of Israel during the time of its transition from a confederation of tribes into a kingdom, was one of the most important figures of the Hebrew Bible between the times of Joshua and David. He was the last of the great Judges and the first of the great Prophets. Samuel was born in the town of Ramat and studied under the priest Eli. He spent most of his adult life wandering the tribal territories of Benjamin, Ephraim and Judah working to improve ties among the Israelite factions. He led a coalition of the tribes to victory over the Philistines at the Battle of Mizpah.

After the battle it was decided that the tribes needed a permanent and uniting leader. Samuel passed on the job for himself, anointing Saul in his stead. He then continued his wandering and work. After many long years of travel he died and was buried in his home city of Ramah. His tomb remained a sacred destination well after the Roman destruction of Judea. According to tradition, when the knights of the First Crusade arrived, they climbed the hill of Ramah, from whence they had their first sight of the city of Jerusalem. The Tomb of Samuel and the surrounding ruins are now incoporated into an Israeli National Park.

Of Interest: Nabi Samuel National Park covers a hill top that is believed to be the former site of the city of Ramah. The shrine which houses the Tomb of Samuel is at the top of the hill surrounded by ruins of older settlements. The building is actually a mosque, but the lower section where the tomb is located houses a synagogue. The tomb is inside the synagogue. The national park is an active archaeological site. The top of the hill affords a spectacular view of the surrounding area, which includes much of the ancient tribal territory of Benjamin.

---

55. TOMB OF THE MACCABEES ARCHAEOLOGICAL SITE

Horbat Ha-Gardi, West Bank

Site Type: Archaeological Site, Burial Site
Dates: Mausoleum originally constructed c. 2nd century BCE
Web: None Available

The Tomb of the Maccabees is an archaeological site near the modern city of Modi'in-Maccabim-Re'ut. Initially excavated in the 19th century, it wasn't until 2015 that archaeologists and academics began to take seriously the possibility that this was in fact the lost tomb of the Maccabee family. The Maccabees, the heroes of the Hanukkah story, were from the area around ancient Modi'in. While the jury is still out on whether or not this is the family burial site, it is a strong candidate.

The region of Modi'in was an important crossroads of ancient Israel. It was a stronghold of the Canaanites when the Israelites first arrived, and several battles were fought in the area during the period of the Judges. The rugged landscape and strategic location between Jerusalem and the sea made it a perfect hideout for fugitives and rebels. The area was a major rallying point for Jewish resistance against the Seleucids in the 2nd century BCE.

The Seleucid Empire, a successor state to the empire of Alexander the Great, was severely disliked by its Jewish subjects. A boiling point was reached in the year 167 BCE when the Seleucid king Antiochus outlawed the practice of Judaism and erected a statue of Zeus in the Great Temple of Jerusalem. A Jewish priest from Modi'in named Mattathias killed a Hellenized Jew who was about to make a sacrifice on a pagan altar. This event kicked off the Maccabean Revolt.

The revolt was carried out by Mattathias' five sons, notably Judah the Maccabee, which means "hammer". From the hills of central Judea the Maccabees waged a guerilla war against the Seleucids. It did not take the Jewish rebels long to drive their enemies from Jerusalem, after which they entered the Holy City in triumph and reconsecrated the Temple. At the height of the revolt Modi'in became not only an important military base, but the burial site of many Jews who died in the war. This included members of the Maccabee family, who later ruled over Judea as the Hasmonean dynasty.

Of Interest: The Tomb of the Maccabees is located in the rugged hills near Modi'in. While academics are not in full agreement that this is for certain the place where the Maccabees are buried, it was really the only major contender at the time of this writing. The site, much of which has been excavated, has numerous buildings and chambers. Remains of columns and pillars may have once supported the pyramidal roofs of the mausoleum. One strange and unexplained feature of the site is the presence of mosaics of crosses. It is possible that these were added to the tomb site by Christians in later centuries.

---

56. RUINS OF TEL SHILOH

Shilo, West Bank

Site Type: Biblical Site, Archaeological Site
Dates: Tabernacle originally set up here c. 13th century BCE
Web: None Available

Shiloh was the religious center of Israel for two and a half centuries following the Israelite conquest of Canaan. Established by Joshua, Shiloh was home to both the Tabernacle and the Ark of the Covenant throughout the era of the Judges. Three times per year every Israelite was required to visit the Tabernacle to leave offerings, a custom that was later assumed by the Temple in Jerusalem. Shiloh continues to be regarded as an important historic and religious site to many Samaritans, and some Jews, in the modern day.

In the years following the initial Israelite conquests in Canaan Joshua decided to give the Tabernacle and the Ark of the Covenant a permanent home in the territory of Ephraim. The place he chose was Shiloh. After the Tabernacle was established there the former Canaanite settlement quickly grew into a thriving town. It became an important seat of the descendents of Aaron, the Israelite high priests, and for centuries served as the religious heart of the new nation.

The Tabernacle and Ark remained in Shiloh throughout the period of the Judges. However following the Battle of Aphek in which the Israelites were routed by the Philistines, the Ark was taken and Shiloh was sacked. It is possible that the Tabernacle was destroyed at this time as there are no indications of its subsequent whereabouts. The Ark of the Covenant was eventually recovered by the Israelites.

After this event Shiloh continued to play a minor role in the history of Israel. Samuel, the last and greatest of the Judges, studied in Shiloh under the priest Eli. Later, in the years following the death of Solomon, it was in Shiloh that the Prophet Ahijah declared the independence of the northern ten tribes of Israel from the southern kingdom of Judah. Although Shiloh remained an important town until the Assyrian conquest, it was eclipsed by Jerusalem in Judah and Samaria in Israel, and never again regained its former importance.

Of Interest: Tel Shiloh has been identified as the site where ancient Shiloh once stood. A small settlement dating entirely from the 20th century now stands on the ancient site. The area in and around the new town is dotted with ruins that date back to the original settelement. Among the archaeological finds are the remains of a public building and grain silos. The location where it is believed the Tabernacle once stood is now home to a Jewish yeshiva.

57. TOMB OF JOSHUA

Kifl Hares, West Bank

Site Type: Biblical Site, Burial Site
Dates: Joshua buried c. 13th century BCE
Web: None Available

The Tomb of Joshua is a Biblical burial site of ancient tradition. Joshua, the last survivor of the Exodus and the first Judge of the Israelites, helped to set the stage for centuries of Jewish history. His death and burial in the city of Timnath-Heres was documented in the book of Joshua. Located in the modern city of Kifl Hares in the West Bank, the tomb is a popular albeit difficult to reach Jewish pilgrimage site.

Joshua was the popular leader of the tribe of Ephraim at the time of the Exodus. He is among the most important figures in the story of the Exodus and was one of Moses' chief followers. Joshua served as both a military commander and a spy for the Israelites, and had a close working relationship with Caleb of the tribe of Judah.

Just before Moses died he chose Joshua to lead the Israelites into Canaan. The subsequent military campaigns of Joshua in Canaan are legendary, beginning with his famous siege of the city of Jericho. Joshua spent the remainder of his years conquering the kingdoms of Canaan and dividing the lands among the Israelite tribes. He established his home at Timnath-Heres where he later died and was buried.

Joshua loosely united the tribes and established Israel geographically as a nation. His tomb was almost certainly a revered place, and was probably a pilgrimage destination during the kingdoms period. The ancient town of Timnath-Heres, believed to now be the Palestian city of Kifl Hares, still receives many visitors who seek Joshua's grave.

Of Interest: The Tomb of Joshua is fairly unassuming. Occupying only a small street corner in the middle of downtown Kifl Hares, it can be easily mistaken for a walled compound of a typical residence of the city. Unfortunately this sacred Jewish site may be recognized by the graffiti that is periodically scrawled on its outer walls. The main building is very simple: a white structure with a small dome, typical of other Biblical tombs in the Holy Land. The grave of Joshua lies beneath the dome. Tradition suggests that Joshua's father Nun and his friend Caleb are buried here as well.

---

58. RUINS OF ANCIENT SAMARIA

Sebastia, West Bank

Site Type: Biblical Site, Archaeological Site
Dates: City established c. 9th century BCE
Web: None Available

The ruins of ancient Samaria are not, strictly speaking, a site of Jewish interest. However, this capital of the Northern Kingdom did play an important role in the history of the ancient Israelites. At its peak Samaria is believed to have surpassed Jerusalem in size and splendor. Today the archaeological site of Samaria, located outside of the modern city of Nablus, remains of great historical importance as it is home to archaeological remnants of the former northern capital.

The united kingdom of Israel lasted for barely more than a century. Soon after Solomon's son Rehoboam was coronated, all but two of the tribes and some of the Levitical cities in the south had seceded. The main cause of the split was a resurgence of the old rivalry between the tribes of Judah and Ephraim. The latter grew tired of seeing the descendents of Judah on the throne in Jerusalem. When Rehoboam continued his father's crushing taxes and other unpopular policies, the northern tribes formed their own nation.

The new kingdom of Israel maintained its hold on the important cities of Shiloh, Gilgal and Shechem, with the latter serving as the capital. War broke out almost immediately, and Israel found itself surrounded by enemies. Shechem, located at the southern end of the kingdom, was extremely vulnerable due to its proximity to Judah. By the time of Omri, the sixth king of the Northern Kingdom, it was decided that a more secure location was needed. Samaria was established with strong fortifications, palaces, and even its own temple. It remained the capital of the Northern Kingdom for the next century and a half. However it was captured and sacked by the Assyrians in 721 BCE.

The conquest of Israel was not the end of the city of Samaria. Like Jerusalem, it was rebuilt in later years. When Israel was divided into provinces under the Romans, the province of Samaria was created, with the city of Samaria as its capital. This became the home city of the Samaritans, the descendents of the northern kingdom who still lived in the area. Under the Byzantines the city of Samaria faded into historical obscurity. It lives on today in the modern day city of Sebastia.

Of Interest: The ruins of the ancient city of Samaria are located just outside of Sebastia, a suburb of modern Nablus. Samaria was sacked on several occasions in ancient times, and little remains of the original settlement of Omri's reign. That said the ruins are extensive and scenic, and boast a number of sites which date back to the Israelite period. These include remnants of the city's walls and fortifications, some of which may have been erected under the direction of Omri. Other sections excavated date from the Seleucid and Roman periods.

59. RUINS OF ANCIENT SHECHEM & TOMB OF JOSEPH

Nablus, West Bank

Site Type: Biblical Site, Archaeological Site, Burial Site
Dates: Joseph buried c. 13th century BCE
Web: http://visitpalestine.ps/nablus-intro (Palestine national tourism website)

The Biblical city of Shechem, located in the modern day city of Nablus, is one of the West Bank's most interesting archaeological sites. Shechem played a minor role in ancient Israelite history, and Nablus is now home to several places of interest. Among these are the ruins of the ancient town, which was assaulted by the sons of Jacob during the age of the Patriarchs; and the Tomb of Joseph.

Shechem was an important settlement in Canaan even before Abraham arrived in the area. He may have lived here for a time before moving on to the south. Shechem periodically appeared in the stories of the Patriarchs. Jacob lived near here with his family before moving to Egypt. According to tradition his daughter Dinah was kidnapped by men from Shechem, and his sons Simeon and Levi took their revenge on the town by killing all of its inhabitants.

Shechem disappeared from the Biblical narrative for several centuries until Joshua captured the city during his conquest of Canaan. Shechem was allocated to the territory of the tribe of Ephraim and was chosen as the burial place of Joseph, whose body had been brought back from Egypt. During the early days of the kingdoms Shechem was one of Israel's most important political centers. After the death of Solomon the ten northern tribes declared their independence from Judah here. The first king, Jeroboam, was coronated in Shechem, and the city served for a time as the new nation's capital.

Following the conquest of the Northern Kingdom by Assyria Shechem more or less disappeared from the Biblical narrative. It remained an important city for the surviving Samaritans, but played no further significant role in ancient Jewish history. Today the city of Nablus stands on the site of ancient Shechem. Access to the Tomb of Joseph is complicated and may require special permission to visit.

Of Interest: Ancient Shechem is one of the best archaeological sites in the northern West Bank. Part of the Bronze Age wall is preserved, and it is easy to make out the general outline of the entire settlement as well some of the buildings. The Tomb of Joseph is located nearby in a different neighborhood. It consists of a small domed building similar to that of other Biblical burial sites. The tomb inside is very old. In addition to Joseph, it is believed that his sons Ephraim and Manessah may be buried here as well.

60. MOUNT GERIZIM

Nablus, West Bank

Site Type: Biblical Site, Archaeological Site
Dates: Temple originally constructed c. 5th century BCE
Web: http://visitpalestine.ps/nablus-intro (Palestine national tourism website)

Mount Gerizim is one of a pair of mountains that overlook the modern day city of Nablus in the West Bank. Located near the heart of what used to be the Northern Kingdom, Mount Gerezim and its twin Mount Ebal were important landmarks of ancient Israel. In the Samaritan tradition, Mount Gerizim remains a major holy site, especially close to its peak where an ancient Samaritan temple once stood.

According to the Hebrew Bible, when Joshua led the Israelites into Canaan, he brought them to the area of what is now Nablus in order to consecrate the newly conquered land. Representatives of six of the tribes ascended Mount Gerezim, where they called down God's blessing for their endeavors. Meanwhile, representatives of the other six tribes ascended the neighboring Mount Ebal, where they called down God's curse upon the enemies of Israel.

Even though the Tabernacle had been erected at Shiloh, and the Temple of Solomon had been erected in Jerusalem, Mount Gerizim remained a special and sacred place in the hearts of the Israelites. It is uncertain exactly when a temple was built on the mountain. But evidence strongly suggests that one was constructed there in the days following the Babylonian Captivity, and was probably destroyed sometime during the Hasmonean era.

Mount Gerizim has remained sacred to the Samaritans since pre-Roman times. The Byzantines constructed a church at the top of the mountain, prompting a massive revolt by the Samaritans in the 5th century CE. Even though the revolt was crushed, the Samaritans continue to regard the mountain as sacred. It remains an important pilgrimage destination to the present day.

Of Interest: Mount Gerizim towers over modern day Nablus. Its slopes are covered in ancient ruins, some of which are active archaeological sites. The most recognizeable landmark is the Byzantine Church which still stands on the mountain's peak. Sections of the ancient temple including the altar are believed to have been identified near the church at the top of the mountain. Samaritan religious festivals and holidays are still celebrated here.

MIDDLE EAST

61. GARDEN OF PEACE

Markou Drakou Street, Xylotymbou, Cyprus

Site Type: Monument
Dates: Dedicated in 2014
Web: None Available

The Garden of Peace is a public space in the town of Xylotymbou that commemorates the role that Cyprus played in the Jewish resettlement of Palestine in the 20th century. During the late 1940s over fifty thousand Jews, many survivors of the Holocaust, were detained here by British authorities while trying to get to Israel. While the internment camps are now long gone, there remains a special bond between Israel and Cyprus and their long shared history.

The story of the Jews in Cyprus is truly ancient. Barely 130 miles away across the Mediterranean Sea, it is likely that Israelites first visited the island as long as three thousand years ago. Jews probably settled on Cyprus during the Hasmonean period, and were certainly established there by the time both Cyprus and Judea were part of the Roman Empire.

The Jewish community of Cyprus may very well have continued without interruption from antiquity all the way until the modern era. During the Ottoman period many Sephardic Jews from the west settled on the island. Even more came during the British Mandate period, especially as anti-Semitism began to reach a fevered pitch in Germany in the 1930s.

After the war Cyprus found itself in the international spotlight when it became the detention location for Jews caught illegally entering into Palestine. Many Jewish immigrants making their way to the Holy Land by boat were stopped by the Royal Navy, taken into custody and held in camps on Cyprus. By 1949 an estimated fifty-three thousand were being held here. After the Israeli War of Independence most of these completed the journey to Israel. Their time on the island is commemorated at the Garden of Peace.

Of Interest: The Garden of Peace is located in the city of Xylotymbou where one of the major detention camps for Jewish refugees once stood. Dedicated in 2014, the garden is relatively new. Several monuments have been erected here, the main one thanking the people of Cyprus for their assistance to Holocaust survivors. Another one commemorates the Jewish children that were born in Cyprus during the later years of the British Mandate.

---

62. SIDON SYNAGOGUE

Harat al-Yahud, Saida, Lebanon

Site Type: Medieval Synagogue
Dates: Originally completed in 833 CE
Web: None Available

The Sidon Synagogue is one of the oldest intact synagogues in the world. Completed in the 9th century CE, it remained in use for over eleven hundred years. It was abandoned in in the 1970s when the last Jews of the community, which had probably been around since Biblical times, finally departed. There has been a renewed interest in the building among Jews and other tourists in the last few years.

The first Israelites to live in what is now Lebanon arrived there during the days of the Judges, possibly as early as the 12th century BCE. The tribal territories of Asher and Naphtali were near the Phoenician coastal cities, and the Hebrew Bible suggests that relations between the Israelites and Phoenicians were cordial. The Jewish community of Lebanon was possibly the oldest in the world outside of Israel.

The Christian New Testament indicates that there were Jews living in Lebanon in the 1st century CE, and new communities were probably founded by Jewish refugees after the revolts against the Romans. The synagogue was completed in the 9th century CE. Although information is incomplete, it appears that Jews have lived in Sidon nearly continuously since the Middle Ages.

During the 20th century the Jews of Lebanon became increasingly caught up in the politics of the region. The community started to come under attack after the creation of the state of Israel. Many left the country in the decades following the Israeli War of Independence. Most of the last Jews left in 1975, at which time the Sidon Synagogue was abandoned. It is estimated that there are fewer than a hundred Jews remaining in Lebanon today.

Of Interest: The Sidon Synagogue is truly old and feels it. The structure has thick fortress-like walls that partially account for the fact that it is still standing. It is believed that the building stands on the site of an even earlier synagogue that may have been constructed during the Roman era. The synagogue interior is very dilapidated, with few Jewish fixtures left. At the time of this writing, the building was being cared for by a Muslim family who moved inside around 1990.

---

63. SHOUF BIOSPHERE RESERVE

Becharre, Lebanon

Site Type: Biblical Site, Nature Reserve
Dates: Established in 1996
Designations: UNESCO World Heritage Site, Lebanon Nature Reserve
Web: http://shoufcedar.org (official website)

The Shouf Biosphere Reserve is the largest nature park in Lebanon and home to many of those trees of Biblical fame, the Cedars of Lebanon. These trees are mentioned many times in the Hebrew Bible, for their wood was prized and used in the construction of the First Temple. Although the cedar forests of the region have been decimated for centuries, a few of the ancient giants still exist. These are now part of a reserve where new trees have been planted and protected since the 19th century.

The Lebanon cedar tree is one of two major species of cedars, and one of the only coniferous species to be found in the Eastern Mediterranean region. Named for the mountain upon which they were first cultivated and harvested, they are native to Lebanon, Cyprus, Syria and Turkey. The wood of the cedar tree has been prized since ancient times, both for its strength and durability in construction as well as for its aroma.

The great cedar forest of Lebanon was considered a sacred place by the ancient Canaanites. The trade in cedar wood reached much of the Mediterranean world, from the cities of Phoenicia where it was used in shipbuilding and construction, to Egypt where its resin was used in the preparation of the dead. It was also prized for medicinal and religious purposes. Demand for cedar wood skyrocketed during the reigns of the kings David and Solomon, who used the trees in their building projects.

In later centuries the cedar forests of Lebanon were plundered by everyone from the Assyrians to the Ottomans. It was only in the 19th century that conservancy efforts were finally introduced. By that time less than twenty trees over a thousand years old were still standing. Today the surviving trees are fiercely protected in a government sponsored nature reserve. Some of the trees can be found in the Forest of Cedars of God UNESCO World Heritage Site.

Of Interest: The Shouf Biosphere Reserve covers a large area in and around Mount Lebanon. It is a highly diverse terrain, with mountains, hills, lowlands, forests and wetlands, and is home to a number of large animal species that are otherwise long gone from the region. The main attraction of the reserve is the three magnificent forests of cedar trees. The most popular site within these forests are the groves which contain the dozen or so ancient giants, cedar trees which tower as high as a hundred and thirty feet and which date back to the days of the Byzantines.

64. CENTRAL SYNAGOGUE OF ALEPPO

Aleppo, Syria

Site Type: Medieval Synagogue
Dates: Current building completed c. 15th century
Designations: UNESCO World Heritage Site
Web: None Available

The Central Synagogue of Aleppo was the main synagogue of the Jewish community in Syria, which tradition dates back to the kingdoms period. For over five centuries it was home to the Aleppo Codex, the oldest known complete copy of the Hebrew Bible. Although Aleppo's Jewish community is virtually gone now, the Central Synagogue remains as their legacy, or at least did before the recent civil war broke out.

A community of Israelites existed in Aleppo at least as far back as the days of the kingdoms. According to tradition the community was established by the Israelite General Joab during the reign of King David in the 10th century BCE. While this can not be verified, Jews were certainly settled throughout Syria long before the Romans arrived.

The Jewish communities of Syria remained active throughout the Roman era, and enjoyed a revival under the various Islamic empires. Aleppo was one of the region's most important centers of Judaism right down to the 20th century. Although the Great Synagogue of Aleppo was destroyed by the Mongols in 1400, it was rebuilt soon afterwards along with the rest of the city.

Around this time a complete copy of the Hebrew Bible written in the 10th century CE was brought here by the descendents of Moses Maimonides. Believed to be the oldest accurate manuscript of the Tanakh, Aleppo became a magnet for scholars who wished to study what is now called the Aleppo Codex. Unfortunately the rebirth of Israel in the 20th century saw the end of this ancient community. The codex disappeared, and most of Aleppo's Jews relocated to Israel. The Central Synagogue of Aleppo is part of the Ancient City of Aleppo UNESCO World Heritage Site.

Of Interest: The exact date when the original synagogue of Aleppo was built is a matter of a conjecture, but there is evidence of a synagogue here as early as the 5th century CE. The current synagogue dates from the reconstruction after the Mongol invasion and a major renovation in the 16th century. The building has an unusual layout that features multiple sanctuaries situated around a central courtyard. There are seven different arks, all of which once housed ancient Torah scrolls. It was in one of these arks that the Aleppo Codex resided for the better part of five centuries. NOTE – The Central Synagogue was badly damaged during the Syrian Civil War which began in 2011. At the time of this writing the extent of the damage was unknown.

65. RUINS OF DURA EUROPAS SYNAGOGUE

Dura Europas, Syria

Site Type: Synagogue Ruins
Dates: Originally completed c. 244 CE
Web: None Available

The synagogue of Dura Europas is what's left of one of the oldest known synagogues in the Middle East outside of Israel. Dating from the mid-3rd century CE, it is not quite as old as some of the ruins to be found in the Holy Land. However these ruins stand out because of the artwork that has survived, or at least did until ISIS occupied the region a few years ago.

Dura Europas was a frontier town of the Parthian, Roman and Sassanian empires from the 3rd century BCE to the 3rd century CE. Originally built by the Parthians, it served as a trading outpost between Persia and Mesopotamia for the better part of five hundred years. Dura Europas reached its height in the 2nd and 3rd centuries CE under the Romans, who greatly expanded the city.

Religious life in Dura Europas appears to have been tolerant, as both a Jewish synagogue and a Christian house church were allowed to be built here in the mid-3rd century. This may have been due to the city's extremely isolated location on the eastern frontier. The city was overrun by the Sassanids in 256 CE, at which time the synagogue was partially destroyed and abandoned.

Of Interest: The Synagogue of Dura Europas archaeological site was, at least up until the Syrian civil war, surprisingly well preserved. This was due to two reasons: first, its walls were part of the city defensive system, and strengthened prior to the Sassanid attack. Second, the city was abandoned and never rebuilt. What survived of the synagogue was left undisturbed for over seventeen hundred years. Because of this the synagogue has what is arguably some of the best surviving examples of Jewish artwork and mosaics from the Roman era. NOTE – Dura Europas was overrun by the forces of ISIS during the Syrian civil war, and much of the site was looted and destroyed. At the time of this writing the state of the synagogue was unknown.

---

66. MOUNT NEBO

Madaba, Jordan

Site Type: Biblical Site
Dates: Moses came here c. 14th century BCE
Web: http://international.visitjordan.com/wheretogo/madaba.aspx (Jordan national tourism website)

Mount Nebo on the east side of the Jordan River was the location of the final moments of the life of Moses. According to the Hebrew Bible it was here that Moses looked out over the Promised Land just before his death, knowing that he could not cross over the river. Despite the fact that the mountain is of great Jewish historical importance, the main shrine commemorating this event is actually a church. Pilgrims come to the peak of the mountain, both for its sacred importance as well as for the magnificent view of the Holy Land it offers.

In the aftermath of the Golden Calf incident at the base of Mount Sinai the Israelites were condemned to wander in the wilderness for forty years, until all who had sinned in the eyes of the Lord had died. Moses spent the better part of this time leading the Israelites from encampment to encampment at the agonizingly slow pace of approximately five to ten miles per year. When at last they reached Mount Nebo, Moses gazed out over the Promised Land, but was prohibited from going further.

There are several traditions regarding Moses' final moments in this world. The Hebrew Bible suggests that he ascended directly to the Heavens. A more secular view holds that he was buried on the mountain in secret by a handful of his most trusted followers. Muslims believe that his body was carried across the Jordan River and buried on the other side near Jericho.

Despite the fact that Moses was arguably the greatest of all Jewish prophets, apparently no effort was made to memorialize the place where he died. Not even a shrine was established at Mount Nebo. Byzantine Christians did erect a series of churches there, the existing one dating from sometime in the 6th century CE. Mount Nebo is perhaps the most important place of Jewish interest in modern day Jordan.

Of Interest: Mount Nebo consists of a long ridge a few miles east of the Jordan River not far from where it empties into the Dead Sea. From its peak the view is impressive. On a good day a large swath of the Holy Land from the Jordan River to Jericho and beyond can be seen. The Moses Memorial Church, the 6th century Byzantine chapel on top of the mountain, is one of the oldest and best preserved churches in the area. An olive tree near the chapel was planted in 2000 by Pope John Paul II. Also nearby the chapel is the Brazen Serpent Monument, a modern day sculpture modeled after Moses' staff which protected the Israelites from snakes during their years of wandering in the wilderness.

67. MOUNT HOR & TOMBS OF AARON AND MIRIAM

Petra, Jordan

Site Type: Biblical Site, Burial Site
Dates: Aaron and Miriam buried here c. 14th century BCE
Designations: UNESCO World Heritage Site, Jordan National Park
Web: www.visitpetra.jo (official website of Petra)

Mount Hor, not to be confused with Mount Horeb, is one of several mountains connected to the Israelites' forty year journey in the Wilderness. It has tradionally been associated with Jebel Harun, a mountain located near Petra in Jordan. According to the Biblical account, the Israelites passed through this area sometime in the 14th century BCE. It was around this time that Moses' siblings, Aaron and Miriam, died and were buried somewhere in the vicinity of Mount Hor.

The area around Petra was settled long before the Israelites arrived. If the Biblical account is correct, the Israelites passed through here towards the end of their journey. According to the Bible, Miriam died before Aaron, and Moses chose a high place for her burial. Aaron died not too much later, though the details regarding his death are unclear. One account suggests that Mount Hor was located in or near Petra, while others believe that it was located elsewhere, and that the body was moved to Petra after his death.

Sometime around the 5th century BCE Nabataean nomads arrived in the area and established a city at Petra. For many centuries Petra was a prosperous stop on the local trade routes. However its importance waned in the latter years of the Roman Empire, until it was largely abandoned by the Middle Ages. During the 20th century adventurous travelers began to rediscover the wonders of Petra. The uniqueness and antiquity of the site have made it an ideal exotic movie location, and it has been featured in several films. Mount Hor is part of Petra National Park which is a UNESCO World Heritage Site.

Of Interest: Jebel Harun, or Mount Hor, is the tallest mountain in the vicinity of Petra. It is not easily accessible from the ruins of Petra, however, and requires at least a full day to get there, climb, descend and return. A well-worn trail leads up the hill. Close to the top is the Ad-Deir Monastery, which purportedly contains the Tomb of Miriam. The peak of the hill is crowned with a small white domed mausoleum. According to tradition this is the Tomb of Aaron. It is sometimes mistaken for a church, but is in actuality a mosque dating back to the 14th century. Also of related interest at Petra is the Spring of Moses, one of many such water sources mentioned in the Torah.

68. RUINS OF BAB EDH-DHRA AND NUMEIRA

Bab Edh-Dhra, Jordan

Site Type: Biblical Site, Archaeological Site
Dates: Original settlements established c. 3rd millennium BCE
Web: None Available

The ruins of Bab Edh-Dhra and Numeira are a pair of archaeological sites in Jordan near the southern end of the Dead Sea. Their significance lies in the fact that these are leading candidates for the sites of the Biblical cities of Sodom and Gomorrah. The story of the destruction of Sodom and Gomorrah has long been considered allegorical. However there is reason to believe that these and the other Cities of the Plains did exist. Archaeological research into this possibility is ongoing.

The aptly named Dead Sea is one of the most desolate bodies of water on Earth. While the shores around the sea are generally inhospitable, the Dead Sea region was home to some of Canaan's earliest settlements. At the time Abraham and Lot arrived in the area, the southern end of the sea was dominated by a confederation of five cities known as the Cities of the Plain. This ancient pentapolis consisted of the cities of Admah, Zoar, Zeboim, Sodom and Gomorrah.

As the Biblical story goes Lot and his family settled in the Valley of Siddim. He spent time in Sodom which was later laid waste by earthquakes and fire from the skies. While Lot and his daughters escaped the devastation, his wife was turned to a pillar of salt for daring to look upon the cataclysm. While the exact location of the Valley of Siddim has long been a mystery, the evidence that points to the Dead Sea region is more or less undisputed.

According to the Hebrew Bible Lot traveled southeast from Abraham's territory to Siddim. If the starting point was Beersheba, Lot would have ended up at the southern end of the Dead Sea. In that area is a city which has been called Zoar since the days of the Israelites. It is likely that this is the same as the Zoar mentioned in the story of Lot as it was the only one of the five cities not destroyed. In addition, this area has evidence of geological activity in the past. Finally there are great salt formations encrusting the cliffs at the southern end of the Dead Sea which may have given rise to the legend of Lot's wife. Unfortunately, hard evidence is inconclusive, and investigations at both locations are ongoing.

Of Interest: The leading contender for the location of Sodom is the ruins of Bab Edh-Dhra, while Gomorrah is associated with Numeira. The surrounding region contains extensive mineral deposits, including sulfur and bitumen. It has been suggested by scientists that the destruction of the Cities of the Plain was initiated by an earthquake that in turn triggered the release of quantities of natural gas which may have turned Sodom and Gomorrah into raging infernos. A number of archaeological discoveries in recent years point to other Bronze Age settlements in the area as well.

69. RUINS OF ANCIENT UR

Nasiriyah, Iraq

Site Type: Biblical Site, Archaeological Site
Dates: Original settlement established c. 7th millennium BCE
Designations: UNESCO World Heritage Site
Web: www.ur-online.org (official website)

The Ruins of Ur, one of the oldest cities on Earth, is believed to have been the original home of the Patriarch Abraham. There was little interest in the site until archaeologists showed up in the area in the mid-19th century. Since then there have been extensive excavations at the ruins, giving glimpses of Ur as it might have existed back in Abraham's day. Because of the decades of conflict that have convulsed Iraq, few foreign visitors are able to get here, making it virgin territory for adventurous pilgrims.

The area around Ur was probably first settled over eight thousand years ago, and reached its height well before any of the great empires arose in the Fertile Crescent. For a while it was the capital of Sumeria and possibly the largest city in the world. From a Biblical perspective Ur was not just any city. According to the Book of Genesis it was here, in the city of Ur of the Chaldees, that Abraham was born.

The Hebrew Bible only gives a limited account of Abraham's life in Ur. At some point around the 18th century BCE Terah, Abraham's father, decided to move his family to Canaan. Presumably Abraham and his brothers Nahor and Haran were alive at the time they left Mesopotamia. After their departure there is no further mention of Ur, except in a referential note in the Book of Nehemiah.

Around the time of Abraham's residency Ur was conquered by the Elamites. It may have been this event that drove Terah and his family to migrate westward. Ur was later absorbed into a succession of Mesopotamian states, including Assyria and Babylon. The city's decline appears to have begun around the time of the arrival of the Persians, and by the Roman era Ur was virtually abandoned. Ur is part of the Ahwar of Southern Iraq UNESCO World Heritage Site.

Of Interest: The Ruins of Ur are fairly extensive, although there is a lot below the surface that remains to be excavated. Among those areas that have been more thoroughly investigated are the royal tombs, which yielded a great wealth of artifacts and which are now on display at several major museums. Another excavated area was part of the city's residential district, which includes a building nicknamed Abraham's House. While it is highly unlikely that Abraham actually resided here, it is representative of the dwellings in the city at the time he is believed to have lived. The star attraction of Ur is its great ziggurat. Completely excavated in the 20th century, much of the structure was restored a few decades ago. This huge and photogenic structure absolutely dominates the archaeological site.

---

70. RUINS OF ANCIENT NINEVEH

Mosul, Iraq

Site Type: Biblical Site, Archaeological Site
Dates: Original settlement established c. 6th millennium BCE
Web: None Available

Ancient Nineveh was the capital city of Assyria, the world's first truly major empire. At its height the Assyrian Empire stretched from what is now Iran in the east to Egypt in the west. Assyria played a significant role in the history of the ancient Israelites, being responsible for the destruction of the Northern Kingdom in the 8th century BCE. The city of Nineveh also appears prominently in the story of Jonah.

According to the book of Genesis, Nineveh was founded by the great hunter Nimrod in prehistoric times. One of the northernmost ancient settlements along the Tigris River, Nineveh was an important trading center from earliest times. It entered the historical stage in the 14th century BCE when it was conquered by the neighboring Assyrians. Nineveh later became the imperial capital. Great walls with fifteen immense gates were constructed, and the city was adorned with dozens of magnificent temples and a royal palace.

As the city grew in size and wealth, so too did its reputation for sin and vice. The Israelites were well aware of the wars of conquest that the Assyrians were waging during the 8th century BCE. It is probable that the people of the Northern Kingdom had a fair idea of what was coming decades before the Assyrian army arrived on their borders. The Prophet Jonah was sent to warn the people of Nineveh, and after a famous detour via a great fish, he eventually completed the journey.

Jonah arrived in Nineveh and gave his warning, and the people there actually listened to him. Despite this Jonah was anxious to see the wrath of God unleashed upon the sinful city, and was disappointed when that wrath failed to materialize. Unfortunately, the repentence of Nineveh did not stop the Assyrians from annihilating the Northern Kingdom a few decades later. The city of Nineveh met a similar fate when the Assyrians were overthrown by the Babylonian Empire, after which it played no further known role in Biblical history.

Of Interest: The ruins of ancient Nineveh outside of modern day Mosul are extensive. They have been investigated over the last two centuries and much of the area has been excavated. The rough outlines of the city wall are discernible, as are several of the city's towers and gates. Within the walls the ruins of temples, residences and other buildings have been excavated. In addition, an effort has been made to actually reconstruct some of Nineveh's buildings, the most famous being the Mashki Gate near the city's northwestern corner. A site locally believed to be the Tomb of Jonah is located in a mosque in nearby Mosul. NOTE – Mosul was overrun by the forces of ISIS during the Syrian civil war, and the mosque was largely destroyed. The Nineveh archaeological site was also badly damaged. The state of the ruins was unknown at the time of this writing.

---

71. GRAVE OF ASENATH BARZANI

Amadiya, Iraq

Site Type: Burial Site
Dates: Asenath Barzani buried in 1670
Web: None Available

The Grave of Asenath Barzani is one of the most obscure Jewish pilgrimage sites anywhere. But this small shrine, located in the city of Amadiya in Kurdistan, attracted visitors for centuries during the Ottoman era. Buried here is Asenath Barzani, a brilliant scholar and religious leader who is considered by some to be the world's first female rabbi. Although never formally ordained, she served as a religious leader for the Jews of Amadiya in the 17th century, and her memory is honored in the city.

Asenath Barzani was born into a prominent and scholarly Jewish family in 1590. Her father, a rabbi, encouraged her to study the Torah, something usually discouraged to women at the time. She was a brilliant academic, and continued her studies even after marriage. This was encouraged by her husband, also a rabbi, and she became a teacher at his yeshiva.

After the death of her husband, Asenath took over the school and achieved renown for her capabilities as a teacher and as a leader in the community. A local legend is told of how she saved the community's Torah scrolls from being burned by a mob. By the time of her death in 1670 she was widely known and respected in the Jewish communities of Kurdistan. For many years afterwards her gravesite was a place of pilgrimage, though few Jews remain in the city today.

Of Interest: The Grave of Asenath Barzani is actually a small mausoleum of stone. It contains her grave as well as that of her father. Her tomb is a small, simple sarcophagus that is sometimes adorned with flowers and other tokens of respect. Although the mausoleum is maintained, there are relatively few Jews left in Kurdistan, and has not received many foreign pilgrims in recent years.

---

72. TOMBS OF ESTHER AND MORDECAI

Ester Alley, Hamedan, Iran

Site Type: Biblical Site, Burial Site
Dates: Shrine completed c. 13th century CE
Web: www.itto.org/iran/city/hamedan (Iran national tourism website)

The Tombs of Esther and Mordecai are one of the major sites of Jewish interest to be found in Iran. The events surrounding the life of Esther are recounted in the Book of Esther, in which she became a wife to the Persian king and used her influence to save the Jewish people from annihilation. Since time immemorial the tombs of Esther and her cousin Mordecai have been a spiritual focal point for the Jews of Iran.

According to Biblical and academic scholars, King Ahasuerus was probably Xerxes I, one of the emperors of ancient Persia. In one of the ancient world's great love stories, Ahasuerus married a Jewish girl named Esther, the cousin of Mordecai. However there was bad blood between Mordecai and Haman, the emperor's chief advisor. Haman sought to punish Mordecai by having all of the Jews of the realm killed. However Esther used her influence to change the king's mind, and the would-be perpetrator of the genocide was put to death instead.

Esther probably died around 500 BCE and was buried in the city of Hamedan along with Mordecai. Later, when the Jews were permitted to return to Palestine, some decided to stay in Persia. Tradition suggests that one of the reasons for this was due to their love for Esther. Although many Jews left Iran in the 20th century, the burial site of Esther and Mordecai remains an important pilgrimage destination for the remaining community.

Of Interest: The shrine where the Tombs of Esther and Mordecai are located is a relatively small structure marked by a domed tower. Although it appears much older, the shrine only dates back to the 13th century CE. The tombs of Esther and Mordecai are far older, and are marked by a pair of large stones similar to the types that sealed off graves in ancient Israel and later Judea. Inscriptions in Hebrew identify the two burials.

------

73. TOMB OF DANIEL

Rajaee Street, Shush, Iran

Site Type: Biblical Site, Burial Site
Dates: Daniel buried c. 6th century BCE
Web: www.itto.org/iran/city/shush-susa (Iran national tourism website)

The Tomb of Daniel is one of the most ambiguous Biblical burial sites. Of all of the great figures of the Hebrew Bible, no one has as many gravesites attributed to them as the Prophet Daniel. More than half a dozen cities in Iran, Iraq and even Uzbekistan make the claim. But the site in Shush, Iran, which was once the capital of the Persian Empire, is easily the most popular. The shrine here is revered by both Jews and Muslims.

The Babylonian Captivity was one of the great traumatic events of the ancient Jewish people. It lasted from 597 until 538 BCE, during which time a large portion of the Jewish population was relocated en masse to the heartlands of the Babylonian Empire. The pivotal event came in 586 BCE, when the Babylonians conquered the city of Jerusalem and destroyed the Temple of Solomon. Daniel lived through much if not all of this period, and was one of the exiles in Babylon.

Daniel was one of the great prophets of ancient Israel, and arguably the most prominent figure of the Babylonian Captivity. He interacted with two of Babylon's greatest leaders, Nebuchadnezzar and Belshazzar, and may have been present when the Persians conquered the city. Daniel went on to serve the Persian emperor Darius I, and probably helped to convince the Persians to allow the Jews to return to their homeland.

Daniel's service to the Babylonian and Persian rulers was likely a key factor in keeping the Jews intact as a people. Undoubtedly he used his influence to mitigate their hardships. However his political achievements were overshadowed by his reputation as a prophet, at least from a religious perspective. Daniel probably spent the last years of his life in the city of Susa, where he died and was buried in the late 6th century BCE.

Of Interest: The exact location of the Tomb of Daniel is uncertain. As of the middle of the 7th century CE it stood along the banks of the Choaspes River in what is now Iran. According to some sources the body was relocated on several occasions. One account even suggests that the final resting place was in the river, with the shrine being built nearby on land. The shrine building is a large structure with early Persian and Islamic influences. The walls and entrances are reflective of the styles common to mosques in Iran, with extensive blue tilework and high pointed archways. The building is crowned with an unusual cone-shaped dome. The ruins of ancient Susa on the outskirts of modern day Shush may have once been home to a Jewish community.

74. DAVID BAAZOV MUSEUM OF HISTORY OF TIIE JEWS OF GEORGIA

3 Anton Catholicos Street, Tblisi, Georgia

Site Type: Museum
Dates: Opened in 1933
Web: https://georgia.travel/en-us/shida-kartli/tblisi (Georgia national tourism website)

The David Baazov Museum of History of the Jews of Georgia is a small but interesting museum in Tblisi. Named in honor of a Georgian Zionist who was active in the early 20th century, the museum tells the story of an ancient Jewish community. Although there are not many exhibits here, the artifacts on display cover centuries of history. The museum is still maintained despite the fact that there are relatively few Jews still living in Tblisi.

According to tradition, the first Jews to settle in Tblisi arrived during the period of the Babylonian exile in the 6th century BCE. However, while there is some evidence to support this, it is more likely that Jews first settled in the region during the Roman era. While Georgia was typically incorporated into larger states throughout its history, it always seemed to be on the geographic perpiphery, far away from centers of power. It is perhaps for this reason that the Jewish community of Georgia remained mostly undisturbed for many centuries.

In the early 19th century Georgia was absorbed into the Russian Empire, and things began to change. Although pogroms were less prevalent here than elsewhere, anti-Semitism was on the rise. Many Ashkenazi Jews relocated to Georgia at this time, reconnecting two distinct Jewish groups for the first time in two thousand years. Life remained difficult for the Jews of Georgia throughout both the tsarist and communist eras.

At its height an estimated one hundred thousand Jews lived in Georgia. Most have steadily emigrated over the last half century, primarily to Israel. Today only about three thousand remain. The Museum of the History of Georgia traces its roots back to 1933, when it was opened as the Jewish Historic-Ethnographic Museum. It was closed for about fifty years during the communist era, and reopened in the early 2000s.

Of Interest: The David Baazov Museum of History of the Jews of Georgia in its current incarnation is only about ten years old. Many of its original artifacts were returned to the museum after its restoration. The museum has a number of major exhibits, the main ones focusing on Jewish history in Georgia beginning as far back as the Bronze Age. There are a number of collections examining different aspects of Jewish culture in Georgia, as well as the history of anti-Semitism in the region.

AFRICA

---

75. MOUNT SINAI

Feran, Egypt

Site Type: Biblical Site
Dates: Moses came here c. 14th century BCE
Designations: UNESCO World Heritage Site
Web: www.sinaimonastery.com (St. Catherine's Monastery website)

Mount Sinai, also called Jabal Musa by the local Bedouins, is the site traditionally identified as the Biblical Mount Sinai. It is a place highly revered by many Jews as well as Christians and Muslims. Because of its out of the way location in the southern Sinai Peninsula it has long escaped the wars and tribulations that have ravaged the majority of holy places in the Middle East. The main site is the mountain itself, and a pilgrimage here is not complete without a hike to its top.

Mount Sinai makes its first appearance in the Bible when Moses found his way there after his expulsion from Egypt. At the end of his journey in the wilderness he made the acquaintance of a Bedouin sheik and subsequently married his daughter. Years later, while attending his flocks, Moses chased a stray sheep up the mountain, only to come across a certain fabled Burning Bush. This was followed by the most famous divine audience in history, in which God ordered Moses to return to Egypt and lead the descendents of Israel to the Promised Land.

Upon securing the freedom of the Israelites, Moses led them through the wilderness, arriving at the base of the Mount Sinai sometime in the 14th or 13th century BCE. There they made a great encampment while Moses spent forty days on the mountain receiving the Ten Commandments. Following the incident with the Golden Calf, the Israelites departed from Mount Sinai, which then mostly disappears from the Biblical narrative.

During the 4th century CE Christians identified what they

believed to be Mount Sinai, possibly based on the traditions of local Bedouins. They constructed St. Catherine's Monastery at its base to accommodate pilgrims. Mount Sinai and its environs appear much today as they have for many centuries. The isolated location has left the area largely pristine. Although the mountain is becoming increasingly popular with religious pilgrims, it is still off the beaten path. Mount Sinai is part of the Saint Catherine Area UNESCO World Heritage Site.

Of Interest: At over a mile in height, Mount Sinai dominates the surrounding plain. The terrain of the mountain is rugged, with virtually no vegetation except for the occasional patch of scrub grass. Its summit can be reached by climbing the Steps of Repentance, a series of nearly four thousand stone carved stairs that meander past a series of chapels and shrines on their way to the mountain's peak. The climb begins at St. Catherine's Monastery and runs past the Springs of Moses and Elijah. Towards the top of the mountain are the Chapel of the Holy Trinity and a small mosque. The latter is located on the site of a cave believed to have been used by Moses to rest in. According to tradition St. Catherine's Monastery is home to a bush that is a descendent of the shrub of Biblical fame. Nearby the Byzantine Chapel of the Golden Calf marks the traditional spot where the idol of the Golden Calf once stood.

76. RUINS OF PI-RAMESES

Qantir, Egypt

Site Type: Biblical Site, Archaeological Site
Dates: Original settlement established c. 14th century BCE
Web: None Available

The Ruins of Pi-Rameses, discovered by archaeologists in the 20th century, is believed to be located in what was once the land of Goshen. According to the Biblical account, Goshen was home to the Israelites from the end of the age of the Patriarchs until the beginning of the

Exodus. Little now remains of their habitation in this region east of the Nile River delta.

The time of Israel's tribulation in Egypt is bookended by the lives of two of the most famous figures in the Hebrew Bible: Joseph and Moses. Joseph, the eleventh son of Jacob, was kidnapped by his jealous brothers and sold as a slave to Midianite merchants. However after years of servitude he found himself in the employment of the Egyptian pharaoh. When his brothers arrived from Canaan in search of provisions, he revealed himself at a tearful family reunion.

Joseph and his family were given the land of Goshen on Egypt's eastern frontier as their own, and their descendents greatly multiplied. At some point after Joseph's death the pharaohs forgot the origins of the Israelites, and whether out of fear of their numbers, or the desire for cheap labor, or both, the descendents of Jacob were constricted to work as slaves. Goshen became a vast forced labor camp. Pi-Rameses, the new capital city of Rameses II, may have been constructed by Hebrew slaves.

Around the 15th century BCE Moses convinced the Egyptians to let the people of Israel go, and in one of the most exciting stories of the entire Bible, the Hebrews departed the land of Goshen under the aegis of some of God's greatest miracles. Their departure probably left the land of Goshen largely depopulated. It is uncertain exactly what led to the downfall of Pi-Rameses, but the city appears to have been abandoned sometime in the 11th century BCE.

Of Interest: The Ruins of Pi-Rameses can be found at Qantir, not too far from the ruins of the city of Avaris. Although the general location of Biblical Goshen is known, its full extent and chief centers of population remain something of a mystery. The cities of Raamses, Pithom and Succoth are mentioned, though there are few details concerning these. Archaeological investigations at Pi-Rameses suggest that it was one of the largest cities ever constructed in ancient Egypt. Recent excavations have found remains of everything from humble homes to grand temples to sprawling palaces. Unfortunately, much of the masonry was removed and reused in other projects. The Ruins of Pithom, another Biblical site, are possibly located at either Tel el-Mashkhuta or Tel el-Rataba.

77. BEN EZRA SYNAGOGUE & CAIRO GENIZA

Kom Ghorab, Old Cairo, Cairo, Egypt

Site Type: Synagogue
Dates: Current building completed in 1892
Designations: UNESCO World Heritage Site
Web: http://egypt.travel/en/regions/nile-valley/cairo (Egypt national tourism website)

The Ben Ezra Synagogue is a relic of the once great Jewish community of Egypt. A synagogue has stood on this spot since at least as far back as the 9th century CE. Cairo was one of the biggest repositories of Jewish knowledge during the Middle Ages, and in the 19th century a long abandoned storage room in the synagogue was found to contain hundreds of thousands of documents. This warehouse, known as the Cairo Geniza, is one of the greatest literary discoveries in Jewish history. The Ben Ezra Synagogue and Geniza are among the most important Jewish historic sites in Egypt.

By the Roman era, Egypt had one of the largest Jewish communities in the world. It reached its height during the days of Philo, the renowned Jewish scholar. Unfortunately the relatively good relationship between Egypt's Jews and Rome collapsed following the Jewish Revolts in Judea at the beginning of the 2nd century CE. In Alexandria alone virtually all Jews were killed or driven out in 117 CE.

The Jewish community of Egypt received new life following the establishment of the Islamic caliphate here. Jews settled in Fustat, now part of Old Cairo, around the same time as the Muslims arrived. In the year 882 CE Abraham ben Ezra, a Jewish native of Jerusalem, purchased a plot of land for the construction of a synagogue. According to local tradition, it was on this spot that the infant Moses was found amidst the reeds. A synagogue was constructed on the site which has, at least in part, survived to the present day.

At some point in the Middle Ages a geniza, a Jewish warehouse for old books, was established here. By the time of the Crusades the collection was considerable. Maimonides made the synagogue his base of operations in Egypt so that he could have access to its immense collection of writings. The collection was forgotten during the Ottoman period, only to be rediscovered centuries later. Solomon Schechter, a future president of the Jewish Theological Society of America, went to Egypt to study the find. Recognizing its importance he had most of the collection removed to England and America. The Ben Ezra Synagogue and Cairo Geniza are part of the Historic Cairo UNESCO World Heritage Site.

Of Interest: The Ben Ezra Synagogue dates back to the 9th century CE, but it has been rebuilt and renovated on numerous occasions. It mostly dates from a reconstruction in 1892. Architecturally it is a mix of Byzantine, Egyptian and Islamic styles. The main sanctuary is a long, narrow building with a tall ceiling, marble fixtures and beautiful tilework. The geniza collection was discovered in the synagogue's attic. The collection included everything from religious texts to personal letters to an assortment of Passover Haggadahs. Fortunately no one ever got around to actually destroying them, and nearly two hundred thousand documents survived. Though the vast majority of the collection has since been removed, the geniza's history is commemorated at the Library of Jewish Heritage in Egypt located next door.

78. NATIONAL MUSEUM OF EGYPTIAN CIVILI-ZATION & MUMMY OF RAMESES II

Ein as Seirah, Old Cairo, Cairo Governate, Egypt

Site Type: Museum
Dates: Opened in 2021
Web: https://nmec.gov.eg (official website)

The National Museum of Egyptian Civilization is, at the time of this writing, a brand new museum in Cairo. Collections from a number of other major museums are being relocated here, most notably from the

Egyptian Museum. Among the most famous artifacts recently moved from the Egyptian Museum to the National Museum of Egyptian Civilization are many royal mummies. One of these is of particular interest to Jewish scholars and theologians: the mummy of Rameses II.

The story of the Exodus of the Israelites from Egypt is one of the epic accounts of the Hebrew Bible. However, for all of its popularity and religious importance, very little evidence of the story of Moses has ever been discovered. There is one major exception, however: the villain, Rameses II. While it is impossible to know for certain if Rameses II was the pharaoh associated with the Book of Exodus, many scholars and theologians consider him to be the leading candidate.

Rameses II was a pharaoh of the Nineteenth Dynasty who ruled over Egypt during the middle of the 13th century BCE. He led the Egyptians in some of the earliest wars in recorded history and was a prolific builder. Egypt probably reached its height during his reign. The idea that he was the pharaoh of the Exodus emerged in the early 20th century, an idea that was popularized in the 1956 film *The Ten Commandments*. If this assertion is correct, then this mummy would be the best surviving remains of any figure of the Hebrew Bible.

Of Interest: The National Museum of Egyptian Civilization is a brand new museum packed with exhibits and artifacts covering the thousands of years of history. Over twenty royal mummies were moved here in April 2021. The mummy of Rameses II is in a state of exceptional preservation. Another artifact of great Jewish interest is still at the Egyptian Museum but may be moved here in the future: The Merneptah Stele. This tablet, dating from around 1200 BCE, contains the earliest known non-Biblical reference to the ancient Israelites.

---

79. EL GHRIBA SYNAGOGUE

Djerba, Tunisia

Site Type: Synagogue
Dates: Current building completed c. 19th century CE
Web: www.elghribasynagogue.com (official website)

The El Ghriba Synagogue is a 19th century synagogue whose congregation may have been founded in pre-Roman times. The Jewish community of Tunisia may be descended from one of the oldest Israelite colonies in the central Mediterranean region. The current synagogue is home to two treasures. One is a stone that, according to tradition, came from the original Temple of Solomon and is embedded somewhere in the structure. The second is a very old handwritten Torah scroll.

From the earliest days of the Israelites in Canaan, relations between them and the Phoenicians appear to have been been friendly and mutually beneficial. The kings of Phoenicia developed strong ties with Israel during the days of Solomon. The northern tribes of Asher, Naphtali and Zebulun probably learned the trade of seafaring from the Phoenicians, and were likely the first seagoing Israelites. When the Phoenicians settled Carthage and the North African coast, it is possible that Israelites were among them.

Whatever their origin, there was almost certainly a Jewish community in Tunisia at the time of the Roman conquest of Carthage. For the most part the Jews of Tunisia had the good fortune of living under a succession of tolerant foreign rulers, and many found refuge here after being driven from other lands, notably from Spain in the 16th century. However in the wake of World War II the Jews of North Africa largely left. From a pre-war population of one hundred thousand, less than two thousand now remain. The El Ghriba Synagogue is an architectural treasure of Tunisia's dwindling Jewish community.

Of Interest: The current incarnation of the El Ghriba Synagogue was built in the 19th century. According to tradition it occupies the same spot as the original synagogue constructed in ancient times. The layout and design are strongly influenced by Moorish styles. The interior of the synagogue is an impressive structure of columns, arches and high ceilings, all decorated in fantastic tilework. Originally the synagogue had both an enclosed and an open prayer area in the manner of a mosque. But the open prayer area was eventually enclosed as well, creating a much larger interior sanctuary. According to tradition, a stone in one of the archways was originally part of the altar of Solomon's Temple. The synagogue is also home to a complete 15th century handwritten Torah scroll.

80. RUINS OF AKSUM

Aksum, Ethiopia

Site Type: Archaeological Site
Dates: Original settlement established c. 1st millennium BCE
Designations: UNESCO World Heritage Site
Web: None Available

The Ruins of Aksum have long been associated with the mysterious and fabled Land of Sheba. From its location to its people to the legends tying this realm to the Israelites, the enigma of Sheba has been slowly unraveling in Ethiopia and Yemen for centuries. From Aksum to Ma'rib, stories persist of the ancient frankincense trade routes; of the hiding place of the long lost Ark of the Covenant; and of ancient royal lines in Ethiopia which can be traced back to King Solomon. All of these legends originate in the traditions concerning the Land of Sheba.

Little is known about the origin or location of Sheba. Some scholars have suggested that Sheba is the same as Saba, the land of the Sabaeans, which is located in what is now Yemen. This would certainly be a logical location as it lay along a major frankincense trade route between Eastern Arabia and Canaan. Ethiopia has an equally strong claim as Sheba's homeland. Historical, cultural and archaeological evidence suggests ties to Israel, including a Jewish presence that dates back thousands of years.

Sheba's major appearance on the Biblical stage took place during the reign of Solomon sometime in the 10th century BCE. According to tradition, the Queen of Sheba traveled to Israel in one of ancient history's most famous state visits. The Bible says little of Sheba after the departure of the queen, and that is where tradition takes over. According to legend, Solomon and the Queen of Sheba's relationship was more than friendly, and at the time of her departure she was pregnant with his child. Her son, Menelik I, was the first Ethiopian ruler of the Solomnic Dynasty. The imperial rule of this family did not end until 1974 when Haile Selassie was deposed.

Another tradition suggests that when the Queen of Sheba returned home she brought the Ark of the Covenant with her. This was apparently done at the behest of Solomon who feared the eventual destruction of the Temple. Whatever the truth is, the fact that Ethiopia has a very ancient Jewish community is not disputed. The Ruins of Aksum are part of the Aksum UNESCO World Heritage Site.

Of Interest: Of all of the places which claim to be the true home of ancient Sheba, the leading contender is arguably Aksum in Ethiopia. A large archaeological site just outside of modern Aksum has revealed extensive, very ancient ruins, including a palace and a large field of stelae that are believed to have been erected by Israelites. The most important artifact, however, is actually located on the grounds of the Orthodox Church of St. Mary of Zion. According to the local priests, there is a secret, highly guarded chapel within the church. The Ark of the Covenant is supposedly kept inside that chapel. Unfortunately, the chapel and the Ark, if it is there, are strictly off limits to anyone but the church leadership.

---

81. ENTEBBE RAID MEMORIAL

Entebbe Airport, 14 Kitaasa Road, Entebbe, Uganda

Site Type: Monument
Dates: Dedicated in 2016
Web: https://caa.go.ug/entebbe-international-airport (Entebbe airport website)

The Entebbe Raid Memorial is a plaque located in the Entebbe Airport commemorating one of the most famous anti-terrorism operations in modern history. It was here in 1976 that Israeli commandoes rescued over a hundred people that had been taken hostage by Palestinian and German terrorists. The raid was a success, with all but a handful of the hostages returned alive.

On June 27, 1976, an Air France flight enroute from Athens to

Paris was hijacked by four gunmen, including two members of the Popular Front for the Liberation of Palestine and two members of the Revolutionary Cells of Germany. The flight and its two hundred and sixty passengers and crew were flown to Uganda where they were held pending an answer to their demands for the release of Palestinian militants.

Although some of the hostages were released, over a hundred were held at the Entebbe Airport. While diplomatic efforts were made to free the hostages, the Israeli government made plans for a rescue mission. A commando raid was planned by various Israeli agencies and executed on July 3-4. The commandos successfully infiltrated the airport, killed the terrorists along several Ugandan soldiers, and safely evacuated all but three of the hostages who were killed in the fighting. The only Israeli soldier to die was Jonathan Netanyahu, the older brother of future Israeli Prime Minister Benjamin Netanyahu.

The Entebbe Raid was a milestone in global anti-terrorism activity. It was generally lauded by western nations and condemned by most African and Middle Eastern nations. A few years later the dictatorship of Idi Amin was overthrown, and eventually relations normalized between Israel and Uganda. In 2016 the governments of Uganda and Israel jointly honored those involved in the raid, and a small plaque of commemoration was installed at the Entebbe Airport.

Of Interest: The Entebbe Raid Memorial is a commemorative marker that can be found at the old terminal of the Entebbe Airport. It depicts the flags of Israel and Uganda and gives a brief overview of the events of July 4, 1776. It also gives the names of those hostages who died, as well as that of Jonathan Netanyahu.

---

82. GARDENS SHUL

88 Hatfield Street, Cape Town City Centre, Cape Town, 8000, South Africa

Site Type: Synagogue, Museum, Holocast Memorial
Dates: Synagogue completed in 1905
Web: http://gardensshul.co.za (official website)

Gardens Shul is a complex of buildings that is home to the oldest Jewish congregation and synagogue in Sub-Saharan Africa. It is also believed to be the second oldest Jewish congregation in the world south of the Equator. Gardens Shul is nicknamed the Mother Synagogue of South Africa, and its congregation helped to spread Judaism throughout the British Empire during the colonial era.

The first Jews to arrive in South Africa probably came in the early 19th century, but no formal congregation existed until the 1830s. The Cape Town Hebrew Congregation was established in 1841. The community met informally in a makeshift compound that included a shul for about two decades. The first synagogue was completed and dedicated in 1863.

By the turn of the century the Jewish community of Cape Town had grown significantly, especially with Jews emmigrating from Eastern Europe. This necessitated a new synagogue to accommodate the growing congregation. The new Great Synagogue was completed in 1905 and is still in use to this day. Gardens Shul is also home to the South African Jewish Museum, which partially incorporates the 1863 synagogue.

Of Interest: Gardens Shul refers to the buildings associated with the Cape Town Hebrew Congregation. Located along Cape Town's Museum Mile, these include the magnificent Great Synagogue as well as the old synagogue. The South African Jewish Museum is accessed through the original synagogue. It includes, among other exhibits, a recreation of a Jewish village in Lithuania where some of the earliest members came from. Also here is the Cape Town Holocaust Center.

This museum, the first of its kind in Africa, has exhibits on discrimination, life in Nazi Germany and the Jewish ghettos. There is also an exhibit on the era of Apartheid in South Africa.

SOUTHEASTERN
EUROPE

83. AHRIDA SYNAGOGUE

Ayvansaray, European Side, 34087 Fatih/Istanbul, Turkey

Site Type: Synagogue
Dates: Dedicated in 1427 CE
Web: https://istanbul-tourist-information.com/en/experience-istanbul/places-of-worship-in-istanbul (municipal tourism website)

The Ahrida Synagogue is the most historic synagogue in a city full of old synagogues. Istanbul is home to the most Jewish synagogues in any city in the Middle East outside of Israel. Dating from the 15th through the 20th centuries, most of these are crowded in and around the old city. Several, including the Ahrida Synagogue, are still in active use.

There have been Jews in Istanbul at least as far back as the early Byzantine era. Up until the end of the 15th century the city's Jews were largely descended from ancient Romaniote communities. Two of the city's synagogues survive from this time period: the Ahrida Synagogue, which dates from the mid-15th century; and the Karaite Synagogue, which was probably built even earlier.

During the 16th century large numbers of Sephardic Jews fleeing the Inquisition settled in Istanbul. They became the dominant Jewish group in the city for most of the Ottoman period, and they constructed the majority of the synagogues still standing in Istanbul. Although the Jewish population in Istanbul has been drastically reduced in recent years, there are still over ten thousand Jews living in this ancient metropolis. The Ahrida Synagogue is among the Jewish community's beloved architectural treasures.

Of Interest: The Ahrida Synagogue dates from the final years of the Byzantine Empire, when the city was still known as Constantinople. Although trace elements of the original structure survive, most of the current synagogue dates from reconstructions in the 15th and 18th centuries. Other historic synagogues in the city include the Bet Avram Synagogue, a beautiful 1940s building which is now closed except by appointment. Across the Golden Horn is the Karaite Synagogue. The ruins of the original Karaite Synagogue date back more than six hundred years, though the current building dates from reconstructions in the 19th and 20th centuries.

84. JEWISH MUSEUM OF TURKEY

Bereketzade, Buyuk Hendek Cd. No:39, 34421 Beyoglu/Istanbul, Turkey

Site Type: Synagogue, Museum
Dates: Synagogue completed in 1863; Museum opened in 2001
Designations: UNESCO World Heritage Site
Web: www.muze500.com (official website)

The Jewish Museum of Turkey, officially known as the Quincentennial Foundation Museum of Turkish Jews, is the largest Jewish Museum in the Middle East outside of Israel. Although it has dwindled significantly over the last century, the Jewish community of Istanbul still has more than ten thousand members and nearly two dozen synagogues. The museum is housed in the old Zulfaris Synagogue.

The history of the Jews in Asia Minor was unusual in that it was, for the most part, relatively uneventful, especially after the collapse of the Byzantine Empire. Jews began migrating into Asia Minor in the 4th century BCE. Based on archaeological evidence as well as writings of the Christian New Testament, Jewish communities existed in Ephesus, Konya, Sardis and other cities as early as Roman times. Although Jews were persecuted here during the Byzantine period, they were largely left alone after the arrival of Islam.

The Jewish communities of Asia Minor enjoyed relative tolerance under the rule of the Ottomans, who recognized and appreciated the benefits of having a stable Jewish population. The Ottomans were also sympathetic to the idea of the restoration of a Jewish state in Palestine, and they allowed many Jews to resettle in Palestine in the 16th and 17th centuries. However these efforts failed to bring about a long-term permanent state.

The Jews remained an important cultural component of life in Turkey up until the 20th century, when under the republic they suffered persecution and forced deportation for the first time. Nevertheless Turkey was the first Muslim-majority nation to recognize the state of Israel, and although less than twenty thousand Jews now live there, it is still the largest Jewish population of any country in the Islamic world. The Zulfaris Synagogue is part of the Historic Areas of Istanbul UNESCO World Heritage Site.

Of Interest: The Jewish Museum of Turkey is housed in the historic Zulfaris Synagogue. Restored and remodeled in the 1990s, the building is one of Istanbul's most beautiful Jewish landmarks. The museum houses exhibits and artifacts relating the history of the Jews in Turkey, as well as artifacts and Torah scrolls from the time the building served as a synagogue. There are also memorial exhibits commemorating Jews who have fought for Turkey during World War I as well as for Turkish Jews who died in the Holocaust.

---

85. RUINS OF SARDIS SYNAGOGUE

Zafer, Belediye Cd. No 124, 45300 Sart, Manisa, Turkey

Site Type: Synagogue Ruins
Dates: Originally completed c. 3rd century CE
Web: www.kulturportali.gov.tr/turkiye/manisa/gezilecekyer/sart (Turkey Culture Portal website)

The Sardis archaeological site is home to one of the best surviving synagogue ruins from antiquity. Believed to have been completed in the 3rd century CE, there may have been an even earlier synagogue in Sardis as the Jewish community here is very ancient. The synagogue is just one of several well preserved buildings and ruins in Sardis that have survived from the Roman era, and offers a glimpse into how the Jewish community was part of the greater Roman community two thousand years ago.

The Jewish community of Sardis is one of the oldest such settlements in Western Anatolia. According to tradition, the first Jews to settle here probably arrived in the 3rd century BCE when the area was still ruled over by the Seleucids. This would predate both the rise of the Hasmonean dynasty in Judea and the arrival of the Romans in the Eastern Mediterranean.

Sardis was devastated by an earthquake in 17 CE, and it is possible that an earlier synagogue was badly damaged or destroyed at this time. The Jewish community in Manisa, the province where Sardis is located, survived all the way up until the 20th century. Almost all of the Jews of the region left in the 1920s after the Greco-Turkish War. The site of the synagogue has been part of ongoing excavations in Sardis since the 1950s.

Of Interest: The ruins of the Sardis Synagogue are extensive, with the floor, courtyard, sections of walls and a number of the columns still intact. The synagogue may have originally been constructed for other uses as it is part of a larger complex of public buildings. Portions of the floor mosaics are still intact, and the site has a number of surviving inscriptions that date from the time that the building was in use as a synagogue.

---

86. JEWISH MUSEUM OF THESSALONIKI

Agiou Mina 11, Thessalniki 546 24, Greece

Site Type: Museum
Dates: Opened in 2001
Web: www.jmth.gr (official website)

The Jewish Museum of Thessaloniki celebrates one of the oldest Jewish communities in continual existence in Europe. Established perhaps as early as the 2nd century BCE, the community is still in existence to this day. The Ets Chaim Synagogue of Thessalonika, which was founded in the 1st century CE and survived for nearly two thousand years, was the oldest synagogue in the world until its unfortunate destruction in a fire in the early 20th century. Today the synagogue, and Thessaloniki's Jewish community, is commemorated at this museum.

In the aftermath of the collapse of Alexander the Great's empire in the 4th century BCE the Jewish people began to spread out into the lands of the Greek speaking world. They probably arrived in Thessaloniki a few decades before the Romans did, and by the 1st century BCE boasted a thriving community. The Ets Chaim Synagogue was established around this time.

Throughout the Roman and Byzantine periods the Jews of Thessaloniki maintained a community here. It was briefly interrupted in the early years of Ottoman rule, when many of the Jews were forcibly resettled in Istanbul. But soon Jews from all over Europe began flooding into Greece, seeking refuge from inquisitions and persecutions in the west. The Jewish population of Thessaloniki soared, peaking in the 17th century, when Jews represented more than sixty percent of the city's inhabitants.

The fortunes of the Jews of Thessaloniki rose and fell, but the community survived more or less intact until the 20th century. The decline began during the political upheavals of the 1800s, accelerated after most of the city's Jewish quarter was destroyed in a fire in 1917, and came to a terrible end during World War II. Of the nearly one hundred thousand Jews that lived in Thessaloniki at the beginning of the century, only about three thousand survived the Holocaust. Less than half of that number now remains in the city.

Of Interest: The Jewish Museum of Thessaloniki documents the long history of this community, and it houses many artifacts that survived the fire of 1917 and the German occupation during World War II. It is located in one of the few Jewish buildings to have survived the 20th century. The museum's various galleries include exhibits on the history of the Jews in Thessalonika as well as the Holocaust. In addition, there are collections of photographs and artifacts documenting the Jewish community in the 19th and early 20th centuries, as well as memorial stones from the old Jewish cemetery which was demolished to make way for public building projects.

---

87. RUINS OF DELOS SYNAGOGUE

Delos, Greece

Site Type: Synagogue Ruins
Dates: Originally completed c. 2nd century BCE
Designations: UNESCO World Heritage Site
Web: www.visitgreece.gr/islands/cyclades/delos (Greece national tourism website)

The Delos Synagogue is part of an archaeological site on the island of Delos off the coast of Greece. Delos is full of the remains of ancient structures, some of which date back to well before the Romans arrived. The ruins identified as the Delos Synagogue are somewhat enigmatic. Dated to the 2nd century BCE, the synagogue may not have been Jewish, but actually Samaritan. Moreover, it might not have even been built as a synagogue. Research into this is still ongoing.

Delos was a well known island long before the arrival of the first Jewish traders. According to Greek myths and traditions, the deities Artemis and Apollo were born here. Other cults were common here as well, including those of Aphrodite, Posedion and Isis. To this day the island is covered in the remains of pagan temples and monuments, some of which remained in use well into the Roman era.

A Jewish or possibly Samaritan community first appeared on the island of Delos around the 3rd century BCE, about the same time such communities were popping up all over the Greek world. The community constructed this synagogue right around the time the Romans showed up in the area, and it likely remained in use for about three hundred years. It stood until the late 2nd century CE and was rediscovered by archaeologists in 1912. The synagogue is part of the Delos UNESCO World Heritage Site.

Of Interest: The ruins of the Delos Synagogue are possibly the oldest such ruins ever discovered in Europe. The question is, was it actually a synagogue? The mosaics depicting menorahs certainly suggest that it was. However, as the building is located in the ruins of the old residential area, it may have simply been a meeting house or private home. There is also the distinct possibility that the building was used by Samaritans, which would be an extremely rare discovery. The ruins of a Samaritan synagogue in Greece would be still of great interest to Jewish scholars.

---

88. SOFIA SYNAGOGUE

Exarch Joseph Street 1800, 1000 Sofia Center, Sofia, Bulgaria

Site Type: Synagogue, Museum
Dates: Completed in 1909
Web: www.sofiasynagogue.com (official website)

The Sofia Synagogue is one of the largest synagogues in Eastern Europe, and one of the grandest to have survived World War II almost entirely intact. Completed in 1909, it is the chief synagogue of a Jewish community that has survived in Bulgaria since antiquity. Today there are only a few thousand Jews left in Bulgaria, but the synagogue is still in use by a small congregation. The Sofia Synagogue is also home to the city's Jewish Museum.

The Bulgarian Jewish community is something of an oddity in Eastern Europe as it was not originally Ashkenazi. The first Jews to settle here came during the Roman era, possibly before the destruction of the Second Temple in the 1st century CE. Many Jews fled from the Byzantine Empire in the early Middle Ages, seeking safety in the lands of the Bulgars. Ashkenazi Jews from central and Eastern Europe did not arrive in Bulgaria until the 14th century.

The number of Jews living in Bulgaria was never large, at least compared to many other places in Europe. It peaked at around fifty thousand prior to World War II. Bulgaria was one of the very few places in Europe which mostly resisted the Nazi efforts to destroy the Jewish population. Although the Jews of Bulgaria suffered during the war, fewer were deported to concentration camps from here than from many other places in Europe.

The massive Sofia Synagogue, constructed in the early 20th century, was designed to accommodate a large number of the capital's Jews. However with the advent of communism most of Bulgaria's Jews relocated to Israel. Today virtually all of Bulgaria's remaining Jews can worship in the synagogue's great sanctuary with room to spare.

Of Interest: The Sofia Synagogue is both immense and stunning. The Moorish building is crowned by an immense dome that dominates the surrounding neighborhood. The synagogue interior is richly decorated, with a huge chandelier dangling from the inside of the dome. Some of the alcove ceilings are done in a deep blue and decorated with points like stars, giving the interior a mystical feel. The synagogue museum has exhibits on the history of the Jews in Bulgaria and the Holocaust.

---

89. RUINS OF STOBI SYNAGOGUE

E75, Stobi, North Macedonia

Site Type: Synagogue Ruins
Dates: Originally completed c. 2nd century BCE
Web: www.stobi.mk (official website)

The Stobi Archaeological Site is the ruin of an ancient town located in the heart of modern day North Macedonia. Founded in pre-Roman times, this small city was for a time home to a Jewish community that left behind a curious legacy: stone ruins engraved with the nearly complete dedication of a synagogue dating from the 2nd century CE. Known as the Polycharmos Synagogue, the inscription is possibly the oldest surviving such record of a synagogue in the world.

According to the inscription, the synagogue was constructed under the patronage of one Claudius Tiberius Polycharmos, who is referred to as the Father of the Synagogue. The elaborate inscription indicates that Polycharmos was a member of the local Jewish community as well as a citizen of the Roman Empire. To date Polycharmos is the earliest patron of a specific synagogue known by name.

The original synagogue at Stobi was replaced by a new synagogue about two centuries later. This was followed by a Christian church in the 5th century. The city and the church were largely destroyed by an earthquake in the 6th century. The church and synagogue ruins were rediscovered by archaeologists in the mid-20th century.

Of Interest: The Stobi Archaeological Site has been extensively studied over the last half-century. The area containing the synagogue is actually referred to as the central basilica, where ruins of the church and both earlier synagogues intermingle. Portions of the floor of both early synagogues have been uncovered and are visible. The columns bearing the famous Polycharmos inscriptions are now kept at the National Museum of Belgrade in Serbia.

---

90. SUBOTICA SYNAGOGUE

Trg Jakaba I Komora 6, Subotica, 24000, Serbia

Site Type: Synagogue
Dates: Completed in 1902
Designations: Serbia Monument of Culture of Exceptional Importance
Web: www.suboticasinagoga.rs/hu (official website)

The Subotica Synagogue is the second largest synagogue in Europe. Originally built in 1902, it was one of the grandest synagogues in the Balkans at the time of its completion. Although it was designed to seat thousands, the Jewish population of Serbia was devastated during and after World War II, leaving a much smaller congregation. Despite this the Subotica Synagogue is still in use and undergoing a restoration at the time of this writing.

The first Jews migrated into what is now Serbia during the Roman era. Historical information about the Jewish communities of Serbia is limited. The Ashkenazi migrations across Eastern Europe seem to have initially bypassed Serbia, although some settled in the region at a later date. Sephardic Jews also immigrated here during the Ottoman period.

The Jewish community of Serbia, never particularly large, was constantly caught up in the struggles between the Hapsburgs, the Ottomans and those Serbs who sought independence. Although pogroms were not regularly experienced in Serbia, there were periodic persecutions depending on who was in charge at any given moment. Things seemed to get better around the turn of the century. The large and prosperous Jewish community of Subotica constructed their synagogue at this time.

World War II was a disaster for the Jews of Serbia. Of the fifty thousand Jews that lived here before the war, around fourteen thousand survived. The dead included four thousand Jews from the city of Subotica. The synagogue survived the war and has since been designated a Serbian Cultural Monument of Exceptional Importance.

Of Interest: The Subotica Synagogue is one of the largest houses of worship in the city. Constructed in the early 20th century in the Art Nouveau style, the synagogue is currently undergoing a major renovation after many years of neglect. The most distinctive feature is the magnificent green and gold dome, with a pair of smaller matching domes flanking the main entrance. The beautiful interior has an unusual color scheme that includes yellow and orange painted ceilings trimmed in floral designs. A stone marker outside the synagogue commemorates the four thousand Jews from Subotica that died during the Holocaust.

91. DUBROVNIK SYNAGOGUE

Zudioska ul. 5, 20000, Dubrovnik, Croatia

Site Type: Medieval Synagogue, Museum
Dates: Originally completed in 1352
Designations: UNESCO World Heritage Site
Web: www.godubrovnik.guide/dubrovnikthingstodo/jewish-synagogue (municpal tourism website)

The Dubrovnik Synagogue is one of the oldest Jewish houses of worship still in use in Europe. Constructed in the mid- to late-14th century, it has survived many wars, pogroms and natural disasters. Today the congregation is very small, but the synagogue is maintained as a cultural site. Worship services are held here periodically.

Jews began settling in what is now Croatia in the Roman era, with evidence of a community dating back to the 3rd century CE. In the 15th century most Jews were forced out of Croatia. However, small numbers of Sephardic Jews fleeing the Inquisition in Spain settled in Dubrovnik in the 16th century. The Jews of Dubrovnik were forced to live in a ghetto under Venetian rule, liberated under French rule, and persecuted again under Austrian rule. The synagogue was damaged in the great earthquake of 1667 and rebuilt.

Although things improved for the Croatian Jews in the 20th century, they were devastated by the Holocaust. What was left of the community suffered again during the Balkan Wars of the 1990s, at which time the synagogue was badly damaged. It was repaired and reopened a few years later. The Dubrovnik Synagogue is part of the Old City of Dubrovnik UNESCO World Heritage Site.

Of Interest: The Dubrovnik Synagogue is a stately and eyecatching building. Mostly rebuilt after the great earthquake, it incorporates Baroque elements that were in style in the 17th century. The interior is dominated by dark wooden furnishings and brass fixtures. An interesting collection of brass lamps and other lighting pieces are suspended from the ceiling. Part of the building is now used to house a small museum with a collection of Judaica from the city's history.

92. GREAT SYNAGOGUE OF ROME
& JEWISH GHETTO

Lungotvere de'Cenci, 00186 Roma, Italy

Site Type: Historic Neighborhood, Synagogue, Museum
Dates: Synagogue completed in 1904
Web: www.romaebraica.it (Jewish Community of Rome website)

The Great Synagogue of Rome is the heart of what may be Europe's oldest continually active Jewish community. It stands on the former site of part of the wall which once enclosed the city's Jewish ghetto. The ghetto in turn is located in an historic district of Rome which has been home to Jews since the 1st century BCE. A number of Jewish families, some of which can trace their lineages back many generations, still live in this neighborhood.

The first Jews to settle in Rome most likely arrived during the Hasmonean period. This was almost certainly the first Jewish community to be established in Western Europe. The Jews of Rome survived despite the revolts of their brethren in Judea, the legalization of Christianity and the collapse of the Roman Empire in the west. Because of their proximity to the seat of the Papacy, the Jews of Rome were alternately protected or persecuted depending on which pope was in power.

Despite the arrival of the Renaissance in Italy, the persecution of the Jews of Rome increased significantly starting in the 16th century. The city's Jewish ghetto was formally established in 1555. The ghetto was overcrowded and its inhabitants subjected to many privations. Although conditions were periodically alleviated by more enlightened popes, the ghetto itself was not outlawed until 1870. The ghetto of Rome was among the last major medieval Jewish ghettoes in Europe to be dismantled.

After the walls came down much of the neighborhood was cleared and rebuilt. A massive new synagogue for the community was completed in 1904. The ghetto was reinstated for several years during World War II. For a few months in late 1943 and early 1944

Rome came under the control of the Nazis, and the Jews of the ghetto suffered great losses to their community. Despite this many of Rome's Jews survived the war, and the neighborhood has continued to be home to a vibrant Jewish community ever since.

Of Interest: The Great Synagogue of Rome is the defining landmark of the city's historic Jewish quarter. Completed in 1904, this building has become a modern day symbol of religious tolerance, a stark contrast to the many earlier centuries of persecutions. The Jewish Museum of Rome, with exhibits covering more than two thousand years of history, can be found in the lower level of the synagogue. While the ghetto of Rome is now gone, there are still remnants to be found. The Jewish Bridge, so named because it led from the central city to the Jewish Quarter, has been in use since Roman times. A number of buildings, mostly shops, date from the ghetto period. Several nearby churches have inscriptions in Hebrew urging the local Jews to convert.

---

93. JEWISH CATACOMBS OF ROME

Via Appia Pignatelli, 2, 00178 Roma, Italy (Vigna Randanini Catacombs)

Via Nomentana, 70, 00161 Roma, Italy (Villa Torlonia Catacombs)

Site Type: Ancient Catacombs
Dates: Originally established c. 2nd century CE
Web: www.romaebraica.it (Jewish Community of Rome website)

In the early 20th century a number of Jewish catacombs were discovered in and around the city of Rome. Jewish catacombs, while not unheard of in the Roman Empire, were something of a rarity. Christian catacombs were almost certainly in use first, more out of the necessity for secrecy, and their use more widespread. Nevertheless Jewish catacombs have been discovered in Rome, as well as in other places including the town of Venosa and on the island of Malta.

Cities throughout Italy and the Mediterranean region began the practice of building extensive burial catacombs during the first and second centuries CE. This was due to increasingly large populations combined with ever shrinking parcels of land made available for cemeteries and mausoleums. The earliest catacombs of Rome were developed for the general population, which was then primarily Pagan. But Christians and Jews eventually started constructing their own.

It is possible that the earliest Jewish catacombs were actually used by both Jews and Christians, as Christianity was still considered by many in the 2nd century CE as being a sect of Judaism. In Malta the famous Catacombs of St. Paul in fact had Christian, Jewish and Pagan burials all side by side. The Jewish Catacombs around Rome, while not really lost, were largely forgotten for over a thousand years, and only explored again in the last century or so.

Of Interest: Of the half-dozen Jewish Catacomb complexes in the area around Rome, two can be explored. The Vigna Randanini Catacombs have extensive artwork and inscriptions that give clues about Jewish life in Rome, as well as pagan symbols that suggest the catacombs might have been taken over by Jews at a later date. The Villa Torlonia Catacombs were incorporated into an air raid shelter complex during World War II.

---

94. ARCH OF TITUS

Via Sacra, 00186, Roma, Italy

Site Type: Monument
Dates: Completed in 81 CE
Designations: UNESCO World Heritage Site
Web: https://parcocolosseo.it/area/foro-romano (Roman Forum website)

The Arch of Titus is an important monument of the old Roman Empire that has special significance for Jews. Constructed by the

Romans to commemorate their triumph over the Jews in the Great Revolt, it depicts the victors making off with the spoils of the Second Temple. The Arch of Titus became a place of celebration for Rome's Jews when the modern state of Israel declared its independence in 1948

In 63 BCE the people of Judea were engulfed in a civil war, even as the Roman Empire was beginning to look for new territories in the Eastern Mediterranean. One of the two claimants to the throne, Aristobulus II, sent an envoy to Pompey asking for his aid. Pompey sent in his legions and restored order. Soon afterward the Romans began playing off the various factions against each other, until Judea's rulers were little more than Roman puppets, and Judea was a client state of Rome.

The Romans were forced to maintain standing armies in the restless province and had to put down several rebellions. The Great Revolt is the one that is most vividly remembered in Jewish history. After some Jewish victories in 66 and 67 CE, the Romans regrouped and invaded Judea with the most powerful army ever assembled in the region. General Vespasian, hand picked by Emperor Nero, systematically crushed the revolt throughout the countryside, then turned his sights on Jerusalem.

The Romans laid siege to Jerusalem. The defenders fought back ferociously but in vain. On Tisha B'Av of the year 70 CE the city fell, the Temple was set on fire and its treasures hauled back to Rome as booty. To commemorate the victory, the Romans constructed a triumphal arch in honor of Emperor Titus. For nearly two thousand years it was tradition among Jews not to walk beneath the arch. This tradition was broken in 1948 when thousands of Italian Jews marched here in celebration of Israel's rebirth. The Arch of Titus is part of the Historic Centre of Rome UNESCO World Heritage Site.

Of Interest: The Arch of Titus is located in what was once the Roman Forum. At fifty feet in height it is one of the largest surviving monuments of ancient Rome. Completed at the end of the 1st century CE, the arch is in remarkably good condition. It is covered with bas-reliefs, scrollwork and engravings celebrating the victory of Vespasian and Titus in Judea. The most famous carving depicts the looting of the Second Temple. In the depiction, Roman soldiers and slaves are seen trampling through the ruins of the city. The building in the background is the Second Temple. The Romans are hauling away treasures, including the giant golden menorah and the sacred trumpets as well as other objects.

95. RUINS OF OSTIA SYNAGOGUE

Via di Tor Boacciana, Ostia, 00119, Roma, Italy

Site Type: Synagogue Ruins
Dates: Originally built c. 48 CE
Web: www.ostiaantica.beniculturali.it (Ostia Archaeological Park website)

The Ostia Synagogue is one of Italy's oldest Jewish historic sites. Located in the Ostia Archaeological Park, it is now part of a vast collection of ruins that was once the chief seaport of the Roman Empire. The synagogue has been reliably dated to the 1st century CE. This makes it one of the oldest known remains of a synagogue in Europe, and one of the oldest in the world outside of the Holy Land.

Ostia Antica was one of the great ports of the Mediterranean Sea during the Roman era. It was in fact the major port for the imperial capital of Rome, with thousands of trade vessels carrying the wealth of the empire to Italy every year. As one of the most important trading centers of antiquity, Ostia Antica became home to an important Jewish community, probably as early as the 1st century BCE.

The history of the port's synagogue is surprisingly well documented. It was constructed during the reign of Claudius around 48 CE, though it is possible that the building was used as a private home before being converted to use as a synagogue a few decades later. Despite the revolts that wracked Judea in the the 1st and 2nd centuries CE, the Jewish community of Ostia appears to not have been significantly impacted. The synagogue probably survived and remained in use until the entire city fell into decline. It was likely abandoned in the mid-9th century along with the rest of Ostia Antica.

Of Interest: The Ostia Synagogue is, along with the rest of the ancient city, largely a ruin. Only portions of the foundations and lower walls have survived, along with a few broken stairs and columns. Inscriptions on the wall indicate the the synagogue once house several Torah arks. Part of one of the remaining columns is decorated with an engraving of a menorah.

---

96. GREAT SYNAGOGUE OF FLORENCE

Via Luigi Carlo Farini, 6, 50121, Firenze, Italy

Site Type: Synagogue, Museum
Dates: Completed in 1882
Designations: UNESCO World Heritage Site
Web: www.firenzebraica.it/sinagoga (official website)

The Great Synagogue of Florence is one of the most magnificent places of Jewish worship in Europe and one of the most beautiful synagogues ever built. Although not completed until the 19th century, it could have easily been one of the city's architectural masterpieces of the Renaissance. It was constructed soon after the emancipation of the Jewish people in Italy and survived destruction at the hands of the Nazis during World War II.

The Jewish community of Florence dates back to the Middle Ages, and may in fact be much older. They were important contributors to the Italian Renaissance, particularly in the areas of literature, science and philosophy. Some of the earliest prominent intellectuals of the Renaissance were Jews who lived in Florence. The first well known Jewish writer of the Italian Renaissance was Isaiah di Trani, a Talmudic scholar who espoused a less severe approach to Jewish Law. His descendents continued to be active literary figures throughout the Renaissance.

The Jewish Renaissance peaked in Florence at the turn of the 15th-16th century under the patronage of the powerful Medici family. In later years, when Jews were expelled from the Papal States and other places, Florence kept its doors wide open. The Jews of Italy were formally emancipated in the mid-19th century. In celebration of this momentous event the Jewish community in Florence constructed the Great Synagogue.

During World War II Florence came under the control of the fascist government of Benito Mussolini and was later occupied by the Germans. As was typical the Nazis utterly disrespected the sanctity of the synagogue and used it for storage. They attempted to destroy the building as the Allies approached the city, but were unable to carry out their plans thanks to the efforts of local resistance fighters. The Great Synagogue of Florence is part of the Historic Centre of Florence UNESCO World Heritage Site.

Of Interest: The Great Synagogue of Florence is a magnificent example of neo-Moorish architecture, a style that was popular among Sephardic Jewish refugees from Iberia. The main dome is one of the largest on a synagogue in Europe. Despite repairs the synagogue still bears the scars of the Nazi occupation. The ark is defaced by the slash-marks of German knives and bayonettes, and a memorial outside of the synagogue commemorates the Jews who were deported from Florence to the concentration camps. The small Jewish Museum of Florence is housed in the synagogue's upper floors. It displays artifacts and photos from Florence's Jewish history.

---

97. JEWISH GHETTO OF VENICE

Cannaregio, Venice, Italy

Site Type: Historic Neighborhood, Museum
Dates: Established in 1516 CE
Designations: UNESCO World Heritage Site
Web: www.ghetto.it (official website)

The Venice Ghetto was the first of the Jewish ghettos that later appeared in many cities throughout Europe. Because of Venice's need for economic and mercantile expertise, as well for its need for go-betweens with the wealthy Islamic lands of the east, Jews were generally tolerated and even welcomed here. Nevertheless the lack of available land as well as the Christian population's discomfort at having so many wealthy Jews nearby led to the establishment of a segregated Jewish district. This was the first true ghetto, and is still an active center of Jewish life in Venice.

The Jewish community of Venice was one of the most unique in Europe. While never a significant religious center of Judaism, Venice's geographic location and mercantile interests made it a major center of Jewish economic life in the late Middle Ages. Venice, which had established itself as a a critical trading and financial center during the Crusades, was interested in the expertise of the Jews in these areas. Because the practical Venetians tended to put economic interests ahead of religious ones, Jews were largely free to come and go, and many settled here.

As the Inquisition began to take root in the west in the early 16th century many Jews fleeing Spain and Portugal relocated to Venice. They were allowed to stay, but to appease the Church they were forced to reside in the Campo Gheto, or iron foundry district. This later became the Gheto district, or simply the "ghetto". The Venice ghetto became something of an architectural wonder. The district was densely populated so the Jews built upwards, creating a rare for the time high rise district.

During the Renaissance Daniel Bomberg established a Hebrew printing press here, making Venice the chief center of Jewish publishing in Europe. However, as the importance of the Venetian Republic waned, so too did the city's Jewish community. Unlike many other places where they were forced out, the Jewish population of Venice merely faded over the years. It is one of the best preserved Renaissance-era Jewish neighborhoods in Europe. The Jewish Ghetto of Venice is part of the Venice and its Lagoon UNESCO World Heritage Site.

Of Interest: Despite its age and relatively small Jewish population, the Venice Ghetto remains surprisingly intact. It is comprised of two areas, the Ghetto Vecchio, or old ghetto, and the Ghetto Nuovissimo, or new ghetto, which are surrounded by canals and accessible by bridge. The gates which once guarded the entrance to the ghetto were destroyed during the occupation of Venice by Napolean Bonaparte. Most of the ghetto sites are clustered around the district's historic center. Among these are five synagogues which date back to the ghetto's early days: the Schola Canton, the Schola Italiana, the Schola Levantina, the Schola Spagnola and the Schola Tedesca. The history of the ghetto is documented at the Jewish Museum of Venice.

---

98. SCOLANOVA SYNAGOGUE

Via Scola Nova, 76125, Trani, Italy

Site Type: Medieval Synagogue
Dates: Completed c. 13th century
Web: www.comune.trani.bt.it/guida/sinagoga-scolanova (municipal tourism website)

The Scolanova Synagogue is believed to be the oldest intact synagogue in Italy and one of the oldest in Europe. Built in the 13th century, it spent most of its existence as a church, and was only recently returned to the Jewish community. Today this medieval building is one of the Jewish historical treasures of southern Italy. While it is an active synagogue, it is only used on a semi-regular basis.

It is uncertain when the first Jews arrived in Trani, but there was a community there at least as far back as the 12th century. Trani was a major port serving pilgrims and crusaders leaving Italy for the Holy Land, which made it a logical base for Jewish travelers and merchants as well. The city was home to several synagogues by the 13th century. However most of these were destroyed or confiscated by the Church in the 16th century.

One of the latter was the Scolanova Synagogue, which was converted into the Church of Santa Maria in Scolanova. The church remained in use until the mid-20th century. By then all of the other former synagogues of Trani were gone. However the Scolanova Synagogue survived. After about a half-century of being abandoned, it was returned to the local Jewish community in 2005.

Of Interest: The Scolanova Synagogue is not only intact after nearly eight centuries of existence, it is essentially unchanged. A relatively small building of cut white stone, the exterior is unassuming, with only a small entrance and a handful of windows. A small bell tower, a relic of its days as a church, is in the front corner of the synagogue. The bell tower is now crowned by a Star of David. The remains of what is believed to have once been a mikveh bath is located beneath the synagogue sanctuary.

---

99. CATACOMBS OF ST. PAUL

Hal-Bajjada, Ir-Rabat, Malta

Site Type: Ancient Catacombs
Dates: Originally established c. 2nd century BCE
Web: https://heritagemalta.org/st-pauls-catacombs (official website)

The Catacombs of St. Paul, named for Paul of the Christian New Testament, is one of numerous ancient subterranean burial sites on the island of Malta. Despite its name the Catacombs of St. Paul appear to have been a Judeo-Christian graveyard at the time of its inception in the 2nd or 3rd century CE. Because of this the catacombs preserve some very ancient Jewish artwork, a legacy of Malta's once large and thriving Jewish community.

The Jewish community on Malta probably dates back to the Hasmonean period. According to the Christian New Testament, Paul, who was then still considered a Jew, visited the island of Malta on one of his missionary journeys in the 1st century CE. In the early years of Christianity Malta's Christian and Jewish populations appear to have lived as one community. This is evidenced by the fact that they shared burial catacombs.

The Jews on Malta appear to have survived for the better part of a thousand years. Unfortunately Malta eventually came under Spanish rule, and the Jews were forced out at the end of the 15th century. Some managed to stay on the island, possibly practicing their faith in secret.

More relocated here after the island became a British territory in the 19th century, and several thousand Jewish refugees found sanctuary here during World War II. The community now is relatively small as most Jews emigrated from here after the founding of the modern state of Israel.

The small island of Malta is home to a surprising number of places of Jewish interest. Most of Malta's cities were home to Jewish neighborhoods and ghettos, with a number of surviving Jewish gates and synagogues on the island. Malta has numerous catacombs where Jews are buried as well as Jewish cemeteries. The Catacombs of St. Paul are merely a starting point to those wishing to explore the ancient Jewish heritage of the island.

Of Interest: The Catacombs of St. Paul, located in Rabat, date back to the late Roman era. Named for the missionary Paul, both Jewish and Christian burial sites can be found in these catacombs. Jewish themes, such as menorahs, can be found in the artwork painted and engraved on the walls. Another popular place of Jewish interest on the island is the Jewish Sally Port in the city of Valletta. This excellent example of a Jewish gate is exactly that: a gate which Jews were required to use when entering or exiting the city.

EASTERN EUROPE

100. HOLOCAUST MEMORIAL SYNAGOGUE

Kutuzovsky Avenue, 53, Moscow, Russia, 121096

Site Type: Synagogue, Museum, Holocaust Memorial
Dates: Completed in 1998
Web: www.poklonnaya.ru (official website)

The Holocaust Memorial Synagogue, also known as the Memorial Synagogue on Poklonnaya Hill, is Russia's national monument to the Jewish victims of the Shoah. It is part of a large complex of monuments in a grand victory park that commemorates Russia's victories over France in the 19th century and Germany in the 20th century. The synagogue houses a large museum with exhibits related to the Holocaust and the Jews who fought against the Nazis.

At the height of World War II the forces of Nazi Germany had overrun huge territories of the Soviet Union. Millions of Jews living in Ukraine, Belarus and the Baltic States came under the control of the Third Reich, and most of these perished as victims of the Final Solution. However the Germans only conquered a relatively small territory of Russia itself. Because of this many Russian Jews escaped the German noose and flocked to join the Soviet war effort against the Nazis.

About a half a million Jews, or roughly one in six Jews living in Russia at the time, served in the Soviet army during World War II. Of these two hundred thousand were killed or captured, with many of the captured subsequently dying in Nazi concentration camps. It was many years before the scale of the Jewish contributions to the Soviet war effort were acknowledged. The Holocaust Memorial Synagogue was dedicated in 1998.

Of Interest: The Holocaust Memorial Synagogue is a large, blocky modern building on a wide plaza. The exterior is ornamented with

stars of David and a huge menorah. A fearsome sculpture of ema-
ciated men and women emerging in a line from the ground captures
the despair of the victims of the Holocaust. Inside the synagogue are
exhibits on the history of the concentration camps and ghettos. Also
here are exhibits on the Jews who fought for the Soviet Union as well
as Jewish partisans who fought behind enemy lines. There is also a
memorial for those Soviet citizens who are members of the Righteous
among the Nations.

101. JEWISH MUSEUM AND
TOLERANCE CENTER

Obraztsova Street, 11, Building 1A, Moscow, Russia, 127055

Site Type: Museum
Dates: Opened in 2012
Web: www.jewish-museum.ru (official website)

The Jewish Museum and Tolerance Center is the largest such institution in Russia and one of the largest Jewish museums in Europe. Completed in 2012, it tells the history of the Jews of Russia and Ukraine.
Funded by both Russian and Jewish supporters, it was conceived as a
project to help strengthen relations between Russia and Israel.

The first Jewish communities in the far east of Europe were to be
found in what is now Ukraine, Georgia and Armenia. These settlements date back to the early Middle Ages, and in some cases as far
back as the Roman era. They largely consisted of Jews who migrated
north from the Byzantine Empire and later the Khazar Empire. However at this time there were few if any Jewish communities established
in what is now Russia proper.

Ashkenazi Jewish immigrants began arriving in Russia in the 15th
century. It was the last part of Europe aside from Scandinavia to see
significant Jewish settlements. Because of this the persecutions associated with the Crusades and the Black Plague were not experienced
here. Nevertheless Russian Jews were regularly exposed to pogroms

during the tsarist period. Persecutions notwithstanding, Jews tended to have more opportunities in Russia than elsewhere in Europe, and beginning in the early 19th century hundreds of thousands of Jews served in the Russian military.

Jews were active in the Russian Revolution and played an important part in helping to overthrow the tsars. However, they then frequently suffered persecutions under the communist regime. After the fall of communism many Jews left. In the early 2000s there was a Jewish renaissance of sorts in Russia. However, Jewish immigration to Israel is once again on the rise and is anticipated to continue for the foreseeable future.

Of Interest: The Jewish Museum and Tolerance Center of Moscow is located in a refurbished bus garage on the north side of the city. It recounts the history of Russian Jews as well as Jewish migrations across Europe. There are also exhibits that focus on Jewish life in both late tsarist and communist Russia. While the museum does have exhibits on persecutions of Russian Jews and pogroms, the focus is more on day-to-day Jewish life in Russia and the former Soviet Union.

---

102. GRAND CHORAL SYNAGOGUE

Lermontovskiy Prospekt, 2, St. Petersburg, Russia, 190121

Site Type: Synagogue
Dates: Completed in 1893
Designations: Russian Registered Landmark
Web: https://sinagoga.jeps.ru (official website)

The Grand Choral Synagogue of St. Petersburg was, for a few decades, the preemnent Jewish house of worship in the old Russian capital, and one of the most important synagogues in the country. Constructed at a time when pogroms against Jews were on the rise throughout Russia, it is surprising that it was allowed to be built at all. Nevertheless the synagogue survived the tsarist period, the World Wars and the communist era.

The Jewish community of St. Petersburg was established in the 18th century, around the time that the city's first major buildings were being constructed. Over time St. Petersburg became home to a number of synagogues, but there was not as yet a great synagogue in the city. In 1869 the tsar personally authorized the construction of a massive new synagogue for the capital.

The Grand Choral Synagogue was completed in 1893. It was in operation for less than three decades when the communists came to power. Most of St. Petersburg's Jews left the city, either by choice or by force. The synagogue was used as a hospital during World War I and was damaged by bombing during World War II. It was rebuilt and renovated in the early 2000s, and is once again in use as a synagogue. The Grand Choral Synagogue is a Russian Registered Landmark.

Of Interest: The Grand Choral Synagogue is one of St. Petersburg's great historic buildings of the late imperial period. A sprawling Moorish structure, it is crowned by an immense grey dome. The main sanctuary is breathtaking and huge, with a magnificent ark. It is large enough to accommodate well over a thousand worshippers.

103. NATIONAL LIBRARY OF RUSSIA & LENINGRAD CODEX

Sadovaya Street, 18, St. Petersburg, Russia, 191069

Site Type: Library
Dates: Opened in 1795
Designations: UNESCO World Heritage Site
Web: www.nlr.ru (official website)

Tucked away in the massive collection of the National Library of Russia in St. Petersburg is an unassuming book of priceless importance to Judaism: the Leningrad Codex, the oldest complete copy of the Hebrew Bible in the world. The Leningrad Codex achieved this status after portions of the Aleppo Codex went missing in the mid-20th century. Just over a thousand years old, the codex has been kept in the National Library of Russia since 1863.

The Leningrad Codex began its long, distinguished history in the workshop of Aaron ben Moses ben Asher towards the end of the 10th century CE. Ben Asher is sometimes called the father of the modern Hebrew Bible. Although it was canonized by Ezra nearly fourteen centuries earlier, it was ben Asher who essentially finalized it in the form that exists today. His family ran a scriptorium in Tiberias which produced authoritative editions of the Tanakh, or Hebrew Bible, for distribution to Jewish communities around the world. In theory, every existing copy of the Hebrew Bible should be identical to these original works.

Aaron ben Moses ben Asher was a master of writing and grammar and spent years perfecting the Tanakh. When Maimonides acquired a copy of ben Asher's work in the 12th century, his positive review made it the favorite version of Jews the world over. According to its own notes, the Leningrad Codex was completed in the year 1008 CE. The text shows corrections that were made based on the older Aleppo Codex. The subsequent history of the codex is something of a mystery. It seems to have passed through the Crimea, and may have been in possession for a time by Karaite Jews. It was acquired by one Abraham Firkovich sometime in the 1830s, and he brought it to Odessa in 1838.

The Leningrad Codex was a great treasure of the Odessa Jewish community until 1863. However, when the avid Russian collector Modest Von Korff discovered the codex, he acquired it and brought it to St. Petersburg where it was housed in the National Library. In the years since it has been used as the basis for several new editions of the Tanakh. It has also been used to supplement the missing sections of the Aleppo Codex. The National Library is part of the Historic Center of St. Petersburg UNESCO World Heritage Site.

Of Interest: The National Library of Russia has moved from its original 19th century location and can now be found in a modern building on the Moskovsky Prospekt. It is home to one of the world's finest collections of books and antiquities. The Leningrad Codex is in good condition for a book that is a thousand years old. It includes all of the books of the traditional Hebrew canon from Genesis to Ezra-Nehemiah. The cover page of the codex contains a beautiful geometric pattern of a Star of David inside a circle, within which are inscribed the names of all those who worked on the book.

---

104. RUINS OF ATIL

Samosdelka, Russia

Site Type: Archaeological Site
Dates: Original settlement established c. 7th century CE
Web: None Available

The Ruins of Atil are an archaeological site connected to one of the oddest chapters of Jewish history: the Khazar Empire, whose leaders converted to Judaism sometime in the 8th or 9th centuries CE, and which may have been the largest Jewish ruled state in history. Archaeologists have only very recently rediscovered what they believe to be the ruins of Atil, the Khazar capital. Research into the site and is currently ongoing.

The Khazars were one of many Turkic peoples who established sprawling empires across the great open plains of Central Asia. They first appeared in history in the 6th century CE and were probably related to the Huns. During the 7th century CE the expansion of the Khazars put them into direct contact with the Muslim Sassanids to the south and the Christian Byzantines to the west. As persecution of Jews increased in both of these empires, the religiously indifferent Khazar Empire seems to have become a haven for Jewish refugees.

The Khazars had a long history of playing the various Christian and Muslim states off against each other. At some point in the late 8th century CE, Bulan, the ruler of the Khazars, decided to emulate the rulers of neighboring countries and adopt the God of Abraham. Since he viewed Judaism as being the older sibling of Christianity and Islam, and therefore superior to both, and since the Jews at that time had no rival monarch, Bulan converted to Judaism and claimed the throne of David for himself.

Amazingly this worked for a time. Although the Khazar king

was never recognized as David's successor by the Jews, Khazaria was a defacto Jewish state, the only one to have existed between 135 CE and 1948. The Jewish-Khazar Empire lasted for about two hundred years. Toward the end of the 10th century CE the Khazar Empire was destroyed in a series of wars. They made their last stand in the Crimea in 1016 CE. While some of the Jews of Khazaria remained in the east, the majority seem to have migrated into Europe where they eventually mingled with Ashkenazi Jews. The Khazar capital of Atil was forgotten until its ruins were rediscovered in the late 20th century.

Of Interest: The ruins of Atil have been ravaged by war and the elements for centuries. Anything that might have survived until the 20th century was probably destroyed during the communist era. It is only in the last few decades that the Khazars became the subject of serious academic investigation. The archaeological dig site at Samosdelka outside of Astrakhan is still in its very early stages. Begun in the 1990s, only a few initial findings have as yet been reported. There is little else in the way of description available at this time, but research is ongoing.

---

105. BRODSKY SYNAGOGUE

Zhukovs'koho Street, 18, Odessa, Odessa Oblast, Ukraine, 65000

Site Type: Synagogue
Dates: Completed in 1863
Designations: Ukrainian State Register of Monuments
Web: www.odessatourism.org/en/do/temples-churches/brodskaja-sinagoga (municipal tourism website)

The Brodsky Synagogue of Odessa is among the most historic synagogues in Ukraine and one of the most interesting Jewish sites in the city. At its height in the 19th century it was one of the largest Jewish houses of worship in Russia. It was home to the first Reform congregation in Ukraine, and was famous for its choir and musical programs. After nearly a century of dispossession, the synagogue has recently been returned to the local Jewish community.

In the early 19th century Jewish immigrants from the Austro-Hungarian Empire began arriving in Odessa in significant numbers. A group of immigrants from the city of Brody established a Reform congregation in Odessa in the 1840s. The congregation was extremely popular among the new immigrants and in the 1860s they constructed a massive new synagogue. It was named the Brodsky Synagogue after the town of Brody.

The community flourished even during the turbulent years of the late 19th century. The synagogue was famous for its concerts, which attracted some of Europe's greatest composers and musicians. The Brodsky Synagogue was seized by the communist authorities in 1927 and put to other purposes. The building weathered both the communists and the Nazi occupation during World War II, one of only a handful of the city's many synagogues to have survived.

Odessa finally returned control of the synagogue back to the Jewish community in 2016. The Brodsky Synagogue is listed on the Ukrainian State Register of Monuments. NOTE – At the time of this writing the interior of the synagogue was in a state of disrepair and off limits to visitors.

Of Interest: The Brodsky Synagogue was a magnificent building at the time of its original completion. Built in the Gothic Florentine style, this huge structure still dominates the surrounding neighborhood. Plans are currently underway for a major restoration of the site.

---

106. JEWISH MUSEUM OF ODESSA

Nizhyns'ka St, 66, Odessa, Odessa Oblast, 65000, Ukraine

Site Type: Museum
Dates: Opened in 2002
Web: www.odessatourism.org/en/do/museums/muzej-istorii-evreev-odessy (municipal tourism website)

The Jewish Museum of Odessa documents the history and culture of one of Europe's largest Jewish communities. There have been Jews in Odessa since at least as far back as the Middle Ages, and possibly since Roman times. During the 19th century Odessa was home to the world's second largest Jewish community after that of Warsaw. Despite being decimated by pogroms, emigration, the Holocaust and communist purges, the community still survives. Their story is told at the city's Jewish Museum.

Odessa had long been a magnet for Jewish immigrants. Jews from the Byzantine Empire may have settled here in the early Middle Ages. The bulk of the community was made up of Ashkenazi Jews who came from Eastern Europe in the later Middle Ages. During the Romanov dynasty Odessa boasted Russia's largest Jewish population. When anti-Semitism began to grow inside the Russian Empire, Odessa became a natural target.

The first major pogroms in Russia took place in Odessa in the 1820s. Over the next century other pogroms broke out here periodically, notably in 1859 and 1871. The assassination of Tsar Alexander II in 1881 was blamed on the Jews. Massive persecutions and riots broke out throughout the Russian Empire, and the Jews of Odessa were among those who suffered the most. It was this pogrom more than any other event that triggered the massive Jewish emigration out of Russia around the turn of the century.

The 20th century was a disaster for Odessa's Jews. Many were killed after the failed uprising against the tsar in 1905, and tens of thousands died in the early communist era. The greatest disaster was the Holocaust, where the majority of Odessa's Jews were wiped out. From its height of two hundred thousand just before World War II, the Jewish population of Odessa now hovers at around a little more than ten thousand. The surviving community opened a museum documenting the city's Jewish heritage in 2002.

Of Interest: The Jewish Museum of Odessa is small but houses a surprisingly large collection, mostly from the late 19th and 20th centuries. The bulk of the artifacts are documents, including newspapers, letters and photographs, as well as all kinds of antiquities, including clothing and everyday items. There are also darker reminders of Odessa's past, including exhibits on pogroms that took place in the city as well as the Nazi atrocities that were perpetrated here during World War II.

107. SHOLEM ALEICHEM BIRTH HOUSE

T1032, Pereiaslav-Khmelnytskyi, Kyivs'ka oblast, Ukraine, 08400

Site Type: Historic Residence
Dates: Solomon Rabinovich born here 1859
Web: www.sholomaleichemmuseum.com (official website)

The Sholem Aleichem Birth House was the childhood home of one of the titans of 19th century literature and arguably the greatest Yiddish writer of all time. Born in Ukraine during turbulent times for the Jews, Sholem Aleichem's writings embraced the experience of Jewish life in Eastern Europe. He introduced both humor and cultural fiction to mainstream Jewish literature. At the time of his death he was an international celebrity. His life and works are celebrated at his home in Pereiaslav.

The identity of the first person to tell jokes about Abram Rabinovich or the wise men of Chelm is lost to the mists of history. But the man most responsible for popularizing Jewish humor and who is most famous for raising it to an art form is undoubtedly the writer Sholem Naumovich Rabinovich, better known as Sholem Aleichem. Sometimes called the Jewish Mark Twain, he was born in 1859 in the small town of Pereiaslav-Khmelnytskyi south of Kiev. He began writing in his teen years, and according to some sources, his first work was a vocabulary book.

Many of his early works drew on his experiences growing up in a small village. Among his most popular writings were his stories of Tevye the Milkman, which consisted of semi-fictional and often humorous accounts of the lives of everyday Jewish peasants. These stories would later become the inspiration for the Broadway show *Fiddler on the Roof.* The fictional village of Anatevka was probably inspired by Pereiaslav. By the time he was in his thirties he was the most popular Jewish writer in the world.

Sholem Aleichem remained in Russia until 1905 when violence against the Jews became so severe that he was forced to leave. He and his family emigrated to Switzerland, and eventually to New York City, where he spent the remaining years of his life. His writings became as popular in the New World as in the Old, and by the time of his death in 1916 he was famous in both the United States and Europe. He is commemorated in several museums, including the one at his birthplace.

Of Interest: The Sholem Aleichem Birth House is a nearly two-centuries old residence that looks almost exactly the same now as it did in the author's day. While small, it was a substantial middle class home by 19th century standards. A small plaque outside explains the building's historical connection to Sholem Aleichem. For those interested in a more comprehensive experience, there is also a Sholem Aleichem Museum in Kiev filled with artifacts from his life, including writings, letters and photos.

---

108. KENESA OF YEVPATORIA

Karaimskaya 68, Yevpatoria, Ukraine

Site Type: Synagogue
Dates: Completed c. early 20th century CE
Web: None Available

The Kenesa of Yevpatoria is the heart of Karaite Judaism in the Crimea. The Karaites, a Jewish sect that originated in Persia, broke off from mainstream Judaism in the years following the arrival of Islam. At its height in the Middle Ages Karaite Judaism represented a significant portion of the Jewish population worldwide, but today there are relatively few Karaite Jews left. Most of these are concentrated in Israel and the United States. However the Crimea is still recognized as an important Karaite religious center.

In the 9th century CE a Mesopotamian Jew, Anan ben David, who was probably a spiritual descendent of the Saducees, started the Karaite movement. The Karaites believed that only the Holy Scriptures were authoritative, and rejected the use of the Talmud or any other rabbinical works. Islamic religious leadership often favored the Karaites because they rejected rabbinical authority.

By the 10th century CE Karaite Judaism was a major Jewish denomination. However the collapse of the Khazar Empire in the 10th century and the Mongol conquest of Persia and Mesopotamia in the 13th century dealt a severe blow to the Karaites. With the Karaites largely gone in the Middle East, the center of Karaitism moved to the Crimea. A small Karaite community has survived in the Crimea since the Middle Ages. NOTE – At the time of this writing, the Crimea was occupied by Russia. It is unknown if the kenesa is still currently active.

Of Interest: The Kenesa of Yevpatoria is a Karaite house of worship. There are only a few dozen traditional kenesas left in the world, though there are some relatively new ones in Israel and the United States. The Kenesa of Yevpatoria is one of the last still in use in the Crimea. Built in the early 20th century, this beautiful old building features a small but elegant sanctuary with a stunning ark. Unlike Jewish synagogues, which are typically oriented east-west, the kenessa is oriented north-south.

---

109. SATANIV SYNAGOGUE

Sataniv, Khmelnytski Oblast, Ukraine, 32034

Site Type: Synagogue
Dates: Completed c. 16th century
Web: None Available

The Sataniv Synagogue is believed to be the oldest surviving synagogue in Ukraine. While the exact date of its construction is uncertain, estimates range from the early 16th century to the mid-17th century. The synagogue is distinguished not only for its age but also for its fortress-like construction. Its incredibly sturdy walls, designed to protect those inside, are probably the main reason the building has survived for so long.

Sataniv is home to one of the oldest Ashkenazi communities in Ukraine. The community dates back to the late 15th or early 16th century when the area was still part of Poland. According to available information, the synagogue was believed to have been constructed in the early 16th century, although some scholars think it may have been completed later.

During the 17th and 18th centuries the synagogue was used as a strongpoint to protect against maurauding Cossacks and other threats. Once the Russians occupied the area the local Jews were subjected to pogroms and persecutions. During World War II virtually every Jew in Sataniv was killed, and the synagogue was converted to use as a warehouse. The building is once again a synagogue and was fully restored in 2012.

Of Interest: The Sataniv Synagogue is one of Ukraine's most interesting places of Jewish interest. Despite the building's average size, its walls were built to withstand a minor siege. Although not the world's only fortified synagogue, it is definitely one of the strongest. The stone walls are over six feet thick in places, enough to keep anti-Semitic mobs at bay, at least for a short period. The majority of the structure remained intact even after years of neglect, and parts of these centuries old walls can still be seen on exposed parts of the building.

---

110. GRAVESITE OF BA'AL SHEM TOV

Baal Shem Tov Street 24, Medzhybizh, Ukraine, 31530

Site Type: Burial Site
Dates: Ba'al Shem Tov buried 1760
Web: None Available

The Gravesite of Ba'al Shem Tov is an historic tomb of great importance to the Hasidic Jewish community. The Hasidic movement was founded by the Rabbi Israel ben Eliezer, more affectionately known as Ba'al Shem Tov, in Eastern Europe in the 18th century. While there are a number of different Hasidic groups, virtually all of them look upon Ba'al Shem Tov as their common founder. The gravesite of Ba'al Shem Tov has become a popular Jewish pilgrimage destination, especially since the end of communism in Eastern Europe.

Israel ben Eliezer was one of the most influential Jews in Europe during the 18th century. He was born in 1698 in Okopy in Ukraine and according to tradition he was a descendent of the Davidian royal line. From his childhood to the early years of his marriage ben Eliezer preferred the outdoor life away from large cities. His views of nature, the universe and God emerged in this period and had a profound effect on his later ideas and philosophies.

Ben Eliezer became respected in the local Jewish communities for his wisdom and fairness, and was often called upon to adjudicate legal disputes. He spent much of his life as a manual laborer, from digging in clay pits to working as a kosher butcher to running a tavern. In his spare time he developed a knowledge of the regional flora and was known for preparing medicinal remedies. For his skill as a healer, his charitable acts and the general respect he commanded, he was awarded the title of Ba'al Shem, which means "Master of the Name".

During his forties he settled down in the village of Medzhybizh where he established a school to pass on his ideas to others. By the time of his death Ba'al Shem Tov was among the most famous Jews in Europe. Although he personally wrote very little his teachings were passed on to his students, and these became the foundation of Hasidic Judaism. The town of Medzhybizh is now home to a number of Ba'al Shem Tove related sites.

Of Interest: The Gravesite of Ba'al Shem Tov can be found in the town of Medzhybizh, which is steeped in Jewish history. He is buried in the Old Jewish Cemetery, along with a number of other graves of early Hassidic leaders. Medzhybizh was also home to Baal Shem Tov's school. The original structure was completely destroyed by the Nazis, but a replica has been built using old plans and photos as a guide. The new building is now part of a museum with exhibits on the life of Baal Shem Tov and the early history of Hasidic Judaism. Finally, there is an old well just outside of the city. According to tradition, it was dug by Baal Shem Tov himself.

111. THE PIT

Alleya Pravednikov Mira, Central District, Minsk, Belarus

Site Type: Holocaust Memorial
Dates: Dedicated in 1947
Web: None Available

The Pit is a monument in Minsk that commemorates the massacre of five thousand Jews by the Nazis in March of 1942. Although a horrific act in and of itself, this event represents only a fraction of those slaughtered by the Nazis in the Soviet Union. The Pit is the most famous Holocaust memorial in Belarus.

Belarus, at the heart of Eastern Europe, was home to over a million Jews when Germany invaded the Soviet Union in 1941. Many of these were refugees who had already escaped from Poland in 1939, only to be caught by the Nazis less than two years later. The Holocaust in Belarus began earlier than in most other areas, before the mass execution facilities were functioning. Because of this countless Jews and other victims in Belarus were killed by firing squads rather than in gas chambers.

One of the most infamous massacres took place in Minsk on March 2, 1942. On that day thousands of inhabitants of the local Jewish ghetto were gunned down and buried in mass graves. Hundreds of thousands of Jews were shot to death in Belarus during the course of the war. The memorial was dedicated in 1947.

Of Interest: The Pit monument is exactly that, a large bowl shaped pit located in a park in downtown Minsk. Steps descend to an open plaza at the bottom marking the location where many Jews were killed. An incredibly moving sculpture depicting about twenty Jews marching down into the pit lines the stairs. An obelisk on the site commemorates the victims of the massacre.

112. GREAT SYNAGOGUE OF GRODNO

Vialikaja Trajeckaja Vulica 59A, Hrodna, Belarus

Site Type: Synagogue
Dates: Originally completed in 1580 CE; current building completed in 1905
Web: www.bhsinagoga.by (official website)

The Great Synagogue of Grodno is one of the largest synagogues in Belarus to have survived the turbulent 20th century. Its congregation was once one of the wealthiest and most influential in Eastern Europe. It stands on the site of an earlier synagogue that had been designed by the Italian Renaissance architect Santi Gucci. While a cultural symbol of the city's Jews, it is not currently active as a synagogue.

Ashkenazi Jews working their way across Europe may have arrived in Belarus as early as the 13th century. The Jewish community of Belarus was closely related to those of Poland and Lithuania, both geographically and culturally. These areas were often under the same rulership, where life for Jews was generally less harsh than in other places across Europe. The community at Grodno completed their first synagogue in the 16th century.

Belarus was conquered by Russia in the late 18th century and incorporated into the region known as the Pale of Settlement. Over the next one hundred years things grew steadily worse under the rule of the tsars. Thousands of Jews emigrated at the turn of the century. Nevertheless many remained in major centers such as Grodno. The original Grodno Synagogue burned down in a fire in the early 20th century. The current building was completed in 1905.

At the outset of World War II it is estimated that there were almost four hundred thousand Jews in Belarus. An estimated quarter of a million were killed in the Holocaust. Since the fall of communism almost all Belarusan Jews have left the country. There are only a few thousand left and only a handful of these remain in Grodno. The Great Synagogue was effectively closed for half a century during the

Nazi and communist eras. It was returned to the Jewish community in the 1990s.

Of Interest: The Great Synagogue of Grodno is a beautiful but run down structure near the old city center. A tan stone building trimmed in white, the synagogue displays an assortment of architectural styles. From the exterior it almost looks more like an old mansion than a house of worship. The interior details of the synagogue feature really exquisite stonework, but the sanctuary is otherwise mostly empty. At the time of this writing the building was in need of repairs.

---

113. OLD VILNA JEWISH CEMETERY & GRAVE OF VILNA GAON

Rinktines g. 1, Vilnius 09200, Lithuania

Site Type: Burial Site
Dates: Vilna Gaon buried 1797
Designations: UNESCO World Heritage Site
Web: None Available

The Old Vilna Jewish Cemetery is the site of the grave of Elijah ben Solomon Zalman, one of the most famous rabbis of the early modern era. Better known as the Vilna Gaon, which means "the genius from Vilnius", he was one of the great Jewish intellectuals of the 18th century. Known for his mastery of the Tanakh, he also promoted the study of science and mathematics as part of a Jewish education. He was most famous for his vigorous opposition to Hasidic Judaism.

The Vilna Gaon was born in 1720 in Sialiec in what is now Belarus. A brilliant child prodigy, he studied both the Tanakh and Talmud and achieved a great knowledge of both when still a youth. He also had an interest in the sciences. According to tradition, much older rabbis came to him for his advice when he was still in his teens. The Gaon spent most of his twenties traveling and visiting Jewish communities throughout Central Europe.

Although he practiced Orthodox Judaism, Elijah ben Solomon Zalman was opposed to the Hasidic movement, which had been growing in popularity since the early 18th century. He rallied the Jewish community of Vilnius to reject Hasidism, even going so far as to excommunicate its practitioners, and inspiring other Jewish communities to do the same. By the time of his death in 1797 he was one of the most famous rabbis in Europe. The Old Vilna Jewish Cemetery is part of the Vilnius Historic Centre UNESCO World Heritage Site.

Of Interest: The Old Vilna Jewish Cemetery is the modern incarnation of Vilnius' original 15th century Jewish graveyard. The gravesite of the Vilna Gaon is actually a mausoleum. The body was moved here when the earlier Jewish cemetery was closed down during the communist era. The Vilna Gaon is also commemorated with a stone memorial marker located at the former site of the Great Synagogue of Vilnius.

---

114. MUSEUM OF THE HISTORY OF THE POLISH JEWS

Mordechaja Anieliwicza 6, 00-157, Warsaw, Poland

Site Type: Museum
Dates: Opened in 2014
Web: www.polin.pl (official website)

The Museum of the History of the Polish Jews tells the story of one of the largest Jewish communities to have ever existed. For nearly five centuries Poland was the heart of Judaism on Earth. It was a place of refuge for Jews fleeing from all other corners of Europe. At its height at the beginning of World War II the Jewish population of Poland approached three and a half million. Today less than a hundred thousand remain.

The earliest documented Jewish settlements in Poland date from the 11th century. During the Crusades increased intolerance and violence against Jews in Western Europe drove many to the relative safety of Poland. In the 14th century King Casimir the Great extended significant protections to the Jews, and large numbers began relocating there. Although there were still difficult periods in Poland, Judiasm largely thrived there.

For centuries the Jewish community of Poland survived and continued to grow, especially as persecutions of Jews elsewhere increased. Things grew more difficult after the dissolution of the Kingdom of Poland in the 18th century. Many Jews actively supported the creation of an independent Polish state throughout the 19th century. When Poland regained its sovereignty following World War I, it once again became a haven for Jews, especially for those fleeing from the Soviet Union.

The great tragedy of the Polish Jews began in September of 1939 when Poland was overrun by the forces of Nazi Germany. Poland was ground zero for the Final Solution. The largest extermination camps were built in Poland, where over three million Jews were slaughtered. After the war most of the survivors left, leaving only a small fraction of this once enormous community. The Museum of the History of Polish Jews opened in 2014.

Of Interest: The Museum of the History of the Polish Jews is one of the largest institutions of its kind in Europe. Originally begun in the 2000s, the construction of the museum was part of a greater Jewish renaissance that started after the collapse of the Soviet Union. The museum traces the entire thousand-year history of this community. Eight galleries cover every major era of Polish Jewish history, from the initial arrivals in the Middle Ages through the present day. One of the galleries is devoted entirely to the tragedy of the Holocaust in Poland.

115. GHETTO HEROES MONUMENT

Ludwika Zamenhofa, 00-153 Warsaw, Poland

Site Type: Holocaust Memorial
Dates: Dedicated in 1948
Web: www.polin.pl (Museum of the History of the Polish Jews website)

The Ghetto Heroes Monument is Warsaw's memorial to the valiant uprising of the city's Jews against the Nazis in 1943. At the height of the power of the Third Reich the ghettos of Europe became prisons from which Jews were organized and deported to concentration camps. There were over a dozen major ghettos and countless smaller ones, most of which were located in Poland. Of these, none are as famous as the ghetto of the city of Warsaw, whose inhabitants fought against the Nazis in one of the most desperate and heroic uprisings of the war.

In the aftermath of Poland's disastrous defeat in 1939 the Nazis went to work. They began by relocating the Jewish populations into the existing ghettoes of the major cities. The ghetto of Warsaw, the largest in pre-war Europe, was home to more than four hundred thousand Jews. In November 1940 the Nazis built a wall around the ghetto and began relocating Jews from the surrounding area there. Perhaps another fifty to one-hundred thousand were added to the existing population. As many as a hundred thousand Jews died in the ghetto just from starvation, disease and violence.

In the summer of 1942 the Nazis began evacuating the ghetto. In two months approximately seventy-five percent of the population was shipped off to the Treblinka death camp. The remaining Jews, realizing that the deportations were to end in their annihilation, decided to fight back. In January 1943 the Warsaw Ghetto Uprising began under the leadership of Mordechai Anielewicz. Less than a thousand Jewish resistance fighters, poorly armed and with only minimal support from the outside, took on the German army.

The Jewish uprising lasted for the better part of four months. By April it was clear to the Germans that it would take a substantial military effort to overcome the insurgency. They systematically destroyed the entire ghetto block-by-block with explosives and flamethrowers. By May 16 it was all but over. More than ten thousand Jews died during the uprising, and almost all of those who survived were subsequently killed at Treblinka. Some escaped to join the Polish resistance and fought in the much larger Warsaw Uprising of 1944. By the time the war ended virtually all of Warsaw had been destroyed. Few traces of the once flourishing Jewish community remain in Warsaw today.

Visiting: The Ghetto Heroes Monument is located near the Museum of the History of Polish Jews. This large stone edifice marks the loction of the uprising's command center and commemorates the leaders of the valiant but ultimately doomed effort. Of related interest in Warsaw are the Pawiak Museum and the Museum of the Warsaw Uprising. The former is located on a former prison compound where forty thousand Jews were killed during the war. The latter commemorates the much larger uprising of the Polish citizens against the Nazis in 1944.

---

116. SYNAGOGUES OF KRAKOW

Several locations along Kupa, Jozefa, Szeroka and Warszauera Streets, Krakow, Poland

Site Type: Historic Neighborhood, Synagogues
Dates: Completed in 1644 (Izaak Synagogue); 1563 (High Synagogue); 1570 (Old Synagogue); 1620 (Popper Synagogue); 1557 (Remuh Synagogue); 1643 (Kupa Synagogue)
Designations: UNESCO World Heritage Site
Web: https://gwkrakow.pl/services/synagogi (website of the Jewish Religious Community in Krakow)

The city of Krakow is home to one of the largest collections of surviving pre-war synagogues in Europe. This is due in large part to the fact that for centuries Krakow was the capital of Poland, which had the largest population of Jews in Europe. Moreover, Krakow escaped the wholesale destruction that was visited on Warsaw during World War II. For these reasons Krakow is now a destination for those wishing to explore one of Eastern Europe's densest concentrations of historic synagogues.

Krakow was founded sometime in the 10th century CE and became the capital of Poland in 1038 CE. Jews first settled here at least as far back as the 13th century. Although they faced periodic persecutions as elsewhere in Europe, the Jewish population of Poland was largely protected by a series of tolerant rulers, especially Casimir. The community flourished in the 15th and 16th centuries, and some of the city's oldest surviving synagogues date from this period.

Krakow ceased to be the royal capital in 1596. Although this led to the beginning of a long decline for the city, the Jewish community remained vibrant. The 17th century saw a wave of synagogue construction. This continued all the way into the 20th century. By the time World War II started there were an estimate seventy thousand Jews in Krakow and nearly a hundred synagogues.

Many of the city's synagogues did not survive the war. Most were ransacked and then put to various uses, largely for storage. Amazingly, some of the city's oldest synagogues did make it to the end of the war at least partially intact. Most of these are clustered near each other in Krakow's historic Kazimierz neighborhood. Kazimierz is part of the Historic Centre of Krakow UNESCO World Heritage Site.

Of Interest: A pedestrian at a reasonable pace can walk past seven of Krakow's major historic synagogues in under an hour. A good order to see them in would be: the Izaak Synagogue, completed in 1644 and still in use; the High Synagogue, completed in 1563 by Sephardic refugees from Southern Europe; the Old Synagogue, originally built in the 15th century, rebuilt in 1570 and renovated in the 1950s, and is now home to a Jewish museum; the Popper Synagogue, originally built in 1620 and now used as a cultural center; the Remuh Synagogue, originally built in 1557; and the Kupa Synagogue, originally built in 1643 and still partially in active use. The oldest, the Remuh Synagogue, seems to be the most popular for visitors. Krakow's Old Jewish Cemetery is located right next door.

117. OSKAR SCHINDLER FACTORY MUSEUM

Lipowa 4, 30-702 Krakow, Poland

Site Type: Factory, Museum, Holocaust Memorial
Dates: Opened in 2010
Web: www.muzeumkrakowa.pl/oddzialy/fabryka-schindlera (official
website)

The Oskar Schindler Factory Museum is among the best known places
in the world associated with the Righteous among the Nations. Made
famous by the 1994 film *Schindler's List*, this factory employed over
a thousand Jews who were subsequently saved from the Nazi death
camps. The factory now houses a branch of the Historical Museum
of the City of Krakow, which in turn houses exhibits from the life of
Oskar Schindler as well as artifacts and props from the film.

Oskar Schindler was born in 1908 in the Austro-Hungarian
Empire, and later lived in Prague. A supporter of German unification,
he joined the Nazis and was actively involved in assisting their efforts
to occupy Czechoslovakia. Although not particularly ideological, his
activities gave him special advantages in business when the Germans
took over.

After the start of the war Schindler moved to occupied Poland
where he took over a formerly Jewish owned factory. At first he
showed an indifference to the plight of the Jews and used them as
slave labor. However, as time went on the brutality of the Nazis trans-
formed Schindler into a sympathizer. Under the guise of his business
interests he used his influence to protect those Jews working for him.
He also worked with the Jewish underground. By the end of the war
he had completely bankrupted himself keeping his workers out of the
concentration camps.

By the time the war ended it was estimated that about twelve
hundred Jews were saved thanks to his efforts. Most of Schindler's
later life was marked by failed businesses and poverty. However, he
was remembered among the Jewish people for his efforts, and in 1962

he became the only former member of the Nazi party to be named one of the Righteous among the Nations. The museum at his factory in Krakow was opened in 2010.

Of Interest: The Oskar Schindler Factory Museum is technically two museums housed inside the old enamelworks building. One is the city's Museum of Contemporary Art. The other is a branch of the Historical Museum of the City of Krakow. The latter is filled with exhibits on Schindler and the Jews that he saved, as well as on the Krakow Ghetto. There are a number of artifacts from the period, including a large display of photos. One room has the names from the list inscribed on the walls. There are also some sets and props that were used in the filming of *Schindler's List*.

---

118. AUSCHWITZ-BIRKENAU MEMORIAL AND MUSEUM

Wiezniow Oswiecimia 20, 32-603 Osciecim, Poland

Site Type: Concentration Camp, Museum
Dates: Concentration Camp opened in 1940; museum opened in 1947
Designations: UNESCO World Heritage Site
Web: www.auschwitz.org (official website)

The Auschwitz-Birkenau Extermination Camp has the dubious distinction of being the most efficient machine of mass murder ever devised by the minds of men. The largest concentration camp built by the Nazis, more than one and a half million innocent people, mostly Jews, were slaughtered here over a five year period. This bleak place resounds with the eternal voices of its victims crying from beyond the grave, "Never Again".

In 1939 Poland became the first country to be conquered by Nazi Germany through military means. Home to a large population of Jews, as well as many Jews who had already fled here from Germany,

Poland became ground zero for the Nazi efforts to extinguish the Jewish people from the European continent. On May 20, 1940, the Konzentrationslager Auschwitz opened its doors to receive its first detainees.

The first camp, also known as Auschwitz I, originally housed prisoners of war and political dissidents. But by 1941 vast numbers of Jews were being brought in. To accommodate them, immense holding facilities were built at Auschwitz II, or Birkenau. Many sub-camps were established for the purpose of exploiting the available slave labor. For those who were not chosen to work in the labor camps, the gas chambers were introduced in 1942.

As the war began to turn against the Germans, the Nazis increased the pace of the killings. The majority of deaths at Auschwitz took place in 1943 and 1944. When the camp was finally liberated, fewer than eight thousand survivors remained. In the end, for every one prisoner who walked out, two hundred had been killed. In 1948 a commemorative museum was erected on the site. The Auschwitz-Birkenau Concentration Camp is a UNESCO World Heritage Site.

Of Interest: Most of the Auschwitz-Birkenau Concentration Camp is now maintained as an open air museum. Numerous buildings have been restored to appear as they did in 1944. The gate at the entrance still bears the mocking inscription "Arbeit macht frei", or "Work will make you free". The saddest sites are the restored gas chamber and crematorium. Numerous exhibits are spread throughout the various buildings of the camp. Some of these focus on the various ethnic groups that died in the camps, including the Jews, Gypsies and Slavs. There are also rooms full of the former inmates' personal effects. Another exhibit shows a film taken by the Soviets when they liberated the camp. There is also a synagogue and Jewish information center on site, with an exhibit on Jewish life in Oswiecim before the Holocaust.

119. CHACHMEI LUBLIN YESHIVA

Lubartowska 85, 20-400 Lublin, Poland

Site Type: Synagogue, Museum
Dates: Opened in 1930
Web: www.hotelilan.pl (official website)

The Chachmei Lublin Yeshiva is an historic Jewish institute of learning. Lublin, once dubbed the Jewish Oxford, was the academic center of Ashkenazi Judaism for the better part of four centuries. From the mid-16th century to the mid-20th century Jewish scholars from all over Europe came to study in Lublin at one of the continent's only state sanctioned Talmudic academies. After languishing for years under the Nazis and communists, the yeshiva has been returned to the Jewish community.

By the beginning of the 16th century Poland was one of the major hubs of European Judaism. Lublin became the defacto capital of European Judaism, and a congress of Jews from all over Eastern Europe met there annually. In 1567 the head of the Yeshiva of Lublin was elevated to equal status with his counterparts at the kingdom's Christian universities.

Unfortunately the Polish Jewish renaissance came to an end in the mid-17th century. In the wake of the Thirty Years War Poland was assaulted on all sides by its neighbors, none of whom were friendly towards the Jews. Neverthless the Yeshiva of Lublin remained the greatest center of Talmudic scholarship in Europe right until 1939. After the war the building was used as a medical school. The yeshiva was returned to the Jewish community in 2003. At the time of this writing the synagogue had already been restored, and a museum for the building was being planned.

Of Interest: Predecessors of the Cachmei Lublin Yeshiva existed at least as far back as the early 16th century. The current building is only a century old. Completed in 1930, this elegant school typifies the architectural style of public buildings of the period. Despite serious damage to the interior during the Nazi regime the yeshiva building survived the ravages of World War II. The renovated exterior appears much today as it did in the 1930s. The yeshiva's synagogue was completed and rededicated in 2007. The restoration effort attempted to recreate the original synagogue based on available plans and photographs. The finished Yeshiva will include a museum.

120. DOHANY STREET SYNAGOGUE

Dohany u. 2, 1704, Budapest, Hungary

Site Type: Synagogue, Museum
Dates: Completed in 1859
Designations: UNESCO World Heritage Site
Web: www.greatsynagogue.hu (official website)

The Dohany Street Synagogue is the largest surviving synagogue in Europe, and for a while in the 19th century it was the largest synagogue in the world. It is among the grandest synagogues to have survived destruction at the hands of the Nazis during World War II. This is perhaps befitting one of the most resilient Jewish communities to be found in Europe.

The origins of the Jews of Hungary are a bit of a mystery. Historically speaking they are primarily descended from Ashkenazi Jews who migrated eastwards from Germany in the Middle Ages. However, it is also possible that Jewish communities existed in the Danube River area as early as Roman times. One tradition suggests that the first Jews here were survivors of the Jewish revolts of the 1st century who came to aid the Dacians, another conquered people trying to drive out the Romans.

The history of the Hungarian Jews was something of a roller coaster. It seemed that once or twice in every generation a new king would ascend the throne, alternately embracing or opressing the Jews. During one period in the mid-14th century the Jews of Hungary were expelled, readmitted, expelled again and readmitted again in the course of just a couple of decades. In spite of this instability, the Jews of

Hungary were generally tolerated by the greater community, perhaps more than any other place in Eastern Europe.

Anti-Semitism in Hungary was historically met with vigorous protests, passive resistance, and sometimes even with force. On at least one occasion the Jews of Hungary escaped deportation simply by ignoring the order to leave. The strange paradoxical existence of the Jews in Hungary continued right up until the 20th century. The synagogue is a testament to the endurance of Hungarian Jews. The Dohany Street Synagogue is part of the Budapest UNESCO World Heritage Site.

Of Interest: The Grand Synagogue of Dohany Street is the largest synagogue in Europe and was the largest in the world until it was surpassed by New York's Temple Emanu-El in 1929. Completed in 1859 this mastepiece of Moorish architecture consists of an enormous walled complex that includes the synagogue, several memorial sites, the Hero's Temple honoring those Jews who fought and died in World War I, a Holocaust Memorial, and the city's Jewish Museum. The interior of the synagogue is breathtaking, and can accommodate up to three thousand worshippers at a time. The synagogue's organ has been played by some of Europe's greatest musicians including Liszt and Saint-Saens. The ark is massive and decorated and crowned in gold leif. The current condition of the synagogue, which was heavily damaged in the war, is the result of extensive restorations that were completed in the 1990s.

---

121. SHOES ON THE DANUBE BANK

Id. Antall Jozsef rkp., 1054, Budapest, Hungary

Site Type: Holocaust Memorial
Dates: Dedicated in 2005
Designations: UNESCO World Heritage Site
Web: www.budapestinfo.hu/shoes-on-the-danube-bank (municipal tourism website)

The Shoes on the Danube Bank is one of the most unusual Holocaust memorial sites anywhere. It commemorates the thousands of victims of the Hungarian fascists who were executed along the Danube River in the last months of World War II. It also commemorates those who attempted to save them, some of whom are members of the Righteous among the Nations.

For most of World War II the Holocaust ravaged the Jewish populations of Axis occupied countries all across Europe. One of the few places bypassed by the Final Solution, at least for the early part of the war, was Hungary. Over eight hundred thousand Jews found refuge here for much of the conflict. That ended when German forces occupied Hungary in 1944.

The Final Solution was immediately implemented in Hungary, and hundreds of thousands of Jews were deported to the concentration camps. Many were also killed by members of the Hungarian Arrow Cross. Over the course of several months in the winter of 1944-1945 thousands of Jews and other victims were marched to the Danube riverfront, stripped of their shoes and shot dead into the river. The monument commemorating the victims of this mass murder was dedicated in 2005. The Shoes on the Danube Bank is part of the Budapest UNESCO World Heritage Site.

Of Interest: The Shoes on the Danube Bank memorial is exactly what it sounds like. It consists of about a hundred sculptures of iron shoes cluttered along a stretch of the river bank not too far from the Hungarian Parliament building. It marks a spot where hundreds, possibly thousands, of Hungarian Jews were massacred in 1944 and 1945. Several plaques on site explain the purpose of the memorial.

CENTRAL EUROPE

122. NEW SYNAGOGUE

Oranienburger Street 28-30, 10117, Berlin, Germany

Site Type: Synagogue, Museum
Dates: Completed in 1866
Web: https://centrumjudaicum.de (official website)

The New Synagogue is one of Berlin's most poignant buildings. Despite the fact that it stood at the heart of the Third Reich, it somehow managed to partially survive the Nazi era. Because of this the New Synagogue is somehow more memorable than many others still standing. Over the last few decades Berlin's New Synagogue has been magnificently restored, a legacy of the city's pre-Nazi Jewish community.

Jews first arrived and settled in Berlin around the 13th century CE. Over time Berlin's Jewish community became quite sizeable, numbering in the tens of thousands by the 16th century. It survived the turbulent years of Europe's religious wars, and was flourishing in the 19th century when Germany achieved nationhood. The New Synagogue dates from this time.

After World War I many Germans in the country's right wing parties blamed the Jews for their defeat. The Berlin Jewish community was immediately targeted as soon as Hitler came to power. On November 9, 1938, on a night that will forever be remembered as the Kristalnacht, or "Night of Shattered Glass", much of the city's Jewish property was wantonly destroyed. Some of the first acts of vandalism took place at the New Synagogue. What was left of the Jewish Quarter of Berlin was spared from destruction due to the efforts of the chief of police.

At the end of the war in 1945 most of the Jewish quarter was in ruins along with the rest of the city. The Berlin Jewish community, which may have numbered over a hundred and fifty thousand at the beginning of the Nazi regime, was all but wiped out. Only a trickle returned during the communist era, but these few made every effort to preserve what they could. After the reunification more Jews returned, and the New Synagogue was restored to its former state. Today it is once again one of the great architectural landmarks of the heart of Berlin.

Of Interest: The New Synagogue was funded by Berlin's wealthiest Jewish families in the 1860s. Built in a magnificent Moorish style, the building is crowned with a great golden dome and two smaller flanking domes. However these were mostly reconstructed in the post-communist era. The new cornerstone was laid down in 1988 on the fiftieth anniversary of the Kristalnacht. In its day the New Synagogue could seat over three thousand congregants. Marble pillars mark the location where the ark and its torah scrolls once stood. The interior is now primarily occupied by the Centrum Judaicum, a museum dedicated to the synagogue and the old Jewish community.

---

123. BERLIN JEWISH MUSEUM

Lindenstrasse 9-14, 10969 Berlin, Germany

Site Type: Museum
Dates: Opened in 2001
Web: www.jmberlin.de (official website)

The Jewish Museum of Berlin is the major Jewish museum of Germany. Opened in 2001, it actually succeeds an earlier museum that was active in the 1930s. At the time of this writing the museum was undergoing a major expansion and renovation, with work to be completed in 2020.

Berlin was home to one of the first Jewish museums in Europe. It originally opened in January of 1933, ironically just a few days before the Nazis came to power in Germany. Located next door to the New Synagogue, this institution amazingly managed to stay open for several years despite mounting pressure from the Nazi government. It finally closed at the end of 1938 following the Kristallnacht pogrom.

This early museum was looted and its contents scattered throughout the Third Reich. Some collections and items have since been recovered and are now on display at the new museum and other Jewish museums around the world. The current museum was opened in 2001, and is now one of the most popular museums in Berlin.

Of Interest: The Berlin Jewish Museum is home to a large collection of Judaica, including an extensive archive of books, documents and photographs. The museum covers a lot of historical ground, with a focus on postwar history. The museum's artistic highlight is an exhibit called the Memory Void, a monument dedicated to all of the innocents who died during World War II.

---

124. MEMORIAL TO THE MURDERED JEWS OF EUROPE

Cora-Berliner-Strasse 1, 10117, Berlin, Germany

Site Type: Holocaust Memorial
Dates: Dedicated in 2005
Web: www.stiftung-denkmal.de/denkmaeler (official website)

The Memorial to the Murdered Jews of Europe is one of the largest Holocaust monuments in the world. It sprawls over a large city block just south of the Brandenburg Gate, close to where the Reich Chancellery and Fuhrer Bunker were once located. Despite the fact that it is a highly moving site, the monument has come under criticism from several groups, including some Jewish organizations.

There is simply no way to separate the history of modern Germany from the Holocaust. Beginning with the imprisonment of political dissidents after the Nazi rise to power in 1933 and building to a horrendous crescendo of slaughter in the mid-1940s, the Holocaust is now and will forever be part of the German identity. And no where is this more keenly felt than in Berlin, the heart of darkness in the Third Reich.

A half-century after the war, work finally began on a monument in Berlin commemorating the victims of the Holocaust. Part of the delay was due to the Cold War, and the project did not move forward until the Berlin Wall came down. The Memorial to the Murdered Jews of Europe took approximately two years to complete and was dedicated in 2005.

Of Interest: The Memorial to the Murdered Jews of Europe is huge and very unique. It consists of a sea of nearly three thousand monoliths of varying heights. The monoliths grow taller the further in visitors go. The monument is somewhat abstract, but clearly gives the impression of confusion and loss. There is a visitor's center adjacent to the site. The memorial has come under criticism from a number of organizations, including some Jewish groups who have pointed out that the site does very little to convey information about the Holocaust itself or any specific details about its victims. Nevertheless the uniqueness and solemnity of the place is worth a visit for those wishing to pay their respects to the lives lost during the Shoah.

125. MENDELSSOHN GRAVESITES

Grosse Hamburger Strasse 26, 10115, Berlin, Germany
(Old Jewish Cemetery)

Schonhauser Allee 25, 10435 Berlin, Germany
(Judischer Friedhof Prenzlauer Berg Cemetery)

Paul-Schneider-Strasse 45, 12247 Berlin, Germany
(Dreifaltigkeits Friedhof Cemetery)

Site Type: Burial Sites
Dates: Moses Mendelssohn buried 1786; Joseph M. buried 1848; Felix M. buried 1847)
Web: www.visitberlin.de/en/alter-judischer-friedhof-old-jewish-cemetery (municipal tourism website)

The Mendelssohn family of Germany was one of the most famous Jewish families of the Enlightenment. Over the course of three generations, the Mendelssohns produced one of the greatest philosophers, one of the greatest bankers and one of the greatest musicians in Europe. The family rose to such prominence that they were considered part of European high society, a difficult achievement for Jews in the 18th and 19th centuries. All three of the famous Mendelssohns are buried in Berlin, and miraculously all three gravesites survived the Nazi era.

The Mendelssohns rose from very humble origins, beginning in Dessau in 1729 with the birth of Moses Mendelssohn. In his earlier years he was given a religious education. At the age of fourteen his family moved to Berlin where he studied foreign languages, philosophy and mathematics. His career as a writer was a successful one, and he became the most prominent Jewish intellectual in Europe since Spinoza. Among his many achievements, Moses Mendelssohn is credited with translating parts of the Hebrew Bible into German. He died in 1786.

Moses Mendelssohn had six children, the most famous being his oldest son Joseph. Born in 1770, Joseph's childhood was a far cry from the poverty of his father's young years. Raised in a house that was always filled with important visitors, Joseph grew up both intelligent and ambitious. In 1795 he founded his own bank in Berlin. Mendelssohn banking interests funded major development projects around Europe during the colonial era. Joseph Mendelssohn was an important fixture of the Berlin financial district until his death in 1848.

Joseph's nephew Felix was born in 1809. Felix was a musical child prodigy, and he grew up to become one of Europe's greatest composers. However his legacy was tainted by the growing anti-Semitism of the age, and he was notoriously disliked by his rival Richard Wagner. Nevertheless when he died in 1847 at the young age of 38, he left behind a legacy of some of the greatest music ever created by a Jewish composer.

Of Interest: The fact that all three of the Mendelssohn gravesites survived World War II is nothing short of a miracle. Moses Mendelssohn was interred in the Old Jewish Cemetery of Berlin, which was destroyed during the Nazi era. His old, faded restored tombstone is one of the only surviving remnants of the graveyard. The grave of

Joseph Mendelssohn is located in the Judischer Friedhof Prenzlauer Berg Cemetery. Felix Mendelssohn is buried in the Dreifaltigkeits Friedhof Cemetery under the name Bartholdy. The use of his father's last name, and the fact that the gravestone is in the shape of a cross, suggests that his descendents made an effort to obscure his Jewish heritage. The Mendelssohn House at 51 Jagerstrasse, which was home to the Mendelssohn & Co. Bank until the 1930, is still in active use as an office building.

---

126. HOUSE OF THE WANNSEE CONFERENCE

Am Grossen Wannsee 56-58, 14109 Berlin, Germany

Site Type: Museum, Holocaust Memorial
Dates: Conference took place in 1942; Museum opened in 1992
Web: www.ghwk.de (official website)

The House of the Wannsee Conference is a beautiful old mansion by a serene lake just outside of Berlin. There, on January 20, 1942, fifteen government officials of the Third Reich met and casually discussed the annhilation of Europe's Jews. This was the official beginning of the implementation of the "Final Solution to the Jewish Question". The villa is now a museum that explains what happened during that fateful meeting and its horrifying consequences.

The persecution of the Jewish people was a keystone of the Nazi party platform from the moment it came to power. Anti-Semitic activity became public policy with the enactment of the Nuremberg Laws in 1935. Over the course of the next few years persecutions of the Jews became increasingly widespread and brutal. By 1941 Germany had overrun much of Europe and millions of Jews were trapped within the borders of the Third Reich. The Nazis decided it was time to move forward with their plans.

Under the orders of Hermann Goering, Reinhard Heydrich began to make prepaprations for Hitler's Final Solution. A few months later the mass deportation of the German Jews began. When the first waves of Jews arrived in the east, those who were healthy were put to work, and the rest were shot outright. However this form of mass murder was too slow and inefficient for the Nazis. Heydrich decided to convene a conference of high ranking German officials to discuss the issue.

The goal was to eliminate the Jewish population of Europe. Since emigration was effectively impossible, that left only one option: genocide. The general idea was to round up every Jew in Europe, ship them off to the east and work them to death. Those unfit to work, or those who survived a bit too long, would be put to death. Within this framework the participants of the Wannsee Conference merely had to discuss the details. The meeting took less than two hours. Three and half years later, six million Jews and five million others were dead. The House of the Wannsee Conference still stands as a stark reminder of the most infamous meeting in history.

Of Interest: The stately Wannsee Conference House on the shore of a tranquil lake utterly belies what took place here in 1942. The villa at 56 Am Grossen Wannsee, owned by the SS, had the dubious distinction of being selected to host the conference. Built in 1914, the beautiful mansion was erected at the very end of Germany's imperial age. The majority of the interior was repurposed as a museum after the war was over. Among its displays are an original copy of the minutes, which escaped destruction in the final, hectic days of the Third Reich.

---

127. OLD SYNAGOGUE

Waagegasse 8, 99084 Erfurt, Germany

Site Type: Medieval Synagogue, Museum
Dates: Completed c. 1270 CE
Web: https://juedisches-leben.erfurt.de/jl/de/mittelalter/ alte_synagoge (official website)

The Old Synagogue of Erfurt is the oldest surviving synagogue in Germany and one of the oldest essentially intact synagogues in Europe.

Largely completed in the 13th century CE, some elements of the Erfurt Synagogue are even older, predating the Staranova Synagogue in Prague. Thanks to the fact that the building was ignored for many centuries, the Old Synagogue preserved many architectural, artistic and actual treasures that are found nowhere else in Europe.

The Erfurt Synagogue was built sometime around the 1270s on the site of an earlier 11th century synagogue. The original synagogue coincides with the time period that Jews are believed to have first settled in Erfurt. The Jewish community survived here for roughly three hundred years. However in 1349, as the Black Plague ravaged Europe, a massacre in Erfurt left most of the city's Jews dead and the survivors driven out.

The city took possession of the building, and in turn sold it to a private owner. For the next six centuries the building had a variety of uses, primarily for storage. Because it was not used as a synagogue, and because it was tucked away in an alley, the Old Synagogue remained anonymous and avoided pretty much all anti-Semitic violence, even during the Nazi era. The building, once again a Jewish property, is currently being used as a museum.

Of Interest: The Old Synagogue of Erfurt and its museum is one of the most historic medieval Jewish sites in Europe. The building itself is an architectural gem, almost intact from its 13th century construction. Archaeological research beneath the synagogue has uncovered a nearly intact medieval mikveh bath which is now on display. The museum houses several exhibits including a priceless collection of Hebrew manuscripts dating from the Middle Ages. Also kept here is the Erfurt Treasure, a recovered horde of silver coins and jewelry that was hidden away at the time of the Jewish massacre.

128. COLOGNE JEWISH MUSEUM
AND ARCHAEOLOGICAL SITE

Obenmarspforten 1, 50667, Cologne, Germany

Site Type: Historic Neighborhood, Archaeological Site, Museum
Dates: Opening in 2021
Web: www.museenkoeln.de/archaeologische-zone (official website)

The Cologne Jewish Museum is, at the time of this writing, a museum to be opened near the Cologne city center in 2021. Unlike most Jewish museums in Europe, which typically house collections of Judaica, this museum's major component will be an underground archaeological exhibit. The site, located in an ancient part of the city, was home to the first significant Jewish community in the Rhineland. It may in fact date back to the Roman era, making it the oldest such community in North-Central Europe.

Cologne was one of the most important cities of the Roman Empire located along the German frontier. Settled in the 1st century CE, it was a critical center of trade between the Germans and the Romans until the empire collapsed in the 5th century. It is uncertain exactly when the first Jews settled in Cologne. There is documentation supporting the existence of a Jewish community here in the early 4th century, but some merchants might have been active here even earlier.

Jews continued to live in Cologne throughout the years of Frankish rule and the early period of the Holy Roman Empire. However like their brethren in France and the Rhineland, the Jews of Cologne were regularly persecuted in the Middle Ages. The worst pogroms took place in the mid-14th century in the wake of the Black Death. The Jews were largely driven from Cologne in the early 1400s, and did not return in substantial numbers for four centuries.

A Jewish community was re-established in the 19th century, and had reached about twenty thousand on the eve of the Nazi rise to power. The majority of these were killed during the Holocaust. However, the city center of Cologne was badly damaged during World War II, and the remains of the ancient Jewish quarter were exposed.

Archaeologists investigated the ruins in the 1950s, and it was preserved as an historic site. The area is currently being incorporated into the city's new Jewish Museum.

Of Interest: The Jewish Museum of Cologne, when finished, has the potential to be one of the most fascinating Jewish museums in Europe. The main museum above street level will house exhibits on the history of the Jews in Cologne and artifacts from the city's Jewish history. The real treasure will be below ground, where a subterranean tunnel will allow visitors to see the ancient archaeological site. The primary points of interest here are the ruins of the medieval synagogue and mikveh ritual bath. Other surviving buildings from the neighborhood include a bakery and a hospital.

129. ROTHSCHILD PALACE & JEWISH MUSEUM

Bertha-Pappenheim-Platz 1, 60311 Frankfurt am Main, Germany

Site Type: Historic Residence, Museum
Dates: Museum opened in 1988
Web: www.juedischesmuseum.de (official website)

The Rothschild Palace in Frankfurt is a former residence of one of the most influential Jewish families in modern history. For more than two centuries the name Rothschild has conjured up visions of fabulous wealth and international prestige. From their ancestral home in Frankfurt, the Rothschilds later expanded into England, France, Austria and Italy, amassing a collection of palatial homes that rivaled those of Europe's great aristocratic families. While their oldest and largest home in Frankfurt was destroyed during World War II, one of their other homes now houses the city's Jewish Museum.

The rise of the Rothschild dynasty was one of the great Jewish success stories of the 18th and 19th centuries. The family's financial empire was founded by Mayer Amschel Rothschild. A resident of the Jewish ghetto in Frankfurt, Mayer Rothschild began with a small banking concern. Recognizing early on the growing importance of international financial firms, he envisioned a family owned company that would eventually spread throughout Europe. Among his innovations was the establishment of new branches in London, Paris, Vienna and Naples, each of which was run directly by one of his sons.

The entire business remained private and within control of the family. The first major branch outside of Frankfurt was the one in London, and together these two banks were instrumental in funding the English and Prussian wars against Napolean Bonaparte. By the end of the Napoleanic wars the Rothschilds were among the richest familes in Europe. During the 19th century the Rothschilds of Austria and England were elevated to the aristocracy. Throughout that period their banks were involved in some of the world's most important development projects, such as the Suez Canal.

As the age of the European empires came to a close and America became the world's new financial center, the wealth and influence of the Rothschilds waned. The Naples office closed in 1861 after the unification of Italy; the Frankfurt office closed when that branch of the family came to an end; and the Vienna office closed in 1938 after the Germans occupied Austria. Most of the Austrian Rothschild's fortune was turned over to the Nazis in order to buy their escape. The Rothschild businesses are now run out of London. Their legacy in Germany survives at the Frankfurt Jewish Museum.

Of Interest: The Jewish Museum of Frankfurt is home to an assortment of collections related to the history of the Jewish community of the city as well as to he Rothschild family. This includes artwork by a number of great artists including Moritz Oppenheimer. At the time of this writing the museum was undergoing a major renovation, with new and updated exhibits planned. Of related interest is the nearby Jewish ghetto museum, which houses exhibits on Frankfurt's medieval Jewish quarter.

130. NEW SYNAGOGUE

Hindenburgstrasse 44, 55118 Mainz, Germany

Site Type: Synagogue
Dates: Completed in 2010
Web: www.jgmainz.de (official website)

The New Synagogue of Mainz is the ultra-modern synagogue of one of Germany's oldest Jewish communities. Constructed in the early 2000s, it stands in place of the city's many historic synagogues that were destroyed by the Nazis in the 1930s. The grounds of the New Synagogue are home to remnants of earlier Jewish houses of worship that are now long gone.

Mainz was one of the medieval cities along that Rhine that gave birth to Ashkenazi Judaism in the Middle Ages. Jews began settling here in the 10th century CE. The community, which survived here for many centuries, experienced the regular persecutions that were typical of the region. There were periodic pogroms, with particularly violent ones during the First Crusade of the 11th century and the Black Death in the 14th century.

The Jewish community of Mainz suffered terribly under the Nazis, with the city's synagogues being badly damaged or destroyed on Kristallnacht in 1938. Few Jews remained in the city after the war, but the community was slowly reestablished in the decades following World War II. By the 1990s there were enough Jews in Mainz to necessitate a synagogue. The New Synagogue was completed in 2010.

Of Interest: The New Synagogue is one of the most architecturally modern houses of worship in Germany. The wildly creative structure is a riotous jumble of walls and elements, none of which appear to share a ninety degree angle with any other element. The roof is roughly designed to resemble a shofar horn. The site where the New Synagogue now stands was occupied by an earlier synagogue prior to Kristallnacht. A portion of a colonnade from the old synagogue is still standing outside of the new building.

131. RASHI SHUL SYNAGOGUE

Synagogenplatz, 67547 Worms, Germany

Site Type: Synagogue, Museum
Dates: Originally completed in 1034 CE; current building completed in 1961
Designations: UNESCO World Heritage Site
Web: www.worms.de/en/tourismus/museen/juedisches_museum
(municipal tourism website)

The Rashi Shul Synagogue, also known as the Worms Synagogue, was among the earliest synagogues founded in Germany. Although it was destroyed on two occasions, once during the Crusades and once during the Holocaust, there are surviving remnants of the synagogue dating back to the early 11th century. Along with other Rhineland cities, Worms was home to the first wave of Jewish settlers that became the basis for Ashkenazi Judaism.

The first Jews to permanently settle in Worms probably arrived in the 10th century CE. The Jewish community of Worms is believed to have been the largest in Germany by the early 11th century CE, and their first major synagogue was completed in the year 1034 CE. In 1096 CE Christian mobs, aroused by the start of the crusades, worked their way along the Rhine bringing terror and destruction to the local Jewish communities. The first Worms Synagogue was destroyed, but rebuilt less than a century later.

The new synagogue stood for well over seven centuries, weathering the rampages of anti-Semitic violence, wars and time. It was still standing and in use when the Nazis came to power in the 1930s. Unfortunately this wonderful Jewish architectural treasure finally met its fate in 1938 on the infamous Kristallnacht, when it was completely destroyed. It was rebuilt in the mid-20th century as accurately as possible. The Rashi Shul Synagogue is part of the ShUM Sites of Speyer, Worms and Mainz UNESCO World Heritage Site.

Of Interest: The current Rashi Shul Synagogue stands on the site of several predecessors. It was completed in 1961 using as much of the original building material as could be recycled. It closely resembles the medieval Romanesque building that stood here for over seven hundred years, though the modern elements are evident. In addition to being an active synagogue, the building is also home to a small museum. Of related interest is the nearby Jewish cemetery, dating from the 11th century, which survived World War II better than the synagogue.

---

132. DACHAU CONCENTRATION CAMP

Alte Romerstrasse 75, 85221 Dachau, Germany

Site Type: Concentration Camp, Museum
Dates: Camp opened in 1933
Web: www.kz-gedenkstaette-dachau.de (official website)

The Dachau Concentration Camp has the dubious distinction of being the first concentration camp created by the Nazis. Due to its proximity to Munich, it is also one of the most visited, especially by foreign tourists. Although not one of the major death camps where executions took place on a monstrous scale, Dachau still witnessed over forty thousand victims in its twelve active years. Most of the original camp grounds and a few the original buildings are preserved.

In March of 1933 the German parliament passed the Enabling Act, which formally authorized the Nazi seizure of power. Within days the first concentration camp was opened at Dachau. This camp, relatively small compared to those that were to come, served initially as an incarceration facility for political dissidents and potential enemies of the Nazis. By the 1940s members of virtually every group targeted by the Nazis could be found imprisoned here, including Jews.

Although not a full-fledged death camp, Dachau was eventually equipped with a crematorium to dispose of the dead. Only a few thousand Jews died here and some, for a very brief period in the beginning, were even allowed to leave provided they turn over all of their possessions to the German government and depart the country. Dachau was liberated on April 29, 1945, ending the longest reign of terror of any concentration camp in the Third Reich.

Of Interest: The Dachau Concentration Camp was arguably one of the less deadly destinations of the Final Solution, although that is a relative measure only. Its historical importance lies in the fact that it was the prototype camp and a training facility for those who unleashed the Holocaust throughout Europe. Some of the camp buildings are still standing or have been recreated, including some of the barracks and the crematorium with two surviving ovens. The main admnistrative building is now home to a museum detailing the history of the Shoah and the terrifying activities that took place at Dachau.

---

133. OLYMPIC MASSACRE MEMORIAL

Spiridon-Louis-Ring 27, 80809 Munich, Germany

Site Type: Monument
Dates: Dedicated in 2017
Web: www.muenchen.de/int/en/sights/parks/olympic-park.html (municipal tourism website)

The Olympic Massacre Memorial is a monument in Munich commemorating the Israeli athletes who were killed at the 1972 Olympic Games. This event, which took place barely a quarter of a century after World War II, left five athletes, four coaches and two officials dead. It shocked and infuriated Jews and countless others all over the world, especially in light of what had taken place during the years of the Third Reich.

Israel's Olympic history began in 1933 when an Israeli National Olympic Committee was formed in Palestine. They had little to do until 1948 when Israel gained independence. The first Israeli athletes participated in the 1952 Summer Olympics in Helsinki. The decision to participate in the 1972 Olympic games in Munich was an important moment in Israel's history. West Germany was awarded the games by an Olympic committee eager to help the Germans reintigrate themselves into a skeptical world. In an effort to distance itself from its terrible past, they presented to the world the "Happy Games".

Unfortunately on the morning of September 5th, terrorists broke into the Israeli athletes' apartments as they slept. Some of the athletes fought back, allowing others time to escape. Within minutes two were dead and nine others hostages. Most of the rest of the day was spent in a standoff between the terrorists and the German authorities. Despite the offer of a large ransom from the German government and the efforts of an Egyptian mediator, the standoff continued.

Eventually the German authorities came up with a rescue plan. Unfortunately the operation was badly mishandled. In the end all of the hostages were killed, along with five of the terrorists and one German police officer. Over eighty thousand spectators and athletes attended a memorial service the next day. The monument to the victims of the massacre was dedicated in 2017.

Of Interest: The Olympic Massacre Memorial, located in Munich's Olympiapark, consists of a peaceful, sheltered space cut into the side of a hill. The walls of the memorial have displays that give information on the events of the massacre as well as the victims. Several other monuments commemorating the massacre can be found elsewhere in Munich. One of these is a stone marker embedded in the pavement of a path which once connected the stadium to the Olympic village. A more personal memorial is mounted on the fence in front of the house where the attack occurred. Here the names of all of the victims are engraved on a plaque in German and Hebrew.

---

134. JOSEFOV GHETTO & JEWISH MUSEM

U Stare Skoly 141/1, 110 00 Stare Mesto, Prague 1, Czechia

Site Type: Historic Neighborhood, Cemetery, Museum
Dates: Museum opened in 1906
Designations: UNESCO World Heritage Site
Web: www.jewishmuseum.cz (Jewish Museum website)

The Josefov Ghetto is one of the better preserved pre-war Jewish neighborhoods in Europe. A full half-dozen synagogues, town hall, community buildings and a very full Jewish cemetery, all located along a single street, paint a portrait of what Jewish life was like in Central Europe in the late Middle Ages. Among the architectural treasures here is the Staronova Synagogue, which is covered in its own section. The buildings of the Josefov Ghetto are now run by the Jewish Museum of Prague.

Prague was visited and mentioned by Jewish travelers from Spain as far back as the year 965 CE. The community's early years were likely peaceful and prosperous, but this did not last long. Prague's first major pogrom took place in 1096 CE, and soon after many of the city's Jews began to gather in the Josefov district for safety.

During the middle ages the population of Josefov soared to nearly twenty thousand, and it became packed with tall houses crowded around narrow lanes. In 1389 over a thousand Jewish inhabitants were massacred here on Easter Sunday. The Prague ghetto reached its peak in the 16th century under its greatest mayor, Mordecai Maisel. Unfortunately things turned bad again when the Bohemian Revolt kicked off the Thirty Years war. Caught between violent Catholic and Protestant rivals, the Jews of Prague suffered at the hands of both. The legend of the Golem, a mythical monster created by a popular rabbi to defend the Jews from their enemies, arose around this time.

As the age of religious wars waned the lives of Jews in Prague became easier. In 1781 the Holy Roman Emperor Joseph II issued the Edict of Toleration, which put an end to many of the more odious laws which had restricted Jewish life. In the early 20th century part of the old Jewish Quarter was demolished to make way for new buildings. Ironically, the Nazis spared most of what was left of the old ghetto to be used as an open-air museum in memory of an extinct race. Because of this the ghetto has some of the best surviving architectural remnants of medieval European Jewry. The Josefov Ghetto is part of the Historic Center of Prague UNESCO World Heritage Site.

Of Interest: The Josefov Ghetto district consists of a handful of city blocks along a single street. It is dominated by the old Town Hall and a half-dozen synagogues dating from the 13th through the 18th centuries. Some of these now function as museums. In addition to the Staronova Synagogue, there are four synagogues dating to the 16th century, including the Pinkas Synagogue and the 19th century Spanish Synagogue. The Jewish cemetery is crowded with tombstones piled one on top of the other. It is estimated that anywhere from ten to twenty thousand people are buried in an area of approximately two city blocks. The Jewish Museum has a collection of tens of thousands of artifacts. Many of these are pieces left here by the Jewish community during the city's occupation by the Nazis, never to be reclaimed.

---

135. STARONOVA SYNAGOGUE

Cervena, 110 01 Prague 1, Czechia

Site Type: Medieval Synagogue
Dates: Completed in 1270
Designations: UNESCO World Heritage Site
Web: www.synagogue.cz/staronova-synagogue?p=15 (official website)

The Staronova Synagogue, also called the Old New Synagogue, is generally accepted as the world's oldest intact and active synagogue. Opened in the 13th century, the Old New Synagogue has remained in use almost continually for over seven hundred years. It is the spiritual heart of the historic ghetto of Prague, one of the most famous Jewish neighborhoods in Europe.

When the Staronova Synagogue was completed in 1270 CE it was simply the "new" synagogue. The Old Synagogue was still standing and in use at the time, but inadequate to the needs of the neighborhood's growing Jewish population. According to tradition, when the New Synagogue was built, stones from the Second Temple in Jerusalem were incorporated into the structure. Unfortunately there is nothing that confirms any of the synagogue's building materials came from the Holy Land.

The New Synagogue survived for seven and a half centuries. This was due in part to the building's fortress-like construction, and possibly due to superstition. According to local legend, the golem, a Frankenstein-like monster, resides in the attic, ready to defend the synagogue and congregation. The Nazis spared the synagogue from destruction as part of the Josefov memorial district. The Staronova Synagogue is part of the Historic Center of Prague UNESCO World Heritage Site.

Of Interest: The 13th century Staronova Synagogue is Prague's most famous Jewish monument. Although not the world's oldest synagogue, it is believed to be the world's oldest continually active synagogue. A hulking gothic building, it appears more like a fortified medieval residence than a synagogue, with thick walls, high vaulted ceilings and few windows. The number twelve is a repeating theme in the synagogue, with artwork and features representing the Twelve Tribes of Israel. A banner on display in the sanctuary commemorates those Jews who helped to defend Prague in the 17th century. Above the main sanctuary is an attic that is inaccessible to the public. Folklore suggests that the fabled golem resides there.

---

136. JUBILEE SYNAGOGUE

Jeruzalemska 1310/7, 110 00 Prague 1, Czechia

Site Type: Synagogue
Dates: Dedicated in 1906
Web: www.synagogue.cz/cs/jerusalem-synagogue-page (official website)

The Jubilee Synagogue, also known as the Jerusalem Synagogue, is Prague's most prominent post-ghetto Jewish house of worship. Constructed in the early 20th century, it was the first synagogue built in Prague after the destruction of most of the old ghetto. It is counted among the most beautiful synagogues built in Central Europe in the 20th century, and the fact that it survived the German occupation and Holocaust is nothing short of a miracle.

In the 1890s and early 1900s most of the old Josefov district of Prague was demolished in an effort to update the neighborhood. A small core of historic buildings was allowed to remain, including several of the most important synagogues. However the loss of some of the synagogues, as well as the disbursement of the Jewish population to new neighborhoods, left a need for a new grand synagogue for the city.

The Jubilee Synagogue was completed in 1906. It was so named in honor of the 50th anniversary of the reign of the Austro-Hungarian Emperor Franz Joseph I. After the Hapsburgs were deposed at the end of World War I, the synagogue was renamed the Jerusalem Synagogue. Like the surviving buildings of the old Jewish ghetto, the Jubilee Synagogue was allowed to remain standing by the Nazis, who used it for storage during the war. Although the synagogues of Josefov are more historic, the Jubilee Synagogue is now Prague's primary Jewish house of worship.

Of Interest: The Jubilee Synagogue is one of the most breathtaking synagogues in Europe, which is saying a lot. Constructed at the height of the Art Nouveau period, the synagogue looks almost more like a Moorish palace than a house of worship. Although not a museum per se, the synagogue is home to artifacts and pieces from the old ghetto that were saved and moved here when the Josefov district was being demolished.

---

137. THERESIENSTADT CONCENTRATION CAMP MUSEUM

Komensheko 148, 411 55 Terezin, Czechia

Site Type: Concentration Camp, Museum
Dates: Camp opened in 1941; museum dedicated in 1991
Web: www.pamatnik-terezin.cz (official website)

The Theresienstadt Ghetto was a hybrid ghetto and concentration camp that served as a propaganda showpiece for the Nazis. Theresienstadt, or

Terezin, was used to convince inspectors, usually from the Red Cross, that life in the camps was not that bad. Because of this the survival rate was higher here than at almost any other camp. Nevertheless the façade of life and culture at Terizin still concealed the horror of the Shoah, if on a smaller scale.

The town of Terezin became a military stronghold for the Third Reich in the early years of the war. The city's fortress was turned into a prison for the Gestapo, and later into a Jewish internment camp. This camp/ghetto received a somewhat privaleged status. Many of the Jews incarcerated here had fought for Germany during World War I, or were otherwise prominent members of society. Conditions at Terezin were less brutal than elsewhere. Regina Jones, the first woman in history ordained as a rabbi, worked in a leadership role at the camp.

The Nazis used Terezin to deceive two different groups. The first was international aid organizations. The second were Jews and other prisoners that were temporarily housed here while enroute to more terrifying destinations. This helped to pacify the latter group and make them less nervous about their final destinations.

Theresienstadt was a haven for those lucky enough to be incarcerated there. Many of those living here were not even aware of how bad things were in other camps until close to the end of the war. Terezin was one of the very last Nazi internment facilities to be liberated, and the only concentration camp where the living outnumbered the dead. After the war the ghetto was maintained as a memorial site. It was formally established as a museum in 1991 after the collapse of communism.

Of Interest: The Theresienstadt Ghetto is one of Europe's best preserved Holocaust sites. It largely avoided destruction both during and after the war. It was mostly intact when the Nazis abandoned it, and the majority of its inmates were still alive. Many artifacts and documents from life in the ghetto escaped destruction at the end of the war. Some of these items are now on display here. The ghetto is now run as the Theresienstadt Concentration Camp Museum.

---

138. TREBIC GHETTO

Leopolda Pokorneho 136, Zamosti, 674 01 Trebic, Czechia

Site Type: Historic Neighborhood
Dates: Ghetto established c. 15th century CE
Designations: UNESCO World Heritage Site
Web: www.visittrebic.eu/sights/jewish-quarter (municipal tourism website)

The Trebic Ghetto is the largest surviving historic Jewish neighborhood in Europe. While there are certainly more famous ghettos that are older and boast more impressive buildings, such as the one in Prague, the Trebic Ghetto has well over a hundred surviving structures. Because of this it is a more comprehensive experience for visitors.

It is uncertain exactly when Jews first settled in Trebic. The original town probably did not exist until the 13th century, and there are no records of a Jewish community here prior to the 14th century. Although the Jews of Trebic undoubtedly suffered the typical pogroms over the centuries, it appears that the community here avoided the worst atrocities.

That ended with the Holocaust. Although the community was never very large, it was almost completely annihilated during the Nazi era. Fewer than a hundred members survived the war. However the city of Trebic itself avoided destruction, and the ghetto was largely spared. Although mostly inhabited by non-Jews today, a majority of the buildings are still standing. The Trebic Ghetto is part of the Jewish Quarter and St. Procopius Basilica UNESCO World Heritage Site.

Of Interest: The Trebic Ghetto stands along the Jihlava River near the old city center. There are over a hundred surviving residences in the neighborhood, many with ground level shops. Two synagogues dominate the neighborhood. One, the Front Synagogue, dates from the 17th century. There are also other community buildings including the town hall and school. Nearby is the city's Jewish cemetery, which is outside of the ghetto. Over four thousand graves dating back as far as the 15th century can be found here.

---

139. JUDENPLATZ

Judenplatz, Vienna, Austria

Site Type: Historic Neighborhood, Museum, Holocaust Memorial
Dates: Jewish quarter established c. 12th century CE; museum opened in 2000
Designations: UNESCO World Heritage Site
Web: www.jmw.at (Jewish Museum of Vienna website)

The Judenplatz is the heart of the old Jewish quarter that once existed in the city center of Vienna. Established in the Middle Ages, the medieval Jewish community was largely driven out in the 15th century and its synagogue destroyed. However the plaza survived, and is now home to several places of Jewish interest. These include an archaeological site associated with the Jewish Museum of Vienna, as well as the city's Holocaust Memorial.

The first Jews to settle in Vienna arrived in the 12th century CE. It is likely that at least some of these were refugees fleeing pogroms in the Rhineland in the years after the First Crusade was declared. The community lived here in relative peace for several hundred years, and they had a synagogue which is believed to have been one of the larger ones in Central Europe at the time. Things started to worsen after the Black Plague.

A major pogrom against the community took place in 1420 and 1421. During this period the Jews of Vienna met various fates, including being starved to death and burned at the stake. Some committed suicide after taking refuge in the synagogue. The rest were driven out, their properties were seized and the synagogue destroyed. For the next three and a half centuries the Jews elsewhere in Austria were regularly persecuted.

In the century leading up to World War II the Jewish community of Austria grew and thrived. While many Jews returned to Vienna, the medieval Jewish quarter was never revived. About a third of Austria's Jewish population perished in the Holocaust. The Judenplatz Holocaust Memorial was dedicated in 2000. In 1995 the ruins of the medieval synagogue were discovered beneath a 17th century house. These have since been excavated and are now part of the Jewish Museum of Vienna. The Judenplatz is part of the Historic Centre of Vienna UNESCO World Heritage Site.

Of Interest: The Judenplatz, or Jewish Plaza, is an open pedestrian zone roughly analogous to the medieval Jewish quarter. It is lined with old buildings, some of which are pre-war. The only structure in the plaza iself is the Holocaust Memorial, a large blocky monument designed to look like an inside-out library. The book spines are facing inward and cannot be read. The door to the monument cannot be opened, suggesting that what is written in the books has been lost forever. One of the buildings, the house at Judenplatz 8, houses part of the Jewish Museum of Vienna. Beneath it is the archaeological site where visitors can see the foundations of the medieval synagogue.

---

140. DANISH JEWISH MUSEUM

Proviantpassagen 6, 1218 Copenhagen, Denmark

Site Type: Museum, Holocaust Memorial
Dates: Opened in 2004
Web: www.jewmus.dk/dansk-joedisk-museum (official website)

The Danish Jewish Museum tells the story of the Jews of Denmark. It is perhaps best known for its exhibit on the Rescue of the Danish Jews during World War II. Not every story of the Holocaust had a heartbreaking ending. Such was the case of the Jews of Denmark, almost all of whom survived the war thanks to the heroic efforts of the Danish people. Many citizens of Denmark, from the Danish resistance to the clergy to the king of Denmark himself, played a part. The event has been memorialized at the Danish Jewish Museum.

Throughout the Middle Ages Jewish migrations largely bypassed northern Europe. Following the Reformation, small numbers of Jews began arriving in Scandinavia, where persecutions and pogroms were incredibly rare. The Jewish community of Denmark was never large. Even at its height numbers probably never exceeded ten thousand.

In April 1940 Denmark was annexed by Nazi Germany. Germany was tolerant of Danish liberties and generally stayed out of Denmark's affairs as long as the Danes did nothing to rock the boat. Because of this the Jews of Denmark remained mostly unmolested for more than three years. However in August 1943 Germany took direct control of the Danish government and moved quickly to begin the deportation of the Jews.

The Danes moved even faster. Thanks to the efforts of Georg Duckwitz, a German diplomat who was sympathetic to the Jews, the people of Denmark were alerted to the imminent action. Virtually the entire Jewish population of Denmark was taken into hiding with barely a day's notice. Over the next few weeks most of the Jews were smuggled out of the country to neutral Sweden. In the end the Nazis captured only four hundred and fifty Danish Jews. Of those captured, four hundred survived thanks to further Danish diplomatic and humanitarian efforts. The survival of the Danish Jews is remembered as one of the miracles of this terrible chapter of European history.

Of Interest: The Danish Jewish Museum is located inside a four-century old building that was once the Royal Boat House of King Christian IV. It was incorporated into the Danish Royal Library in the early 1900s, and later made available for use as a Jewish Museum which opened in 2004. Architecturally the museum is eclectic, blending modern Scandinavian styles with the original stone construction. The lightness of the place reflects the promise of the survival of Denmark's Jews. The museum houses a collection of artifacts highlighting the life and history of Danish Jews. The main exhibit tells the story of the great rescue of 1943.

141. GREAT SYNAGOGUE OF STOCKHOLM

3, Wahrendorffsgatan Norrmalm, 111 47, Stockholm, Sweden

Site Type: Synagogue
Dates: Completed in 1870
Designations: Swedish Registry of Historic Buildings
Web: https://jfst.se/judendom-judar/det-judiska-stockholm/
stockholms-stora-synagoga (official website)

The Great Synagogue of Stockholm is the largest Jewish house of worship to be found in the Scandinavian Peninsula. Located near the royal gardens in Stockholm's old city center, the synagogue is a standout in an historic neighborhood. It is home to one of the oldest and largest Jewish congregations in the far north of Europe.

Scandinavia, or at least the peninsular countries of Sweden, Norway and Finland, was the last place in Europe to see Jewish communities established. Although likely visited in the Middle Ages, the first permanent Jewish settlements were not founded in Scandinavia until the early 18th century. This was well after Jews had started to settle in European colonies around the world.

Even today there are relatively few Jewish communities in Scandinavia, and most of these live in Sweden. The biggest community was at the capital city of Stockholm, which had a series of synagogues established during the 18th century. The Great Synagogue, home to the largest Jewish congregation in Scandinavia, was completed in 1870.

Of Interest: The Great Synagogue of Stockholm is a breathtaking structure that is a 19th century architectural masterpiece. From the sides this stately building could be mistaken for a grand turn-of-the-century government building or museum rather than a house of worship. However the magnificent façade unmistakenly evokes images of the Second Temple of Jerusalem. The synagogue also houses a Jewish library. Next door to the building is Sweden's national Memorial to the Victims of the Holocaust.

WESTERN EUROPE

142. KAZERNE DOSSIN MEMORIAL, MUSEUM AND DOCUMENTATION CENTER

Goswin de Stassartstraat, 2800 Mechelen, Belgium

Site Type: Prison, Museum, Holocaust Memorial
Dates: Museum opened in 2012
Web: www.kazernedossin.eu (official website)

The Kazerne Dossin Memorial, Museum and Documentation Center is a complex dedicated to commemorating the victims of the Holocaust that came from Belgium. It is partially housed inside the Mechelen Concentration Camp, a relatively small transit camp from which the Jews of Belgium were deported to the death camps further east. It is estimated that approximately twenty-five thousand Jews and others passed through here during the war.

Prior to the German invasion of 1940 there were probably fewer than fifty thousand Belgian Jewish citizens, and perhaps another twenty thousand Jewish refugees from Germany. After the Nazi occupation of Belgium the Germans set up a transit camp at Mechelen in that city's former Dossin Barracks building. Mechelen was active from 1942 through 1944, during which time over twenty thousand Jews passed through the camp.

Although only around three hundred were killed on site here, almost everyone who was shipped out from Mechelen died elsewhere. Only around fourteen hundred people who passed through Mechelen survived the camps. After the war a memorial was set up in the old barracks building. The museum and documentation center opened in a new facility nearby in 2012.

Of Interest: The Kazerne Dossin Memorial is located in the former Dossin Barracks building, which is largely intact. A prison more than a true concentration camp, visitors here can see the facilities and appreciate the cramped conditions in which the inmates were incarcerated. The museum houses a number of Holocaust related exhibits, with a focus on the rise of fascism during the interwar years, the rounding up and deportation of Jews from Mechelen and the Jewish resistance movement in Belgium.

143. PORTUGUESE SYNAGOGUE & JEWISH HISTORY MUSEUM

Mr. Visserplein 3, 1011 RD Amsterdam, Netherlands

Site Type: Synagogue, Museum
Dates: Synagogue completed in 1675; museum opened in 1932
Web: www.esnoga.com (official website)

The Portuguese Synagogue of Amsterdam is the oldest synagogue in the Netherlands, and one of the oldest active synagogues in west-central Europe. It is named for the Jews who came here from Portugal in the early 16th century. Right across the street is the Jewish History Museum, with an excellent collection of Judaica from the city's history. The two buildings form the core of the Amsterdam Jewish Cultural Quarter.

There have been Jews in what is now the Netherlands since the Middle Ages. Like other Jewish communities in Central Europe, they were periodically persecuted, especially around the time of the Black Plague. In 1579 the Netherlands became the first place in Europe to nominally grant freedom of worship to the Jewish people.

About a century earlier the Inquisition ravaged the Jewish communities of Portugal. Many Jews had long since been driven out, though a few remained, some pretending to have converted to Christianity. In 1581 the Netherlands became independent of the Hapsburg Empire, and thousands of Jews who had remained in Iberia relocated to the safety of the Low Countries. By the late-17th century the Jewish community of Amsterdam was among the largest in Western Europe.

In addition to religious freedom the Netherlands offered economic opportunities thanks to the wealth flowing in from the Dutch colonies around the world. The prosperous Jewish congregation constructed the magnificent Portuguese Synagogue in 1675. The Jewish community of Amsterdam flourished right up until World War II. Today the community, with the Portuguese Synagogue at its heart, is growing again thanks in part to the Jewish immigration from Eastern Europe.

Of Interest: The Portuguese Synagogue is a large red brick building that dominates the surrounding neighborhood close to Amsterdam's old city center. The interior of the building soars on massive columns to an impressively arched wooden ceiling. The entire sanctuary is filled with beautiful woodworked fixtures. The synagogue houses a nice collection of Judaica from the congregation's history. Additional pieces can be found across the street at the Jewish History Museum. Originally opened in 1932, it took many years for the museum to recover from looting during World War II. The museum was renovated in 2007 and now houses thousands of artifacts.

---

144. ANNE FRANK HOUSE

Westermarkt 20, 1016 GV Amsterdam, Netherlands

Site Type: Historic Residence, Museum, Holocaust Memorial
Dates: Museum opened in 1960
Web: www.annefrank.org (official website)

The somewhat misnamed Anne Frank House is actually a former office-warehouse building where the famous young Jewish girl lived in hiding with her family for two years. She chronicled her experience in one of history's most famous diaries. Though there were many places throughout Nazi-occupied Europe where courageous people helped to protect their Jewish neighbors, there is perhaps no other place as famous as the Anne Frank House in Amsterdam. The site is now operated as a museum dedicated to the memory of its inhabitants and Anne Frank's writings.

In May 1940 German armies swept through the Netherlands on their way to France, humbling the Dutch army in a whirlwind campaign that lasted less than a week. On May 15 the government surrendered, leaving the Dutch people, and its Jewish community, at the mercy of the Nazis for the next five years. The widescale persecution of Amsterdam's Jews began almost immediately.

Seven years earlier Otto Frank, a Jewish businessman, had relocated his family to Amsterdam from Frankfurt following the Nazi rise to power in Germany. He went with his wife and two daughters and resettled in the Netherlands. In 1942 Otto Frank was forced to give up his business, and when his older daughter was ordered to report to a work camp the family decided it was time to go into hiding. With the help of trusted friends they moved into the attic above his former warehouse.

Anne Frank, the younger daughter, had received a diary for her birthday shortly before going into hiding. Within its pages she diligently recorded the goings-on of their lives. The Frank family, and four other fugitives, survived in the small attic until August 4, 1944 when they were betrayed and discovered. Anne, along with her mother and sister, died soon afterwards in Nazi concentration camps. Her diary, and the small attic over the warehouse where they lived, has been preserved in her memory.

Of Interest: The Anne Frank House is located in the warehouse building where Otto Frank's business was located. It was constructed in the mid-17th century as a residence along the Prinsengracht canal. The building has been partially preserved as it appeared in the early 1940s. Offices and warehouse space are located on the lower floors, while the attic residence occupies the upper floors. The attic rooms have largely been restored to appear as they did during the war. The lower floors have been completely converted into a museum which tells the story of the Frank family. Many artifacts of their residency are on display here including Anne Frank's actual diary.

145. SPINOZA HOUSE AND MUSEUM

Spinozalaan 29, 2231 SG Rijnsburg, Netherlands

Site Type: Historic Residence, Museum
Dates: Museum opened in 1897
Web: www.spinozahuis.nl (official website)

Baruch Spinoza is regarded as one of the great Jewish intellectuals of the modern era. His philosophical ideas and writings were among the most important of his day, and he is credited by both Jews and non-Jews as having been a key philosophical figure of the Enlightenment. His teachings challenged established Jewish dogma of the time, and as a result Spinoza was excommunicated from Judaism. Today he is a national hero of the Netherlands, and while he is technically still in a state of excommunication, modern day Jews have come to see him in a much more positive light. His former home in Rijnsburg is now a museum.

Spinoza was a Sephardic Jew whose family fled to the Netherlands from the turmoil in Iberia in the early 16th century. Originally Marranos, the family moved to the Netherlands in 1615 where they openly reverted to Judaism. Baruch was born in Amsterdam in 1632. While he had a traditional Jewish upbringing and education, his intellectual and philosophical interests led him to pursue a career that lay outside of both the family business and traditional Jewish scholarship.

Spinoza took up lensmaking in his teen years and pursued this as his official trade for the rest of his life. His true calling was as a philosopher and writer, and it was for these that he attained both fame and notoriety. By his early twenties his writings were already well known in Amsterdam. Many of his ideas were provocative to both Jews and Christians. Despite warnings from Jewish and civic leaders, Spinoza continued with his work, and at the age of twenty-four he was issued a Writ of Cherem, the Jewish equivalent of excommunication. This did little to discourage Spinoza.

His writings became famous throughout Western Europe. Other

than a short career in public life he maintained himself on the proceeds of his lensmaking business. As well known as he was at the time of his death, it was not yet imagined how immense the impact his ideas would have as the Age of Enlightenment dawned. He was particularly concerned with ethics, which was the topic of one of his most famous essays. His views on the oneness of God, the universe and nature were extremely controversial at the time. Spinoza's work is considered an integral part of Enlightenment thinking, and he is highly regarded in the Netherlands.

Of Interest: The Spinoza House, where Baruch Spinoza spent several years in Rijnsburg, is still standing and has been preserved as an historic site. The house, which is now run as a museum, looks much the same as it did in the 17th century when the philosopher resided there. The rooms have been restored as best as possible to the way they were in Spinoza's time. Of particular interest is the study where some of his personal library books and artifacts are on display.

---

146. CORRIE TEN BOOM HOUSE

Barteljorisstraat 19, 2011 RA Haarlem, Netherlands

Site Type: Historic Residence, Museum, Holocaust Memorial
Dates: Museum opened in 1988
Web: www.corrietenboom.com (official website)

The Corrie Ten Boom House in Haarlem is the former residence of Corrie Ten Boom, a woman who helped to save the lives of hundreds of Jews and others trying to escape the Nazis. Many of those she aided hid out in this building until 1944 when her activities were discovered and she was arrested. Corrie Ten Boom survived the war and she became a national hero of the Netherlands. The museum honors her legacy and commemorates those who she saved.

Cornelia Ten Boom was a watchmaker living in Haarlem when the Nazis overran the Netherlands in 1940. A devout Christian, she and her father and other family members turned their home into a refuge for those trying to escape the Nazis. It was not only a hideout, but also a transit point that could be used from which refugees could flee to other safe locations. It is estimated that eight hundred people hid out here during the course of the war.

The Ten Booms actively worked with others in their efforts to protect the innocent, including the Dutch underground. They used their connections to provide those in need with food and supplies. They were able to keep up the operation for three years before they were finally caught. Corrie Ten Boom, along with her father and sister, was arrested. Before the war ended her father died in prison and her sister was killed at Ravensbruck. Corrie was also sent to Ravensbruck but survived.

Corrie Ten Boom spent the last few months of the war aiding who she could during the horrible winter conditions of early 1945. She resumed her activities protecting those who sought refuge from the Nazis. After the war her efforts were recognized by the Dutch government and many organizations. She was named one of the Righteous among the Nations in Israel. Her home was renovated and opened as a museum in 1988.

Of Interest: The Ten Boom Museum occupies the family home where the Ten Booms had resided since the 1830s. The building itself is a stately brick affair originally constructed in the early 17th century. It looks much like it did in the 1940s, with a watch and jewelry shop on the first floor and residence on the second floor. The residence houses a very small museum with artifacts and photographs. Visitors can also see the hidden room, constructed by members of the Dutch resistance, where refugees hid when the Nazis came by.

147. LE MARAIS & MUSEUM OF JEWISH ART AND HISTORY

Hotel de Saint-Aignan, 71 Rue du Temple, 75003 Paris, France

Site Type: Historic Neighborhood, Museum
Dates: Museum opened in 1998
Web: www.mahj.org (Museum of Jewish Art and History website)

Le Marais, which means The Marsh, is the historic Jewish neighborhood of Paris. Unlike most other Jewish districts spread out across Europe, Le Marais did not begin as a medieval Jewish ghetto, but rather as a popular residential area for the upper classes. Still home to a sizeable Jewish community, the modern neighborhood has numerous Jewish businesses. Le Marais is also very popular with artists.

The area north of the Seine opposite the Isle de la Cite is one of the oldest districts of Paris. Nevertheless it wasn't until the Later Middle Ages that it became popular with the aristocracy. In the 13th century the Templars set up a church in the area. This was followed by the palaces and mansions of the royal courtiers. By the 18th century it was one of the wealthiest neighborhoods in France. However during the French Revolution most of the Marais district's population was killed or driven out.

During the 19th century Le Marais became a Jewish neighborhood. Many Jews fleeing pogroms and persecutions that were taking place in Eastern Europe settled here. By the time World War I broke out the Jewish community here was one of the largest in Western Europe. Le Marais also became home to a sizable community of Chinese immigrants in the 1910s.

After the fall of France in 1940 the Nazis occupied Paris, and the usual calamnity befell the Jews of the city. Many perished in the Holocaust. The Jewish community here did rebuild after the war but never really fully recovered. Nevertheless there has been a Jewish renaissance in the neighborhood since the 1990s. The Museum of Jewish Art and History at the heart of the neighborhood opened in 1998.

Of Interest: Le Marais is a busy, popular neighborhood located close to the city center in the 3rd and 4th arrondissements. Thanks to the fact that Paris was largely spared during World War II, Le Marais looks much like it did more than a century ago. A number of old Jewish buildings are still evident, including the hundred year old Agoudas Hakehilos Synagogue. In the 1990s the historic 17th century Hotel de Saint-Aignan became home to the Museum of Jewish Art and History. This truly excellent collection of Judaica includes over a dozen major exhibits which cover millenia of Jewish history and culture.

---

148. MONTPARNASSE CEMETERY & GRAVESITE OF ALFRED DREYFUS

3 Boulevard Edgar Quinet, 75014 Paris, France

Site Type: Cemetery
Dates: Dreyfus buried in 1935
Web: www.paris.fr/equipements/cimetiere-du-montparnasse-4802 (official website)

Alfred Dreyfus was a Jewish officer who served in the French army in the late 19th century. Framed and tried for treason, Dreyfus became a major figure in the struggle against anti-Semitism. France was one of the first nations in the world to officially embrace religious tolerance. Nevertheless the road was a rocky one. The Dreyfus Affair ultimately led to the seperation of church and state in France, formally ending state sponsored anti-Semitism in that nation.

In the wake of the Thirty Years War France began to distance itself from the Roman Catholic Church. This led to a gradual increase in acceptance of people of different faiths, not only of Protestants but of Jews as well. In 1785 the first anti-Semitic laws in France were struck down. Jews were allowed to live wherever they wished and would henceforth be taxed in the same manner as their countrymen. A few years later when the Revolution broke out many Jews joined the armies of the Republic. Despite setbacks the condition of the French Jews steadily improved.

During the reign of Napolean Bonaparte Jews were permited to serve in the national government as well as the officer corps of the army. Even after the monarchy was restored the Jewish community retained these new rights. Once again this caused a conservative backlash, especially in the circles of the French upper classes, and they worked diligently to undermine Jewish progress. In the army a systematic effort was made to discredit and remove Jewish officers. The crisis came to a head in 1894 when Alfred Dreyfus was framed for an act of treason.

Dreyfus was court-martialed and falsely found guilty for passing top secret information to France's enemies. However the entire plot was uncovered through the efforts of the writer Emile Zola and others, and the ensuing public outcry led to the condemnation of the reactionaries and calls for further reforms. Drefus was pardoned in 1899 and fully exonerated in 1906. In 1905 the French government enacted the Law on the Separation of Church and State. Dreyfus went on to a distinguished career in the army and was the first person of Jewish origin awarded the Legion of Honor. He died in 1935, and his funeral procession was part of the Bastille Day celebration of that year.

Of Interest: Alfred Dreyfus was buried in the prestigious Montparnasse Cemetery, where hundreds of France's most prominent leaders and distinguished citizens have been interred since the 19th century. The relatively modest tombstone of Alfred Dreyfus is almost lost in a veritable sea of spectacular monuments. The writing on his tomb simply states his name, rank, and dates of birth and death. Dreyfus is also honored with a public statue which stands in front of the city's Museum of Jewish Art and History.

149. MEMORIAL OF THE DEPORTATION MARTYRS

Square de l'Ile-de-France, 7 Quai de l'Archeveche, 75004 Paris, France

Site Type: Holocaust Memorial
Dates: Dedicated in 1962
Web: www.onac-vg.fr/hauts-lieux-memoire-necropoles/memorial-des-martyrs-de-la-deportation (official website)

The Memorial of the Deportation Martyrs is the national monument to all French citizens who were sent off to Nazi concentration camps, from which many never returned. The largest such monument in France, it is also one of the most evocative. The memorial is meant to honor all of the French victims of the Holocaust, including Jews and many others.

In the summer of 1940 France was defeated by the German army in just a matter of weeks. By September of that year the restrictions and persecutions of the Jews in France had begun. The roundups and deportations started the next year. During the war tens of thousands of French Jews were packed onto trains and sent off to the concentration camps.

However, thanks to the efforts of the French people, the relatively light occupying presence of the Nazis in France and advantageous geography, the Jews of France had many more opportunities to hide from and evade the Germans. Of the roughly three hundred and thirty thousand Jews living in France during the war, over a quarter of a million avoided deportation.

Unfortunately, this still meant that more than seventy five thousand were shipped off, along with over a hundred thousand Jews from other countries who were staying in France as refugees. After the war France was among the first countries in Europe to commission a monument commemorating the victims of the Holocaust. The Memorial of the Deportation Martyrs was dedicated in 1962.

Of Interest: The Memorial of the Deportation Martyrs is among the most visited Holocaust monuments in Europe. Located just behind the Notre Dame Cathedral in the heart of Paris, this giant mausole-um-like structure is only partially visible above ground. The entrance is through an extremely narrow and foreboding gate. The interior features a long, dim corridor decorated with prison-like structures and chapels. Two-hundred thousand small crystals represent those from France who perished in the Nazi camps.

150. LOUVRE MUSEUM & MOABITE STONE

Rue de Rivoli, 75001 Paris, France

Site Type: Museum
Dates: Opened in 1793
Web: www.louvre.fr (official website)

The Louvre Museum is one of the greatest museums in the world. It has one of the finest collections of art and antiquites to be found anywhere. Among the latter is a spectacular exhibit of Near Eastern Antiquities; and among the pieces in this collection is one of the most important archaeological finds of ancient Jewish history: the Moabite Stone.

The Moabite Stone, also called the Mesha Stele, is a nearly three-thousand year old tablet that has what is believed to be the oldest recorded extra-Biblical reference to the Kingdom of Israel. Discovered in Jordan in the mid-19th century, it specifically mentions the conflict between Israel and Moab during the reign of King Omri. It also mentions the men of Gad, a part of the Northern Kingdom located close to Moab, as well as Mount Nebo. It also states the name of the Israelite god Yahweh.

Unfortunately the tablet is incomplete. According to documenta-tion from the original expedition, the Moabite Stone had been found in a nearly perfect state of preservation. Unfortunately, it was later broken into pieces during a dispute over its ownership. About half of the fragments were later recovered. What is left is now on display at the Louvre Museum in Paris.

Of Interest: The Near Eastern Antiquities department of the Louvre Museum is home to hundreds of artifacts discovered in the Middle East. While there are a number of items of Biblical interest, the Moabite Stone is easily the star attraction. The recovered pieces of the stele were partially reconstructed, and a cast that had been taken of the stone was able to fill in some of the missing sections. What is on display at the Louvre constitutes about half of the stone and around sixty percent of the text.

---

151. MARC CHAGALL NATIONAL MUSEUM

Avenue Dr Menard, 06000 Nice, France

Site Type: Museum
Dates: Opened in 1973
Web: https://musees-nationaux-alpesmaritimes.fr/chagall (official website)

The Marc Chagall National Museum in Nice is home to the largest collection of artwork by one of the world's most celebrated Jewish artists. A giant of European Modernism, Chagall was one of the most influential artists of the 20th century. His work spanned the better part of eight decades and was inspired by the experience of Jews in Czarist Russia, Communist Russia, Nazi Germany and modern Israel. His artwork can be found in museums, public buildings and houses of worship around the world.

The Jewish people have long flourished in many cultural mediums. However, visual artistic expression tended to lag even during the Renaissance. This is due in part to a reticence to produce anything that might break the commandment against the making of graven images. It was not until the Modern art movements of the 20th century that Jews began to make real strides in the visual arts; and in no person was this more true than Chagall.

Born in Russia during the final years of the tsars, Chagall lived through nearly a century of upheavals. His artistic career was influenced by his early life in Eastern Europe. He studied for years in St. Petersburg and then later in Paris. He was actively involved in the Russian Revolution, though he turned his back on communism and moved to Paris where he spent the interwar years. After World War II he traveled around the United States, Europe and Israel, leaving a trail of artistic masterpieces in his wake. He ultimately settled in Nice where he lived until his death.

Marc Chagall was respected by his contemporaries from his earliest days as an artist. He was accomplished both as a painter and as a designer of stained glass windows. Chagall's art is indelibly tied to the architecture of the 20th century, and is prominently displayed in such places as the United Nations General Assembly Building, the Metropolitan Opera in New York House, the Paris Opera House, St. Stephens Cathedral in Mainz, the Hadassah Ein Kerem Hospital in Jerusalem and the State Hall of the Knesset. The largest collection of his work can be found at the Marc Chagall National Museum in Nice.

Of Interest: The Marc Chagall National Museum, also known as the Chagall Biblical Message, is one of several major art museums in art rich Nice. In addition to the numerous works of Chagall on display, the museum has exhibits on the history of the artist's life. The most famous exhibit at the museum is a cycle of seventeen paintings collectively titled the *Biblical Message* for which the museum is named. These paintings depict a series of scenes from the Hebrew Bible and collectively are considered one of his greatest masterpieces. Marc Chagall is buried in the St. Paul Town Cemetery in nearby St-Paul de Vence outside of Nice.

152. EXODUS 47 MONUMENT

Promenade du Marechal Leclerc, Sete, France

Site Type: Monument
Dates: Dedicated in 1982
Web: None Available

The Exodus 47 Monument overlooking the sea near the port of Sete commemorates a very special chapter in the history of the modern state of Israel: the 1947 voyage of the SS Exodus. The Exodus famously attempted to ferry over four thousand Jews to Israel in 1947. Although the mission was not initially successful, almost all of the passengers, many of whom had survived the Holocaust, eventually made it to become some of the first immigrants to the newly formed state of Israel.

Completed in 1928, the Exodus, formerly known as the SS President Warfield, was an American steamship that worked along the Atlantic coast of the United States during the interwar period. In the mid-1940s it was put to use for the war effort. Later the ship was acquired by Israeli interests, renamed the Exodus, and moved to the Mediterranean to transport Jewish immigrants to the Holy Land.

In 1947 the Exodus departed from the port of Sete in southern France packed with over four thousand Jewish refugees. However the British navy intercepted the Exodus and detained its passengers as illegal immigrants. They were held on the island of Cyprus until 1948, when Israel declared independence. Most of the refugees later completed the journey to the Holy Land.

Although the Exodus was only one of many ships that transported Jewish refugees to Israel, it was arguably the most famous. The voyage was immortalized in the 1960 film *Exodus*. Sadly, the remains of the ship were destroyed in an accidental fire in the 1950s. The remains are now on the sea floor just offshore from the city of Haifa. The voyage of the SS Exodus is commemorated both in Israel and in France.

Of Interest: The Exodus 47 Monument in Sete is a small commemorative plaque set into the seawall near the harbor from where the ship departed in 1947. It was dedicated in 1982, thirty-five years after the famous voyage. Another small monumuent commemorating the journey of the Exodus can be found in the port city of Haifa in Israel.

---

153. GREATER SYNAGOGUE OF BARCELONA

Carrer de Marlet, 5, 08002 Barcelona, Spain

Site Type: Medieval Synagogue, Museum
Dates: Originally completed c. 4th century; museum opened in 2002
Web: www.sinagogamayor.com (official website)

The Greater Synagogue of Barcelona, also referred to as the Ancient Synagogue, is counted among the oldest synagogues in Europe. Forgotten for centuries, the building's former use as a synagogue was rediscovered in the 1980s. While part of the building has been dated to the Roman era, it was not likely used as a synagogue until the Middle Ages. Recently renovated, the building is now home to a museum.

It is uncertain exactly when the first Jews arrived and settled in Spain, but it was almost certainly during Roman times. One of the earliest Jewish settlements is believed to have been in the coastal area near Barcino, or modern day Barcelona. Sometime around the 4th century CE the initial building now called the Greater Synagogue was constructed, which does coincide with the existence of an early Jewish community here.

The Jewish community of Barcelona is believed to have survived continually through the eras of Visigothic, Muslim and early Christian rule. The synagogue as it now exists largely dates from the 13th century when Barcelona was a Christian city. However, anti-Semitism increased across Spain during the Reconquista, and in 1391 many of Barcelona's Jews were killed or driven out. The synagogue appears to have been converted to other uses at this time.

During the 1980s a researcher was able to identify the probable location of the synagogue based on records from the Middle Ages. The building was subsequently restored and reopened to the public in the early 2000s. Although technically active as a synagogue, it is only generally used on special occasions.

Of Interest: The Greater Synagogue is one of Barcelona's most important architectural treasures. Regardless of whether or not it was originally used as a synagogue, the fact that some of the original Roman-era building is still in use is impressive. Part of the reason for its long survival is the fact that the building is lost in a jumble of alleys and does not call much attention to itself. Most of the building is of medieval origin, with thick stone walls, arched ceilings, and a glass floor that reveals the original foundations.

---

154. SYNAGOGUES OF TOLEDO

Calle de los Reyes Catolicos, 4, 45002 Toledo, Spain
(Ibn Shushan Synagogue)

Calle Samuel Levi, s/n, 45002 Toledo, Spain
(Samuel Halevi Abulafia Synagogue)

Site Type: Medieval Synagogues, Museum
Dates: Ibn Shushan Synagogue completed c. 1180 CE; Samuel Halevi Abulafia Synagogue completed c. 1350 CE
Designations: UNESCO World Heritage Site
Web: https://toledomonumental.com/santa-maria-blanca (Ibn Shushan Synagogue website)

Toledo is one of the oldest cities in Spain. It is unknown exactly when Jews first settled in Toledo, but it might have been as early as the Roman era or during the years of Visigothic rule. There was at least a small community of Jews here by the time the Spain was conquered by the Muslims in the 8th century. During the years of Islamic rule the Jewish community of Toledo thrived, with a population that supported at least ten synagogues.

In 1085 CE a Christian army from the Kingdom of Castile conquered Toledo. While the Muslim population of the city suffered, the Jewish community was mostly left alone, at least for a while. In 1180 CE the Ibn Shushan Synagogue was built. It remained in use for over two hundred years before being seized and converted to use as a church under the name of Santa Maria la Blanca. It is believed that Conversos might have worshipped here under the guise as Christians.

Toledo's other historic synagogue, the Samuel Halevi Abulafia Synagogue, was built in the late 1350s. Its namesake was a high ranking Jewish official who served the royal house of Castile. Constructed in the wake of the Black Plague, it is a miracle that this synagogue was built at all in the face of the anti-Semitism of the era. It remained in use as a Jewish house of worship until 1492 CE when it was converted to use as a church under the name El Transito de Nuestra Senora. Both Synagogues are part of the Historic City of Toledo UNESCO World Heritage Site.

Of Interest: The Ibn Shushan Synagogue is one of the oldest essentially intact synagogues in Europe. However, it has not been used as a Jewish house of worship in over six centuries. Despite this it has been very well preserved, ironically thanks in part to its former use as a church and monastery. The Samuel Halevi Abulafia Synagogue, now known as the El Transito Synagogue, is a similarly well preserved building despite the fact that it has not been used as a synagogue for over five hundred years. It is now home to the Sephardi Museum.

---

155. PLAZA DE ZOCODOVER

Plaza de Zocodover, Toledo, Spain

Site Type: Historic Neighborhood
Dates: Inquisition activities took place here late 15th century
Designations: UNESCO World Heritage Site
Web: www.spain.info/en/destination/toledo (Spain national tourism website)

During the latter years of the 15th century the Plaza de Zocodover in Toledo witnessed numerous atrocities perpetrated by the Spanish Inquisition. From 1485 to 1492 Toledo was the headquarters of Tomas de Torquemada, the Grand Inquisitor of Spain, and it was here that he personally presided over one of the darkest chapters in Spanish history. Over the course of six years, many Jews and other victims of the Inquisition were tormented and killed in this square.

The institution known as the Inquisition did not exist until the 13th century when it was created to address the Albigensian Heresy in France. Originally designed to reconcile heretics with the Catholic Church, it soon degenerated into an instrument of terror. In 1242 CE, under the orders of the Inquisition, thousands of copies of the Talmud were destroyed throughout Western Europe. In 1288 CE the first Jews were burned at the stake by the Inquisition. Similar activities quickly spread throughout France, Italy, Spain and Portugal.

The persecution of Jews in Spain began long before the Inquisition. As the Moorish cities of Spain fell to the Christians during the Reconquista, the native population of Jews and Muslims faced ever increasing persecution. Tens of thousands of Jews were forced to convert to Christianity, the alternative being deportation, imprisonment or death. These Christians came to be known as Conversos. However, most Conversos continued to practice Judaism in secret. Eventually the monarchy and the church learned of this practice, and by the late 15th century the problem of backsliding had become so pervasive that the government decided to take drastic action.

In 1481 the Inquisition was formally established in Spain. Torquemada, who was himself partly Jewish, took it over in 1483, and things quickly turned ugly. In 1485 a headquarters was established at Toledo, where twenty five Autos de Fe, or Acts of Faith, were held. At these public events every Converso was required to confirm their Christian faith or face burning at the stake. Nearly five hundred chose the latter. The end of the first Spanish Inquisition came in 1492, when all remaiing Jews were simply evicted from the country. The Plaza de Zocodover is part of the Historic Center of Toledo UNESCO World Heritage Site.

Of Interest: The Plaza de Zocodover is Toledo's main square and a major tourism hub, adorned with scenic buildings, outdoor cafes and street vendors, with the city alcazar just to the south. Over the centuries the Plaza de Zocodover has seen its share of blood and violence, from the Autos de Fe to bullfights to street clashes during the Spanish Civil War. A small memorial plaque mentions the Autos de Fe. The alcazar is one of the oldest castles in Europe, with parts of it dating back to Roman times. During the Inquisition, many of its victims were imprisoned in the alcazar where they awaited trials and executions.

---

156. CORDOBA JEWISH QUARTER

Calle Judios, 20, 14004 Cordoba, Spain

Site Type: Historic Neighborhood, Medieval Synagogue
Dates: Synagogue completed in 1315 CE
Designations: UNESCO World Heritage Site
Web: www.turismodecordoba.org/the-jewish-quarter (municipal tourism website)

Cordoba was one of the greatest centers of Judaism in Western Europe in the early Middle Ages. From the time the Umayyad Caliphate reached its height in the 10th century until the late Reconquista, the Jewish community of Cordoba flourished. This was due in large part to the generally cordial relations with the Muslim rulers of Spain. Remnants of the old Jewish Quarter survive to this day.

Early in the 8th century a Muslim army from North Africa arrived in Spain and quickly overran much of the peninsula. Cordoba was conquered in 711 CE, and in 756 became the capital of a new independent Islamic caliphate. Under the caliphate the Jewish community of Cordoba grew and thrived, with Jews serving in prominent positions under various governments. Moses Maimonides was born in Cordoba in 1138 CE.

In 1236 CE five centuries of Muslim rule in Cordoba came to an end when the Christian forces of the Reconquista captured the city. Muslims were persecuted, and their grand mosque converted to a church. The city's Jewish community was left alone, albeit in a lesser position than they had enjoyed under the Muslims.

In the late 15th century the Jews of Cordoba came under increasing persecution by the country's Christian rulers. The Spanish Inquisition led to the end of the community, with the city's Jews either converting or forced to flee. A small Jewish community began to return to Cordoba in the 20th century as part of a greater Jewish renaissance in Spain. Today the Jewish Quarter is part of the Historic Center of Cordoba UNESCO World Heritage Site.

Of Interest: The Cordoba Jewish Quarter largely looks today like it has for centuries. The Cordoba Synagogue, the only surviving Jewish house of worship in the city, is built on the site of an earlier synagogue. The strong Moorish influence is reflected in the architecture and style of this building, and it probably appears much like its predecessor did during the Islamic golden age of Spain. The synagogue underwent a major restoration in the 1980s and was rededicated on the 850th anniversary of the birth of Maimonides. The plaza outside is now called Tiberias Square in honor of the city in Israel. A statue of Moses Maimonides was erected in Cordoba in the 1930s in honor of the city's favorite Jewish son.

---

157. SEVILLE JEWISH QUARTER

Barrio de Santa Cruz, Seville, Spain

Site Type: Historic Neighborhood
Dates: Synagogue completed in 1180 CE
Web: www.visitsevilla.es/en (municipal tourism website)

The Seville Jewish Quarter, also known as the Santa Cruz district, is one of the most beautiful former Jewish neighborhoods in Europe. The entire area is a labyrinth of narrow whitewashed alleys leading to secluded plazas filled with fountains and orange trees. Jews lived here for many centuries, first under the Muslims and later under the Christians. Like elsewhere in Spain the Jews were driven out in 1492, and today there is very little left of their former presence. Their legacy is this magnificent quarter.

The first Jews to settle in the region of Seville probably arrived during the Roman era. In 587 CE the Visigoths, who had conquered Spain in the 5th century, converted to Christianity, after which conditions for the Jews in Spain deteriorated rapidly. The Visigoths were particularly violent towards the Jewish population, so by the time Muslim invaders arrived in the 8th century, the Jews welcomed them as liberators.

Under the Umayyad caliphate the Jewish community of Spain reached its zenith. Jews became highly regarded as merchants, scholars, physicians and other professions. However in 1031 CE the caliphate collapsed, and within a few decades Spain had gone from being a place of safety to being a place where Jews lived in fear of the sudden violent outbursts of their neighbors. After thousands of Jews were slaughtered in Granada in 1066 CE, many began relocating to the relative safety of the northern Christian kingdoms.

By the early 13th century the Jewish community of Seville was the second largest in Spain after Toledo. In 1248 CE Christian forces of the Reconquista captured Seville. The Jews of the city were relocated into their own quarter and separated from the Christian population by a wall. Despite this the community enjoyed a brief renaissance. Unfortunately many of the Jews were killed here during the pogrom of 1391, and the survivors forced to convert or leave by the Spanish Inquisition a century later.

Of Interest: The Jewish Quarter of Seville is a walker's delight. There is not much left of Jewish interest per se, but there are a few things for intrepid explorers to hunt down. Some of the original streets of the quarter have been preserved as they were in the 14th and 15th centuries, and the Church of Santa Maria la Blanca was the city's former Great Synagogue. One favorite site of the quarter is a house with a picture of a skull painted on the front. This was once the home of a Jewish woman named Susona, who fell in love with a Christian man. In true Romeo and Juliet fashion their story did not end well. Also in the quarter is the small but interesting Jewish Museum of Seville.

158. STONE SYNAGOGUE

Old Town, Obidos, Portugal

Site Type: Medieval Synagogue
Dates: Possibly completed c. 8th century CE
Web: www.visitportugal.com/en/node/73768 (Portugal national tourism website)

The Stone Synagogue of Obidos is arguably the most historic Jewish architectural treasure of Portugal. This tiny building on the western fringe of Europe is believed to date to the Visigothic era. Although this dating is not completely without problems, if true it would make this synagogue the oldest standing in Europe.

The history of the Jews in Portugal is roughly parallel to the history of the Jews in Spain. Although the first Jewish communities here were established later, possibly in the 5th century CE, the overall timeline beginning with the Islamic caliphate is basically the same. The Jews suffered persecution under the Visigoths, then flourished for a while under the Muslims before being persecuted again, then flourished for a while under the Christians before being persecuted yet again.

According to tradition the Stone Synagogue of Obidos was originally constructed in the 8th century CE. The Jewish community of Obidos is believed to have survived more or less continually for the better part of a thousand years. However towards the end of the 15th century the Inquisition reached Portugal, and the Jewish population was forced to either convert or flee. Despite being damaged by the great earthquake of 1755, the building has survived, a monument to this ancient Jewish neighborhood.

Of Interest: The Stone Synagogue is a very old building. However, tradition aside, it is more likely that it dates from much later, possibly even as late as the post-Muslim period. Moreover, there are also questions as to whether or not it was purpose built as a synagogue, or even when and for how long it was used as a synagogue. That said it is a very distinctive building, with hewn stone brick walls and gothic features. The idea that it formerly served as a synagogue is a very strong tradition in the local Jewish community.

---

159. BEVIS MARKS SYNAGOGUE

4 Heneage Lane, London EC3A 5DQ, United Kingdom

Site Type: Synagogue
Dates: Completed in 1701 CE
Designations: English Heritage Listed Building
Web: www.sephardi.org.uk/bevis-marks (official website)

The Bevis Marks Synagogue, officially the Kahal Kadosh Shaar Asamaim Synagogue, is the oldest standing Jewish house of worship in the British Isles. It is also one of the older continually active synagogues in Europe, having been open for worship continually since its completion in 1701 CE. For about a century it was considered the most important synagogue in the English speaking world, and it was instrumental in helping to found new Jewish congregations as the British Empire spread around the globe.

From the late 13th century until the late 17th century there was no Jewish community to speak of in England. However by the 1690s there were several hundred Jews in London. The congregation acquired a rabbi and went about building a synagogue. The synagogue, the first to be built in England in centuries, was dedicated in 1701 CE. There are several traditions associated with its construction. One holds that the queen of England personally donated at least some of the roofing materials. Another is that the contractor for the construction, a Quaker, refused to take full payment for work on a house of God.

During the early years of Britain's colonial empire the congregation of Bevis Marks Synagogue frequently acted as a contact for Jewish communities in the colonies with the British government. They offered assistance to Jews in the Caribbean colonies and brought attention to persecutions in Continental Europe. During the 1990s the Bevis Marks Synagogue was damaged in several terrorist bombings. In the last few decades the synagogue has been visited by such luminaries as Prime Minister Tony Blair and Prince Charles. Bevis Marks is an English Heritage Listed Building.

Of Interest: The Bevis Marks Synagogue is a stately Georgian brick building located on an ancient lane just off of Bevis Marks Street. Its design is believed to have been influenced by the Portuguese Synagogue completed in Amsterdam a few years earlier. A magnificent ark dominates the eastern wall. As of the time of this writing, a new building was being constructed nearby to house a Jewish cultural center.

---

160. JEWISH MUSEUM OF LONDON

Raymond Burton House, 129-131 Albert Street, London, NW1 YNB, United Kingdom

Site Type: Museum
Dates: Predeccesor museum opened in 1932
Web: https://jewishmuseum.org.uk (official website)

The Jewish Museum of London is the oldest and largest such institution in the British Isles. It is actually the result of a merger of two earlier museums: the Jewish Museum of London, opened in Bloomsbury in 1932; and the London Museum of Jewish Life, opened in the East End in 1983. The combined museum opened at the current facility in Camden Town in 2010.

Jewish communities likely existed here in the British Isles in Roman times, but had largely disappeared by the early Middle Ages. They returned with the Normans in the 11th century, but after a period of persecutions were driven out again in 1290 CE. It wasn't until the late 17th century that a permanent Jewish population was established in England, and another two centuries before they achieved full emancipation and the right to citizenship.

Nevertheless Jews in England generally enjoyed freedoms and

privelages long before their counterparts in much of the rest of Europe. Prominent Jews received knighthoods and served in high government offices. There was even a Jewish volunteer corps that served in the British army. Thanks to the fact that the Nazis were not able to conquer the British Isles, the Jews of England escaped the horrors of the Holocaust. Today the Jewish community of England is one of the largest in Europe. Their story is told at the Jewish Museum of London.

Of Interest: The Jewish Museum of London opened in 2010 in a former piano factory. It has several permanent exhibits, with a focus on the history of Jews in Britain. A medieval mikveh bath, discovered at a construction site, was moved here and is on permanent display. There is also a large collection of Judaica, as well as exhibits on the Jewish LGBTQ community and the Holocaust.

---

161. BRITISH LIBRARY & HEBREW COLLECTIONS

96 Euston Road, London, NW1 2DB, United Kingdom

Site Type: Library
Dates: Opened in 1973
Web: www.bl.uk (official website)

The British Library is the national library of the United Kingdom and one of the largest and most comprehensive libraries in the world. Home to an estimated 170 million items, the British Library has an enormous collection of writings and important historical documents. Among the latter are several items of particular Jewish interest: the Hebrew Collections, which includes tens of thousands of books, manuscripts and periodicals which date back centuries; and the original copy of the Balfour Declaration.

In 1917 the worldwide Zionist movement picked up momentum when the British Foreign Secretary, Arthur James Balfour, issued one of the most controversial documents of the 20th century: the Balfour

Declaration. This document formally acknowledged the support of the British government for the creation of a Jewish homeland in Palestine. It was hoped that this might encourage American Jews to pressure their government to send more troops to France, appeal to Jewish revolutionaries in Russia to keep the war going in the east, undermine the morale of Jews serving in the enemy armies, and encourage Jews in Palestine to take up arms against the Ottoman Empire.

On November 2, 1917 the Declaration was signed by Balfour and sent on to the Zionist Federation. The entire letter consisted of a short paragraph, with the key statement summed up in a single sentence: "His Majesty's Government views with favour the establishment in Palestine of a national home for the Jewish people, and will use their best endeavours to facilitate the achievement of this object, it being clearly understood that nothing shall be done which may prejudice the civil and religious rights of existing non-Jewish communities in Palestine, or the rights and political status enjoyed by Jews in any other country."

The Balfour Declaration did indeed increase Jewish support for the war, but in the end it also created major headaches for the British Empire. Nevertheless, despite the tangled diplomatic mess it created, the Balfour Declaration was a major contributing factor to the creation of the modern state of Israel three decades later. It is still regarded as a critical document supporting Israel's right to exist as a state.

Of Interest: The British Library began as an adjunct of the British Museum in 1753, but became an independent institution in 1973. The current facility on Pancras Road opened in 1997. The original copy of the Balfour Declaration is part of the library's special collections. Unfortunately the declaration is not on regular display. The library's Hebrew Collections is substantial. There are between eighty and a hundred thousand items in the collection, and includes documents from the Cairo Geniza and the Samaritan Manuscripts. The oldest major item in the collection is the 10th century London Codex, one of the oldest surviving books written in Hebrew.

162. HYDE PARK HOLOCAUST MEMORIAL

38 A4, London W2 2AR, United Kingdom

Site Type: Holocaust Memorial
Dates: Dedicated in 1983
Web: www.royalparks.org.uk/parks/hyde-park (Hyde Park website)

The Hyde Park Holocaust Memorial is the United Kingdom's national monument to the Jewish victims of the Nazis. Completed and dedicated in 1983, it is a quiet, simple reminder of the horrors that raged across Continental Europe not too far away. But for the bravery of the British military and the narrow waters of the English Channel, the Holocaust might have ravaged the United Kingdom as well.

In the years leading up to World War II Jewish refugees began to flee to the west. One popular destination was the British Isles. Roughly eighty thousand Jews were allowed into the United Kingdom in the years immediately before the war broke out. This included ten thousand Jewish children who arrived through the Kindertransport program.

Although Great Britain was in the fight against the Germans from the beginning of the conflict, it is not believed that they were aware of what was going on in the concentration camps for several years. It wasn't until late 1942 and early 1943 that eyewitness accounts began to emerge. Despite this the British military took little direct action to stop the slaughter.

After the war the British government was criticized for its inaction to help the Jews both before and during the conflict. This criticism was further stoked by Britain's hostility towards Jewish settlers in the British Mandate of Palestine. It took the United Kingdom several decades to come to terms with the consequences of its inactions. The Holocaust Memorial in Hyde Park is a symbol of that effort.

Of Interest: The Hyde Park Holocaust Memorial is a relatively sub-dued monument. It is a small, secluded tree-lined spot that focuses on solitude and contemplation. Several large stones serve as markers, and are engraved with words of mourning from the Old Testament. At the time of this writing the Imperial War Museum of London also had a more comprehensive exhibit on the Holocaust.

---

163. PLYMOUTH SYNAGOGUE

Synagogue Chambers, Catherine Street, Plymouth PL1 2AD, United Kingdom

Site Type: Synagogue
Dates: Opened in 1762
Designations: English Heritage Listed Building
Web: www.plymouthsynagogue.com (official website)

The Plymouth Synagogue is home to the oldest Ashkenazi congregation in England, and by extension the English speaking world. Opened in 1762, it is also the second longest continually active synagogue in Great Britain after Bevis Marks in London. Today it is one of the historic landmarks in the old city center of Plymouth.

Up until the 18th century, Jews living in Western Europe and the Americas were almost entirely of Sephardic background. This was due in large part to the activities of the Inquisition, which drove the Sephardic Jews from their homes in Spain and Portugal. Many relocated to the Netherlands, and from there to England in the 1600s. When persecutions and pogroms began to increase in Eastern Europe, Ashkenazi Jews began to flee west, with many arriving in England in the early 18th century.

By the 1740s a community of Ashkenazi Jews had settled in Plymouth. They came via Central Europe and the Netherlands. Interestingly those seeking religious freedom commonly made their way from the Netherlands to the city of Plymouth, just as the Seperatist Pilgrims of Christianity had done a century earlier before heading to the Americas. By the 1750s the community had grown large enough to necessitate a synagogue, which was opened in 1762. The Plymouth Synagogue is an English Heritage Listed Building.

Of Interest: The Plymouth Synagogue is a simple white brick building somewhat reminiscent of the Christian meetinghouses that were commonly built in England in the 18th century. It was designed so as not to attract attention, which is the reason the main door is tucked away on a side street. The interior is also reminiscent of a traditional meeting house, with benches facing inward towards a central bimah rather than forward towards the ark. An old mikveh bath, no longer in use, can be found on the premises.

164. CLIFFORD'S TOWER

Tower Street, York YO1 9SA, United Kingdom

Site Type: Castle
Dates: Originally completed in 1069 CE
Designations: English Heritage Listed Site
Web: www.english-heritage.org.uk/visit/places/cliffords-tower-york (official website)

Clifford's Tower, a small castle that dominates the city of York, was the site of one of the most tragic events of the Jewish people in the Middle Ages. There, in 1190 CE, most of the city's Jews committed mass suicide rather than die at the hands of an angry mob. This act was the most gruesome event in Jewish history in England in the Middle Ages. Clifford's Tower has since become something of a memorial site, and the victims of 1190 CE are now commemorated at the castle.

The history of the Jews in England in the Middle Ages was a short and tumultuous one. The first significant numbers of Jews arrived in England along with the armies of William the Conqueror in the 11th century CE. William's interest in the Jews was primarily economic. Jewish trading networks were already well established in his territories in northern France, and William was desirous of putting Jewish expertise to use in England.

For a while the Jews enjoyed the protection of the crown. However this did not last long. Throughout the second half of the 12th century persecutions increased in frequency. These took on a fevered pitch as Richard the Lionheart whipped the country into a religious frenzy in preparation for the Third Crusade. On March 16, 1190, the Jews of York, fearful of a gathering mob, took refuge in York Castle. Unfortunately the sherrif and his soldiers were clearly outmatched and were forced to abandon the Jews to their fate.

The mob laid siege to the tower. Inside were about a hundred and fifty Jews under the leadership of their rabbi. Realizing that there was no way to keep the mob out, and fearful of the impending mass torture, rape and slaughter of his charges, he led the trapped Jews in a mass suicide. A handful refused, deciding to accept the mob's offer to convert to Christianity, but these were betrayed and slain anyway. None survived the massacre. All remaining Jews were driven out of England in 1290 CE. In 1980 a ceremony was held in which the Jews formally forgave the incident. Clifford's Tower is an English Heritage Listed Site.

Of Interest: The current incarnation of Clifford's Tower is not the same as the York Castle of the time of the massacre. The original fortress was a wooden motte-and-bailey castle that was constructed during William's reign. It was actually destroyed in a fire that started on the day of the massacre. The tower has been rebuilt several times, with the current structure dating mostly from the 13th and 17th centuries. Shortly after its reconstruction in 1245 CE it is said that the walls turned red as if running with blood. This has occurred several times in the tower's history, and the phenomenon has never been explained. The walls still bear a slightly pinkish tint, a reminder of the events of 1190 CE.

FAR EAST

165. JEWISH QUARTER OF SAMARKAND

Abu Laiz Samarkandi, Samarkand, Uzbekistan

Site Type: Historic Neighborhood
Dates: Synagogue completed in 1891
Designations: UNESCO World Heritage Site
Web: www.uzbek-travel.com/about-uzbekistan/monuments/old-city-jewish-quarter (Uzbekistan national tourism website)

The Jewish Quarter of Samarkand is a very old place. It was inhabited by Bukharan Jews for many centuries, though there are now few left. Thanks to its isolation in Central Asia, the Jewish community here was largely left alone until the Russians conquered the region in the 19th century. The remnant of the old Jewish Quarter is one of the most unique that can be found anywhere.

Archaeology confirms that Jews have lived in what is now Uzbekistan since at least the 4th century CE. However tradition suggests that they may have arrived even earlier. Some believe that the first Jews to settle here were actually Israelites of the Northern Kingdom captured by the Assyrians in the 8th century BCE. The city of Samarkand was founded around this time, and its name bears a striking similarity to "Samaria", the former capital of Israel.

Despite this possibility, it is more likely that the first Jews settled here a few centuries later under the Achaemenids or the Sassanians. This would make sense as Samarkhand was one of the most important stops on the Silk Road from China to Europe. The city reached its peak under the Timurids, when it served as the capital of one of the Mongol kingdoms.

At its height the Jewish population of Uzbekistan probably numbered in the tens of thousands, with most living in major cities like Bukhara and Samarkand. When Uzbekistan came under the control of the Russian Empire some Ashkenazi Jews relocated here as well.

The Jewish community of Uzbekistan peaked at around a hundred thousand in the 1970s, but most emigrated after the collapse of the Soviet Union. The Jewish Quarter of Samarkand is part of the Samarkand UNESCO World Heritage Site.

Of Interest: The Jewish Quarter of Samarkand is one of several ancient Jewish communities in Uzbekistan, and arguably the one most worth visiting. Lost in the tangle of streets in the old town center, the quarter can be surprisingly difficult to find. Those who do can explore the beautiful 19th century Gumbaz Synagogue where a handful of Jews still worship. Of perhaps greater historical and cultural interest is the Jewish cemetery, with crowded gravestones dating back centuries. Many of these are ornamented with engravings of the faces of those who are buried here.

---

166. PARADESI SYNAGOGUE

Synagogue Lane, Jew Town, Kappalandimukku, Mattancherry, Kochi, Kerala, 682002, India

Site Type: Synagogue
Dates: Completed in 1568
Web: www.keralatourism.org/kochi/paradeso-synagogue-mattancherry.php (municipal tourism website)

The Paradesi Synagogue is one of the oldest Jewish sites in the Far East. Although not definitively proven, there is evidence that Jews may have settled in India around the time of the fall of the kingdom of Judah. It is more likely that Jewish traders were established here at a later date, possibly during the Roman era. The community's greatest legacy is the 16th century Paradesi Synagogue, the oldest east of Iran.

According to tradition the first Jewish immigrants to India arrived in the 6th century BCE. These were the Cochin Jews. According to their own history they arrived at the port of Cranganore in southern India in 562 BCE, approximately twenty-five years after the fall of

Jerusalem. These settlers almost certainly came by sea, though whether directly from Judah or from Babylon is uncertain. The Cochin Jews spent the better part of over a thousand years living a quiet existence in the south of India.

Because of the area's isolation from both Christians and Muslims, India's Jews were largely left alone. A synagogue was constructed by the community in the 14th century. Until the 16th century there is no record of any deliberate acts of anti-Semitic violence in Southern India. Muslim persecutions of the Jews of Cranganore began in 1524, forcing them to move south to safety in Cochin. However the Portuguese arrived soon afterward and proceeded to oppress the Jews in Cochin. The old synagogue was destroyed, but a new one was completed in 1568.

By the time the Dutch arrived in 1660 the community had dwindled considerably. A new wave of Jewish immigrants arrived in the 18th century, where they lived under the protection of the British Empire. However, most of India's Jews relocated to Israel in the second half of the 20th century. The Paradesi Synagogue is the architectural legacy of this ancient Jewish community.

Of Interest: The current Paradesi Synagogue was constructed on land donated by the Raja of Kochi and with funds donated by Dutch merchant interests. It stands adjacent to the Mattancherry Palace with which it shares a wall. A blend of Indian and Colonial architecture, the exterior of the synagogue is unusual. The most striking exterior feature is the clock tower with four faces which feature Hebrew, Arabic, Hindi and Roman numerals. An engraved stone from the original 14th century synagogue is part of the walls. The interior of the synagogue is appointed with hand painted floor tiles, brass fixtures and glass chandeliers. A series of paintings depict Jewish life in Cochin. The synagogue's treasures include an ancient pair of copper plates and an oriental rug. The former was a gift to the Jewish community in the 10th century by the local raja. The latter was a gift to the synagogue by Haile Selassie of Ethiopia.

167. SHANGHAI JEWISH REFUGEES MUSEUM

62 Changyang Road, Hongkou District, Shanghai, China

Site Type: Historic Neighborhood, Museum
Dates: Museum opened in 2007
Web: www.shhkjrm.com/node2/n4/n6/index.html (official website)

The Shanghai Jewish Refugees Museum showcases the history of the Jews who lived in China in the early 20th century and who fled here during the war years. Even under the Japanese occupation, the city's Jewish community fared much better than in German-occupied Europe. Parts of the old Jewish quarter survived both the war and the postwar era, and can still be visited.

Jews began arriving in China's port cities such as Hong Kong and Shanghai in the late 19th and early 20th centuries. After the electoral victory of the Nazis in 1933, Jews all over Central Europe began to look abroad for places of safety; and it was just at this same time the nations all over the world began closing their borders to Jewish refugees. There was one noteworthy exception: China.

By 1937 China and Japan had been at war for several years. Shanghai, though surrounded by territory occupied by Japan, received a special status under an International Settlement which essentially allowed the European dominated city to be left alone. This settlement allowed westerners, including Jews, to enter and settle in Shanghai without a visa. Between 1937 and the outbreak of the war in Europe in 1939, somewhere around twenty five thousand Jews fled to Shanghai.

Even after the war started and Shanghai was occupied, the Jews were generally left alone. Most of the Shanghai Jewish community survived the war. After the communist takeover of China virtually all of the surviving Jews left and went to Israel and the United States. The Shanghai Jewish Refugees Museum opened in 2007 on the one hundredth anniversary of the founding of the first congregation in the city.

Of Interest: The Shanghai Jewish Refugees Museum is located in the former Ohel Moshe Synagogue and is the central place of interest for those visiting the Jewish Quarter. The museum has exhibits documenting the history of the Jews in Shanghai, including a collection of personal items and photographs from those who lived here. A monument outside of the museum is inscribed with the names of nearly fourteen thousand Jewish refugees who made Shanghai their home in the 1930s and 40s. A few other buildings survive in the old Jewish Quarter including the Ohel Rachel Synagogue, one of the largest synagogues built in the Far East during the Colonial era.

---

168. KAIFENG MUSEUM & JEWISH STELAE

26 Yingbin Road, Gulou District, Kaifeng, Henan, China

Site Type: Museum
Dates: Opened in 1962
Web: None Available

The Kaifeng Museum is a prominent regional museum of Chinese history, culture, archaeology and art. It is home, among other things, to a collection of Judaica related to the city's old Jewish community. In particular there is a trio of stone monuments, or stelae, that are kept here that document early Chinese Jewish lore and religious practices. It is only in very recent years that visitors to China have begun to rediscover this wonderful treasure.

The origin of the Jews of China is nearly impossible to reconstruct with any certitude. There are some traditions that suggest Jews might have become established here along the Silk Road in ancient times. A Jewish community in China can only be traced as far back as the Middle Ages. One of the stelae of Kaifeng mentions the construction of a synagogue in China sometime around the year 1163 CE.

It is likely that another wave of Jewish settlers arrived in China around the 14th or 15th centuries. The exact relationship of this group of newcomers to the earlier Jews is unknown. They might have merged with the older community or formed an entirely new one. Over the centuries the Jewish community tended to grow smaller, in part due to intermarriage with the local population. However, as of the 19th century the remaining Jews still had their own synagogue and maintained many of their customs.

The Jews of China historically suffered little in the way of religious persecution, at least until 1850, when their synagogue was destroyed and the population temporarily dispersed. Many Jews left China following the communist revolution. Nevertheless a few Jewish communities remain. A tiny bit of their history can be found at the Kaifeng Museum.

Of Interest: The Kaifeng Museum primarily focuses on the history of the Song Dynasty, of which Kaifeng was the capital city from 960-1279 CE. It was during this period that Jews became established in Kaifeng. The museum's Jewish collection is tiny but consists of the museum's greatest treasures: the Jewish stelae. Although these stone monuments are very worn, there are rubbings displayed in the museum that make the writing clearer to read. The stelae have been dated to the years 1489, 1512 and 1663, respectively. Featuring a blend of Chinese and Hebrew styles, they document, among other things, the construction of an early synagogue in Kaifeng as well a list of the prophets from Abraham to Ezra.

169. PORT OF HUMANITY TSURUGA MUSEUM

23-1, Kanegasaki-cho, Tsuruga-shi, Fukui 914-0072, Japan

Site Type: Museum, Holocaust Memorial
Dates: Museum opened in 2008
Web: https://tsuruga-museum.jp (official website)

The Port of Humanity Tsuruga Museum commemorates Chiune Sugihara, a Japanese diplomat in Europe who aided thousands of Jews escape from the Nazis. This story is particularly fascinating considering that Japan was Germany's primary ally during the war, and the fact that those Sugihara helped escape had to cross thousands of miles of

Eurasia by railroad. The museum is located in Tsuruga, the destination of many of the refugees.

Chiune Sugihara worked at the Japanese consulate in Lithuania when World War II broke out. For the first two years of the war Lithuania was part of Soviet territory. Many Jews and other refugees desperate to get out of Eastern Europe sought exit visas in Lithuania. Sugihara was sympathetic to the plight of these refugees, and in the summer of 1940 he began churning out exit visas.

He worked nearly around the clock for over a month. He prepared so many visas that the actual count was lost, although the estimated figure is about six thousand. According to witnesses, when time was running out, he signed and stamped over a thousand blank visas and tossed them to the desperate refugees. In September the consulate was closed and Sugihara left Lithuania. He may have left the consular stamp behind so that others could forge more visas.

It is unknown exactly how many people were saved through Sugihara's efforts. Many of the visas covered whole families. Several thousand, and perhaps as many as ten thousand, Jews and other refugees survived the war thanks to Sugihara. He was later honored as a member of the Righteous among the Nations and is commemorated in Japan at the Port of Humanity Tsuruga Museum.

Of Interest: The Port of Humanity Tsuruga Museum is named for the port, which received its nickname following World War II. Many refugees fleeing the war in Europe arrived here after a long journey on the Trans-Siberian Railway and a sea voyage. From here they continued on to safe sanctuaries elsewhere in Japan and China. The museum has exhibits on the history of the port and on the Russian railway. There is a section devoted entirely to the Jews who took refuge here as well as on the life of Chiune Sugihara.

170. MANADO MENORAH

Manado, Indonesia

Site Type: Monument
Dates: Completed in 2009
Web: www.indonesia.travel/gb/en/destinations/sulawesi/manado
(Indonesia national tourism website)

In a world full of strange and incongruous religious sites, the Manado Menorah can be counted among the most unusual. The presence of the world's largest permanent menorah, one of the definitive symbols of the Jewish people, in the middle of the country with the world's largest Muslim population is strange to say the least. But this menorah is in Indonesia, where there are well over two hundred million Muslims and, at last count, approximately one hundred Jews.

Indonesia never had a particularly large Jewish population. Most that came here arrived with the Dutch during the Colonial era. Most were Sephardim from Western Europe. At its height in the interwar period there were perhaps two thousand Jews living in Indonesia. The majority of these left the country following World War II and the end of Dutch colonial rule in the East Indies.

While the Jewish population of Indonesia virtually vanished, a handful of familes remained, mostly on the island of North Sulawesi, which was also home to a sizeable Christian community. In 2009 the government constructed the gigantic menorah as a symbol of religious friendship between Muslims and Christians and, presumably, Jews as well. The people of the city love the menorah and are happy to show it off.

Of Interest: The immense Manado Menorah is more than sixty feet in height. It stands on a sizeable platform on top of a hill, making it appear even bigger. It is a standard seven branch candelabram menorah, as opposed to a nine-branch menorah that would be used during the Hanukkah holiday.

171. SYNAGOGUES OF SYDNEY

166 Castlereagh Street, Sydney, NSW 2000, Australia (Great Synagogue of Sydney)

15 Bon Accord Avenue, Bondi Junction NSW 2022, Australia (Central Synagogue of Sydney)

Site Type: Synagogues
Dates: Great Synagogue completed in 1878; Central Synagogue current building completed in 1998
Designations: New South Wales Heritage Register
Web: www.greatsynagogue.org.au & www.centralsynagogue.com.au (official websites)

Sydney, the largest city in Australia, is home to some of the oldest and most historic synagogues in the Australasia. The Great Synagogue of Sydney is the oldest synagogue on the Australian mainland. The Central Synagogue of Sydney is not only the largest synagogue in Australia, it also claims the record of being the largest synagogue anywhere in the world south of the Equator. The congregations of these two synagogues anchor one of the largest Jewish communities in Australasia.

The Jewish community in Sydney was established by the first Jews to arrive in Australia in 1788. The Jewish population remained relatively small well into the 19th century, and the community did not have a synagogue until 1844. A few decades later there were enough Jews in Sydney to necessitate a major house of worship. The Great Synagogue was completed in 1878.

Around the turn of the century large numbers of Jewish immigrants from Eastern Europe were arriving in Australia, with many settling in Sydney. The community grew much more quickly, and soon yet another synagogue was needed. Moreover, most of the new arrivals were Ashkenazis who wanted their own place to worship. The first Central Synagogue was completed in 1912. The community has since moved twice, and has been at its current location since the 1960s. The Great Synagogue is listed on the New South Wales Heritage Register.

Of Interest: The Great Synagogue of Sydney is a classic late-19th century building in a mixed Gothic-Byzantine style. The façade is flanked by a pair of towers crowned with onion domes. The sanctuary is breathtaking, with a particularly beautifully designed gallery supported by graceful columns. The huge vaulted ceiling is painted to like like a starry blue sky. The Central Synagogue of Sydney, specifically the current building of the congregation, was completed in 1998. This masterpiece of modern architecture is enormous, and can seat well over three thousand worshippers at once.

---

172. JEWISH MUSEUM OF AUSTRALIA

26 Alma Road, St. Kilda VIC 3182, Australia

Site Type: Museum
Dates: Opened in 1982
Web: www.jewishmuseum.com.au (official website)

The Jewish Museum of Australia is one of the best Jewish museums in the Far East. Located in Melbourne, it is part of the historic St. Kilda District, which is home to one of Australia's oldest and largest Jewish communities. While not as big as other major national Jewish museums, the Jewish Museum of Australia has a comprehensive collection that ranges from historical artifacts to art.

Australia was the last settled continent to become home to a Jewish population. The first Jews arrived in 1788 as convicts forced to relocate to the Botany Bay colony. Several small Jewish communities formed early in the 19th century. These communities grew considerably larger as more immigrants arrived in the 1850s. The first congregation in the city of Melbourne formed in 1841.

By the beginning of the 20th century there were well over ten thousand Jews living down under. When Australia achieved independence from the British Empire in 1901, a few of the new country's leaders were Jewish. Several thousand Jewish refugees managed to flee to Australia from Europe prior to the outbreak of World War II. Today there are nearly a hundred thousand Jews living in Australia, more than in many countries in Europe. The Jewish Museum of Australia opened in 1982.

Of Interest: The Jewish Museum of Australia moved to its current building in 1995. It houses several collections containing thousands of artifacts. There are a number of exhibits on history and culture that cover thousands of years of Jewish history. The most unique exhibit here focuses on the history of the Jews of Australia, from their arrival at the Botany Bay penal colony in the 18th century to modern Jewish life in the land down under.

---

173. HOBART SYNAGOGUE

59 Argyle Street, Hobart, TAS 7000, Australia

Site Type: Synagogue
Dates: Completed in 1845
Designations: Tasmanian Heritage Register
Web: www.hobartsynagogue.org (official website)

The Hobart Synagogue in Tasmania is the oldest synagogue on the the western side of the Pacific Rim. Constructed in 1845, it is famous not only for its age but also for its unusual construction style. The synagogue is also unusual in that it hosts both Reform and Orthodox worship services.

It is uncertain exactly when the first Jews arrived in Tasmania. Like those who arrived in nearby Australia they were convicts who came to help settle the island. Among these convicts were the brothers Judah and Joseph Solomon, who were criminals in England but successful entrepreneurs in Tasmania. By the mid-19th century there was a small Jewish community on the island. It soon required a synagogue, which was completed in 1845.

Many of the founding members of the congregation were former convicts who had been freed following the end of their sentences. Because of this the synagogue was something of a symbol of their freedom. Over the years the Hobart Synagogue remained continually active despite fluctuations in the size of the congregation. The Hobart Synagogue is listed on the Tasmanian Heritage Register.

Of Interest: The Hobart Synagogue is an interesting example of Egyptian Revival architecture, a rarity in synagogue construction. This style was chosen as a call back to the convicts receiving their freedom, just as the ancient Israelites had been freed from Egypt. The primary Egyptian feature is the main entrance, which resembles a columned gate into an ancient temple.

AMERICAS

174. KAHAL ZUR ISRAEL SYNAGOGUE MUSEUM

R. do Bom Jesus, 197-Recife, PE, 50030-170, Brazil

Site Type: Museum
Dates: Opened in 2001
Web: http://museubrasil.org/en/museu/museu-sinagoga-kahal-zur-israel (official website)

The Kahal Zur Synagogue was founded by the first Jewish congregation on the mainland of the New World. The first Jews to arrive here came as refugees from the Inquisition in Portugal. Jews practiced here more openly under Dutch rule, and also spread from here to other locations in the Americas. The original Kahal Zur Israel Synagogue was unfortunately torn down, but a Jewish museum now exists at the same location.

The history of the Jews in Brazil, and in the New World in general, began in 1500. The first Jewish person to arrive in Brazil was Gaspar de Gama. Technically a Catholic, his conversion was forced on him by the Inquisition, and historians believe that he was a Converso who practiced Judaism in secret. Distrusted by the Church, these New Christians were still persecuted by both religious and secular authorities. One of the few safe places for them to go was the New World.

Although things were generally better for the Jews in Brazil, religious persecution was still the order of the day. Things improved considerably with the arrival of the tolerant Dutch, who conquered the northern part of Brazil in the early 1600s. The Kahal Zur Israel Synagogue was constructed at this time in the colonial capital at Recife. From 1630 to 1654 the Jews of Brazil practiced openly. However, Portugal soon reconquered the territory, and the persecutions resumed.

A hundred years later Portugal formally ended religious persecution of non-Catholics. Jews began to relocate to Brazil. Immigration peaked at the beginning of the 20th century before the World Wars.

Throughout its history Recife remained the center of Judaism in Brazil. In the late 20th century archaeological research identified the former location of the city's original synagogue. Recife's Jewish Museum now occupies a building which stands upon the site.

Of Interest: The location where the Kahal Zur Israel Synagogue once stood was excavated around the turn of the century. Archaeological investigations revealed the old building's foundations as well as a ritual bath. The local Jewish community constructed a new building on the site, to be used both as a museum and cultural center. The museum houses a few small exhibits and shops on the lower level. The upper level is a reconstruction of a typical 17th century synagogue interior, offering a glimpse of what the original synagogue might have looked like in its heyday. Bom Jesus Street, formerly known as the Street of the Jews, is home to traditional Jewish residences and shops.

---

175. RUINS OF SINT EUSTATIUS SYNAGOGUE

Oranjestad, Sint Eustatius, Netherlands Territory

Site Type: Synagogue Ruins
Dates: Originally completed in 1737
Web: www.statia-tourism.com (municipal tourism website)

The Sint Eustatius Synagogue was one of the earliest synagogues built in the Caribbean region. Constructed nearly three hundred years ago, it fell out of use in the 19th century. By the 1990s there was little left. However the synagogue ruins have recently been partially restored. Today it is part of the island's fascinating old historic district.

Sint Eustatius is one of the islands that formerly constituted the colonial territory of the Dutch West Indies. Despite the fact that the the population was tiny, it still attracted a small Jewish community. By the 1730s the Jewish population was large enough and a synagogue was constructed. The Jews were generally tolerated by the Dutch. Unfortunately the island was occupied by the British for a time in 1781.

Angry at their misfortunes in the American Revolution, the British took some of their anger out on the Jews, which was unusual. There were confiscations of Jewish property as well as deportations. In the end these injustices were redressed, but the social damage to the community was done. Many left and the synagogue was no longer in use by the 1810s. Today the Sint Eustatius Synagogue is a scenic ruin.

Of Interest: The Sint Eustatius Synagogue has not been in use for over two hundred years. Largely dilapidated and in places completely wrecked, the ruins were partially restored in 2001. Today all that is left are the stone walls surrounding a carpet of grass. Although not functional, it is nevertheless a tranquil and pretty place. A short distance away is the old Jewish cemetery, with graves dating back to the early 18th century.

---

176. MIKVE ISRAEL-EMANUEL SYNAGOGUE

Hanchi Snoa, Willemstad, Curacao, Netherlands Territory

Site Type: Synagogue
Dates: Completed in 1730
Designations: UNESCO World Heritage Site
Web: https://snoa.com (official website)

The Mikve Israel-Emanuel Synagogue, also known as the Curacao Synagogue, is the oldest essentially intact synagogue in the New World. It is also the oldest in the Western Hemisphere that is still in use. Constructed in 1730, it serves a congregation that was founded in 17th century and which is still active after more than three and a half centuries.

The island of Curacao was one of the earliest Spanish colonies in the Caribbean. It was annexed by the Dutch in 1634. Among the original settlers here were Sephardic Jews from Europe. These were joined by additional Jewish exiles from Brazil when that territory was lost to the Portuguese. The community established a makeshift house synagogue in 1674.

The Jews of Curacao became important members of the island's population, and were successful as traders in the Caribbean. They constructed a permanent synagogue in Willemstad in 1730. The community survived centuries of colonial wars in the region, though many began to leave in the early 19th century following a British occupation of the island.

Curacao played an interesting role during World War II as a safe haven for Jews fleeing from Eastern Europe. The island was one of only a handful of places that allowed refugees to come without a visa. Working with the Japanese consulate in Lithuania, many Jews were able to escape Europe to Curacao via Russia and Japan. The Curacao Jewish community, though small, remains active. The Mikve Israel-Emanuel Synagogue is part of the Historic Area of Willemstad UNESCO World Heritage Site.

Of Interest: The Mikve Israel-Emanuel Synagogue, now approaching its three hundredth birthday, is a truly beautiful and elegant building. Architecturally it looks much more like an 18th century colonial-style church. The sanctuary is a stunning mix of brilliant white walls and columns offset by dark mahogany wooden fixtures. Of particular interest is the floor which is covered with sand. Although symbolic of the Israelites' forty year journey in the wilderness, the real purpose of the sand is to muffle the sound of footsteps, a tradition that dates back to Conversos hiding their faith from the Inquisition.

177. NIDHE ISRAEL SYNAGOGUE MUSEUM

Synagogue Lane, Bridgetown, Barbados

Site Type: Synagogue, Museum
Dates: Opened in 1831
Designations: UNESCO World Heritage Site
Web: https://synagoguehistoricdistrict.com (official website)

The Nidhe Israel Synagogue is an historic Caribbean house of worship that is associated with the first Jewish congregation established in the British colonies in the Americas. Although constructed in the 1830s, it replaced an earlier 17th century synagogue that was the first built in an English speaking territory outside of England. The building is now home to a small museum.

Barbados was claimed as a colony and settled by the British in the 1620s. In 1654 the Dutch were driven out of Brazil by the Portuguese, and the Jewish community there faced renewed persecutions. Most fled, with some relocating to Barbados where the island was undergoing an economic boom from the sugar trade. Around three hundred Jews settled here and founded what is believed to be the first Jewish congregation in the English speaking colonies.

An early synagogue was constructed in the mid-17th century and stood until it was destroyed by a hurricane in the 19th century. After the hurricane the synagogue was rebuilt, but the community began to undergo a long, slow decline. The Jewish population was largely gone by the 1920s. A small number of Jews resettled here after World War II, at which time efforts were made to preserve the old synagogue. The Nidhe Israel Synagogue is part of the Historic Bridgetown UNESCO World Heritage Site.

Of Interest: The Nidhe Israel Synagogue is a part of historic old Bridgetown, which includes a number of places of Jewish interest. The synagogue dates almost entirely from its reconstruction in the 1830s. The interior has largely been restored to the way it looked two centuries ago. A short distance from the synagogue are two related sites: the old Jewish Cemetery, with hundreds of graves dating as far back as 1658; and a mikveh bath, which was rediscovered during an archaeological dig in 2008.

178. SIERRA JUSTO SYNAGOGUE

Justo Sierra 71, Centro Historico de la Cdad. De Mexico, Centro,
Cuauhtemoc, 06020 Ejido del, CDMX, Mexico

Site Type: Synagogue
Dates: Completed in 1938
Web: www.sinagogajustosierra.com (official website)

The Sierro Justo Synagogue is one of the most historic synagogues in Spanish-speaking Latin America. Its exterior architecture is interesting as the building is almost indistinguishable from an average residence of the neighborhood. Even though it is not yet a century old, it is still among the oldest surviving synagogues to be found in the territories of the former Spanish Empire in the Americas.

During the early colonial era Jews from Western Europe settled in colonies all over the New World. By the end of the 17th century Jewish communities could be found in North America, South America and the islands of the Carribean. Most set down roots in areas ruled by the Dutch and British, but there were also a small number in the French territories and even, for a brief time, Portuguese Brazil. But there were few Jews to be found in the Spanish colonies, and almost none of these practiced openly.

The Spanish Inquisition worked diligently to keep the Jews out of their empire in the Americas. Undoubtedly a number of Conversos managed to slip in, but these practiced their faith in secret for centuries. Even after many of these territories achieved their independence, Jewish immigrants rarely found a welcome. It wasn't until the late 19th century that Jews were able to practice their faith here, if only semi-openly.

Many Jews, mostly Ashkenazi, immigrated to Mexico at the turn of the century. The Jewish community of Mexico City grew large enough by the 1910s to require synagogues. The Sierra Justo Synagogue, which was constructed in the late 1930s, was the second to be completed in the city. Today it serves as the secretive heart of Mexico City's Ashkenazi community.

Of Interest: The Sierra Justo Synagogue is definitely an architectural oddity as synagogues go. From the outside it looks like nothing more than a three story apartment building on a quiet neighborhood street. The interior, however, is a true Jewish treasure. White walls and lightly stained woodworked fixtures give the stunning sanctuary a light and airy feel. The ceiling is wonderfully painted in cheerful colors and features images of Torah scrolls, the Ten Commandments and Stars of David.

179. CANADIAN MUSEUM OF IMMIGRATION AT PIER 21

1055 Marginal Road, Halifax, NS B3H 4P7, Canada

Site Type: Museum, Holocaust Memorial
Dates: Opened in 1999
Web: https://pier21.ca (official website)

The Canadian Museum of Immigration at Pier 21 is an institution that commemorates Canada's maritime immigration history. Located in a former ship terminal, many immigrants arrived here during the interwar and postwar years of the 20th century. The museum is home to the Wheel of Conscience monument. This memorial commemorates the MS St. Louis and the infamous Voyage of the Damned, in which a shipload of Jewish refugees trying to flee Nazi Germany were denied safe harbor in a number of western nations.

The Voyage of the Damned was one of the greatest avoidable tragedies of the Holocaust. In May of 1939 the ocean liner MS St. Louis departed Germany with nearly a thousand passengers, almost all of them Jewish. Bound for Havana, virtually everyone on board had an entry visa for Cuba, where they hoped to find asylum from the Nazis. However, unbeknownst to anyone on the ship, the Cuban government revoked the visas before the St. Louis arrived. Only a handful of passengers were permitted to disembark.

The captain, Gustav Schroder, who was sympathetic to the plight of his passengers, endeavored to find them an alternative port of disembarkation. Over the course of the next month the passengers of the St. Louis were denied entry into the United States, Canada and the United Kingdom. Schroder even contemplated grounding the ship on purpose, thereby forcing the passengers to be evacuated. Eventually the St. Louis was finally able to dock in Belgium, barely three hundred miles from Hamburg.

The Jewish passengers found asylum in France, Belgium and the Netherlands, and some were even allowed into the United Kingdom. Unfortunately, a year later France and the Low Countries were overrun, and most of the MS St. Louis Jews found themselves once more in Nazi territory. According to estimates, roughly two hundred and fifty former Jewish passengers of the St. Louis subsequently perished in the concentration camps. Nevertheless between six and seven hundred survived, and for his efforts Captain Schroder was named one of the Righteous among the Nations. The Voyage of the Damned is remembered at the Canadian Museum of Immigration.

Of Interest: The Canadian Museum of Immigration at Pier 21 is similar to the Ellis Island Museum in New York Harbor. Exhibits tell the story of centuries of immigration into Canada. There is also a monument to those Canadians who served overseas during the Second World War. The MS St. Louis Monument is a memorial to the passengers of the Voyage of the Damned. The names of the passengers are inscribed on the monument.

---

180. CONGREGATION EMANU-EL SYNAGOGUE

1461 Blanshard Street, Victoria, BC V8W 2J3, Canada

Site Type: Synagogue
Dates: Completed in 1863
Designations: Canadian National Historic Site
Web: www.congregationemanuel.ca (official website)

The Congregation Emanu-El Synagogue in Victoria, British Columbia is one of the oldest standing synagogues in Canada. It is also one of the oldest surviving synagogues on the Pacific coast of the Americas. Completed in 1863, it has been in continual use since its dedication, and is one of the city of Victoria's historical gems.

The first Jews arrived in the far west of Canada in the 1850s. They mostly came here during the gold rush of 1858. In fact many of these early Jewish arrivals came from California, where they had participated in the San Francisco gold rush of 1849. It only took a few years for the Jewish community of Victoria to grow large enough to require a synagogue.

The Jews of Victoria were very involved in city affairs. Victoria produced Canada's first Jewish mayor as well as the first Jewish MP. Even well after the gold rush ended, the Jewish population grew and remained active. Congregation Emanu-El is a Canadian National Historic Site.

Of Interest: The Congregation Emanu-El Synagogue is a landmark of the historic old center of Victoria. A red brick Romanesque building on a peaceful tree lined street, the synagogue looks exactly as it has since the 19th century. A time capsule containing artifacts from when the synagogue was under construction is buried beneath the building.

UNITED STATES

181. SPANISH AND PORTUGUESE SYNAGOGUE

8 West 70th Street, New York, New York, 10023

Site Type: Synagogue
Dates: Completed in 1897
Designations: New York City Historic Landmark
Web: https://shearithisrael.org (official website)

The Spanish and Portuguese Synagogue in New York, also known as Congregation Shearith Israel, is home to one of the most historic Jewish congregations in the United States. Closely tied to the founding of the Touro Synagogue in Rhode Island, there is some question as to which one is technically older, but there is no doubt that Shearith Israel has been continually active and is the better known of the two.

The first Jews to come to New York arrived in the 17th century. Fleeing from lands where the Inquisition was persecuting Jews, a popular destination was the Dutch colonies of the New World. Arriving in 1654 these Jewish immigrants were at first denied entry into New Amsterdam, and briefly settled in what is now Newport, Rhode Island. The next year they were allowed to settle in what is now New York, where they established the Congregation Shearith Israel.

While they could not at first setup a synagogue, the congregation did establish a Jewish cemetery in 1656. Interestingly, this cemetery is the last surviving remnant of the original Dutch colony. The community's first synagogue was constructed on Mill Street in 1730. Throughout the late 18th and 19th centuries the congregation grew rapidly, requiring four moves. They constructed the current synagogue in 1897.

Congregation Shearith Israel was instrumental in founding some of America's most important Jewish organizations. Among these was the Jewish Theological Seminary near Columbia University. The Spanish and Portuguese Synagogue was named a New York City

Historic Landmark in 1974. The Graveyard is listed on the National Register of Historic Places.

Of Interest: The Spanish and Portuguese Synagogue was completed in 1897 and is a neo-Classical masterpiece well suited to Central Park West. The magnificent façade is replete with a quartet of columns and a tall, peaked roof. The synagogue interior is equally impressive, from its beautiful crystal chandeliers to the stained glass windows. Among the synagogue's treasures are its archives which chronicle three and a half centuries of Jewish life in New York City. The adjoining worship area, known as the Little Synagogue, is actually a replica of the congregation's former house of worship on Mill Street. The cemetery of the synagogue, located in lower Manhattan, is the oldest surviving man-made structure of any sort in New York City.

---

182. TEMPLE EMANU-EL

1 East 65th Street, New York, New York, 10065

Site Type: Synagogue
Dates: Completed in 1929
Web: www.emanuelnyc.org (official website)

Temple Emanu-El is the largest synagogue in New York City and was, until recent years, the largest in the world. Its congregation grew out of the massive influx of Jewish immigrants from Central and Eastern Europe in the late 19th century. Temple Emanu-El was one the founding synagogues of Reform Judaism in the United States and is counted among the great houses of worship that line Fifth Avenue in Midtown Manhattan.

Most of the early Jewish arrivals in New York City were Sephardic immigrants coming from Spanish and Portuguese colonies in the New World. This began to change dramatically in the 1830s, when large waves of Ashkenazi Jews began arriving from Europe. The first Ashkenazi Jews to arrive in New York were from Germany, with many others from Eastern Europe following soon after.

The Ashkenazis introduced a strong secular element to Jewish life in America, with a focus on intellectual professions and the arts, as well as the use of Yiddish. In 1845 the German Jews established Congregation Emanu-El, one of the earliest Reform Jewish congregations in America. Congregation Emanu-El moved several times. Beginning in the Lower East Side, which was home to many European Jewish immigrants in the 19th century, the congregation built a succession of synagogues up Fifth Avenue, each one larger than the last.

In 1927 Emanu-El merged with another New York congregation, Beth-El. In 1929 the consolidated congregation moved into its current home at the Temple Emanu-El Synagogue on the Upper East Side of Manhattan. From its inception Emanu-El espoused Reform Judaism, and has been a cornerstone of the American Reform Jewish community ever since.

Of Interest: Temple Emanuel has recently undergone a massive renovation that has restored it to it its early 20th century magnificence. The immense synagogue is home to the world's largest vaulted sanctuary in a Jewish house of worship. The interior is decorated with some of the best mosaic artwork to be found in New York City. There is also a small museum on site with exhibits containing centuries of Judaica on display.

---

183. JEWISH MUSEUM OF NEW YORK

1109 5th Avenue, New York, New York, 10128

Site Type: Museum
Dates: Opened in 1944
Web: https://thejewishmuseum.org (official website)

The Jewish Museum of New York is the oldest and largest institution of its kind in the United States. Founded in the early 20th century, it inspired the creation of Jewish museums around the world. An integral part of New York City's famous museum mile, it houses a collection of well over twenty thousand artifacts and pieces of art from thousands of years of Jewish history. It is among the most visited Jewish museums in the world.

In 1904 Mayer Sulzberger, a prominent New Yorker, donated twenty-six pieces of artwork to the Jewish Theological Seminary with the idea that it might one day form the basis of a future museum collection. In the decades leading up to World War II the collection grew rapidly. Donations and purchased items were acquired, and by the 1940s the collection had become too large for the seminary. In 1944 Frieda Warburg donated a mansion at the corner of Fifth Avenue and 92nd Street for use as a new museum.

Almost from its inception the Jewish Museum has been a work in progress, with its focus occasionally shifting between history, art, culture and archaeology. The museum has added hundreds of pieces to its collection every year, with new acquisitions reflecting changing trends in the museum's focus. The expansion of the collections has been matched several times by the expansion of the museum itself, including substantial increases of space in 1963 and 1993.

In the years following the Holocaust the importance of the Jewish Museum of New York took on a new urgency. The realization that European Judaism had been brought to the brink of total annhilation highlighted the critical importance to more aggressively protect Jewish culture and heritage. Jews around the world looked to New York for guidance. In the second half of the 20th century Jewish museums proliferated in many countries. There are now well over a hundred such museums around the world.

Of Interest: The Jewish Museum of New York is housed in the Neo-Gothic Warburg Mansion. Subsequent additions to the museum matched the style so as to maintain the architectural integrity of the original building. The Jewish Museum's primary permanent exhibit is Culture and Continuity: The Jewish Journey. This exhibit, which displays over eight hundred pieces from the museum's permanent collection, traces centuries of Jewish history. The majority of the museum's galleries are set aside for the display of temporary exhibits. In the past these galleries have featured pieces from the museum's collection as well as traveling exhibits.

184. MUSEUM OF JEWISH HERITAGE

36 Battery Place, New York, New York, 10280

Site Type: Museum, Holocaust Memorial
Dates: Opened in 1997
Web: https://mjhnyc.org (official website)

The Museum of Jewish Heritage, not to be confused with the Jewish Museum of New York, is the city's Holocaust museum. Built in the 1990s after many years of delays, it is the second largest Holocaust museum in the United States. Located near Battery Park, it is now part of New York City's downtown historic district.

At the outset of World War II New York City was home to the largest Jewish community in the United States. By the time the war was over, it was the largest Jewish community in the world. Almost every major Jewish population center in Europe emerged from the Nazi reign of terror a fraction of its former size. The Jewish community of New York was horrifically impacted as almost all American Jews lost family and friends that still lived in Europe before the war.

Efforts to build a memorial to the victims of the Holocaust in New York began in the 1960s. However, political and financial concerns delayed the project until the 1990s. The museum was finally completed and opened in 1997.

Of Interest: The Museum of Jewish Heritage is a huge modern building crowned with a pyramid that dominates the northwest corner of Battery Park. It directly overlooks the Hudson River and is in site of Ellis Island and the Statue of Liberty. The building houses tens of thousands of artifacts related to the Holocaust, many of which are on display in the main exhibit areas. There is also an extensive collection of artwork by those who personally witnessed the horrors of the concentration camps, from those who had been incarcerated as well as those who liberated them.

185. JEWISH THEOLOGICAL SEMINARY LIBRARY

3080 Broadway, New York, New York, 10027

Site Type: Library
Dates: Seminary opened in 1886
Web: www.jtsa.edu/library (official website)

The Jewish Theological Seminary of America is the primary college of Conservative Judaism in the United States and one of the most imporant Jewish universities in the world. A successor to the Jewish Theological Seminary of Breslau in Poland, it has been a major institution in New York since the late 19th century. The library of the seminary is home to one of the greatest collections of Jewish documents anywhere. Jewish scholars and theologians from all over the world come to the seminary library in order to study the treasures kept therein.

The Jewish Theological Seminary of America was founded in the late 19th century in response to the growing popularity of Reform Judaism. In 1902 Solomon Schechter was made the president of the seminary. Schechter, a Romanian Jew who served on the faculty of Cambridge University in England, became well known in the 1890s for his studies of the Cairo Geniza. During his time at Cambridge he arranged for the acquisition and transport of the contents of the Cairo Geniza to England. Much of this collection later found its way to New York City when Schechter took up his position at the seminary. Many of the documents in the library's collection of rare books date from this time.

Throughout much of the early 20th century the Jewish Theological Seminary received considerable donations of documents and other artifacts of Jewish interest. This began in 1904 when Mayer Sulzberger donated a collection of art to the seminary. By the late 1930s the collection had grown so large that a museum was created to house and display much of the seminary's collection. Most of the non-document pieces were moved out in the 1940s.

In 1966 tragedy struck the seminary library. A fire broke out, and while nobody was seriously hurt, it took nine hours to put the fire out. By the time it was through more than seventy thousand written works had been destroyed. Thankfully the fire did not reach the area where the rarest and most valuable writings were stored, sparing the best of the collection. The library was rebuilt in the 1980s. There are now nearly four-hundred thousand books, papers and manuscripts available here. The seminary library is among the most important repositories of Jewish written records in the world.

Of Interest: The Jewish Theological Seminary and Library occupy a complex of buildings on the Upper West Side of Manhattan. The library collection is immense, and includes everything from books, manuscripts and scrolls to postcards, photographs and prints. Among the library highlights are over thirty-thousand surviving documents from the Geniza library, including an extensive collection of Passover Haggadahs. Several hundred were recovered from the Geniza, including a fragment of one which dates back to the 11th century.

---

186. ERUV OF MANHATTAN

New York, New York

Site Type: Eruv Enclosure
Dates: First created in 1999
Web: www.jewishcenter.org/manhattan-eruv.html (The Jewish Center website)

The Eruv of Manhattan is one of the most unique structures, for lack of a better term, in modern Jewish culture. It essentially is an eighteen mile long wire, suspended from poles and other available structures, that physically surrounds most of the island of Manhattan. The purpose of the wire is to designate Manhattan as a single domain for the purposes of Shabbat obvservances, and is relevant primarily to Orthodox and some Conservative Jewish communities.

An eruv chatzerot, or eruv for short, is a designated enclosure within which certain Shabbat prohibitions are waived. The idea for the eruv goes back centuries. On Shabbat there is an extensive list of activities that are prohibited to observant Jews. Many of these involve the moving of certain types of objects between different types of places. An example of a transgression would be carrying a set of keys from one house to another house. Obviously this can be very restrictive.

At some point someone came up with the idea that a large enclosed area could consist of a single domain, and therefore mitigate some of the rules. These enclosures could consist of walls, fences, or in some cases, a wire. Over time such enclosures became more common and larger. Over the last century many Jewish neighborhoods in major cities around the world have erected eruv wires. The largest of these is the eruv wire which surrounds Manhattan.

Of Interest: The Eruv of Manhattan is approximately eighteen miles long and encloses roughly eighteen square miles of area. Almost all of Manhattan Island is included except for Washington Heights and a few other places here and there. The wire is elevated at approximately fifteen feet above the ground and is regularly maintained. It costs roughly $100,000 a year to maintain the eruv wire.

187. KANE STREET SYNAGOGUE

236 Kane Street, Brooklyn, New York, 11231

Site Type: Synagogue
Dates: Completed in 1855
Web: https://kanestreet.org (official website)

The Kane Street Synagogue, officially known as Congregation Baith Israel Anshei Emes, is home to the oldest Jewish congregation in Brooklyn. Originally constructed as a church, it is one of the oldest buildings in New York still in use as a synagogue. It has served the congregation since 1905. The Kane Street Synagogue is an important historical landmark of one of the largest Jewish communities in America.

The first Jewish congregation in Brooklyn was formed in the 1850s. Their first synagogue was constructed in 1862. The congregation suffered significant growing pains stemming from the fact that its members came from a variety of backgrounds and traditions. In 1905 they moved to the current building after their former synagogue was destroyed in a fire. Interestingly, the former use of the building was as a church that dated from the mid-19th century.

Israel Goldfarb, one of the most prominent American rabbis of the early 20th century, helped the congregation to grow significantly. Goldfarb is credited with writing the music to the popular Jewish song *Shalom Aleichem*. Composer Aaron Copland was a member of the congregation in his childhood. Congregation Baith Israel Anshei Emes has historically been an early adopter of policies that allowed women to serve in official capacities in the synagogue, and is known for its tolerance and progressive policies.

Of Interest: The Kane Street Synagogue is a brownstone Romanesque structure with a belltower that hints at the building's former use. The sanctuary is both elegant and artistically interesting. A recent renovation saw the addition of an education center courtesy of philanthropist Lilian Goldman. The building is a landmark of one of Brooklyn's oldest neighborhoods.

---

188. TOURO SYNAGOGUE

85 Touro Street, Newport, Rhode Island, 02840

Site Type: Synagogue
Dates: Completed in 1763
Designations: U.S. National Historic Site, National Register of Historic Places
Web: www.tourosynagogue.org (official website)

Touro Synagogue is the oldest intact synagogue in the United States, and among the oldest still in use in the Western Hemisphere. Built in 1763, it is one of the most historic Jewish places of worship in America. It was home to a thriving congregation, then abandoned and left in trust to Christian neighbors, reopened, and, at the time of this writing, caught in a custody battle between rival congregations.

The Jewish community of Newport can be traced back to refugees fleeing Spain and Portugal in the 16th century. Some of these early Jewish colonists traveled first to South America, where for a time they received some protection under the Dutch on the northern coast of Brazil. When the Dutch lost this colony to Portugal in 1654, some of the Jews living here fled to New Amsterdam. However due to bureaucratic issues they were not permitted to settle there, and instead moved on to what is now Newport.

Surviving the initial trials of getting established, as well as the British takeover of the Dutch territory a few years later, the Newport congregation grew and thrived well into the 18th century. In 1763 they constructed the Touro Synagogue. Unfortunately the Jewish community here waned in the late 18th century when the state capital was moved from Newport to Providence. The synagogue was closed, its important documents sent to the Congregation Shearith Israel in New York for safekeeping, and the keys entrusted to local Quakers, who cared for the property for over half a century.

The synagogue was reopened in 1883, when immigrants from Eastern Europe significantly increased the Jewish community of Rhode Island. In an arrangement that goes back to the 17th century, the Touro Synagogue has special ties to Congregation Shearith Israel in New York. The Touro Synagogue was declared a National Historic Site in 1946 and listed on the National Register of Historic Places in 1966.

Of Interest: One of the most iconic synagogues in the United States, the Touro Synagogue was designed by famed architect Peter Harrison. Among its features are twelve magnificent columns representing the Twelve Tribes, all carved from a single tree. A letter from George Washington to the Jews of Newport expressing his support for religious freedom is kept in the synagogue and is read before the congregation annually.

189. RODEPH SHALOM SYNAGOGUE

615 North Broad Street, Philadelphia, Pennsylvania, 19123

Site Type: Synagogue
Dates: Completed in 1927
Designations: U.S. National Historic Landmark, National Register of Historic Places
Web: www.rodephshalom.org (official website)

Rodeph Shalom Synagogue is home to the oldest Ashkenazi congregation in America. Established by Jewish immigrants from Central Europe, it predated all of the other German-rite congregations in the United States, including those in New York City. Congregation Rodeph Shalom was instrumental in introducing Reform Judaism to the United States.

Philadelphia already had a long established Sephardic Jewish community dating back decades before the first Jewish immigrants from Germany and Poland began arriving in America. The earliest of these joined Congregation Mikveh Israel. But by 1795 the growing Ashkenazi population, which largely spoke Yiddish, decided to break with Mikveh Israel and establish their own synagogue using Central European worship rites.

During its first seventy years the congregation made use of various buildings for worship until constructing their own synagogue in 1866. By the second half of the 19th century the Jewish Reform movement was underway, and many of the German and Polish congregations began embracing the new style of worship. Rodeph Shalom was among the earliest congregations to embrace Reform Judaism.

By the 1920s Rodeph Shalom was the largest Jewish congregation in Philadelphia, and in 1927 they completed a new synagogue. Rodeph Shalom has since played a key role in the Philadelphia Jewish community. In 2008 it hosted future president Barack Obama who delivered a speech there at Passover. The Rodeph Shalom Synagogue was designated a National Historic Landmark and listed on the National Register of Historic Places in 2008.

Of Interest: The Rodeph Shalom Synagogue is a Moorish Revival building with a façade that evokes images of the Second Temple. The magnificent interior features soaring arches, a rotunda-like ceiling and phenomenal mosaics. Much of the interior is decorated in rich golden colors that converge on the synagogue's breathtaking ark.

190. NATIONAL MUSEUM OF AMERICAN JEWISH HISTORY

101 South Independence Mall East, Philadelphia, Pennsylvania, 19106

Site Type: Museum
Dates: Opened in 1976
Web: www.nmajh.org (official website)

The National Museum of American Jewish History is dedicated to telling the story of Jews in the United States. Originally opened in 1976, the museum is closely associated with Philadelphia's Congregation Mikveh Israel, which played an active role in the American Revolution. The museum moved to its current location in 2010, and is now one of the major sites of Philadelphia's Independence Mall.

Congregation Mikveh Israel, one of the earliest Jewish congregations established in the northern American colonies, was founded in 1740. On the eve of the American Revolution the Jewish community here numbered around three hundred. Some of the congregation members joined up with their fellow patriots to fight against the British, while one, Haym Solomon, was instrumental in helping George Washington finance the war effort.

For its contributions to the American cause, the congregation has been nicknamed the "synagogue of the American Revolution". For over two centuries the congregation of Mikveh Israel has been a prominent fixture of the historic Philadelphia cityscape. In 1976 members of the congregation founded the National Museum of American Jewish History.

Of Interest: The National Museum of American Jewish History, an affiliate of the Smithsonian Institute, houses a substantial collection of American Judaica. The main exhibit halls trace the history of the Jewish people in America, starting with 17th century origins on the 4th floor and working down to the modern day on the 2nd floor. The 3rd floor houses exhibits that feature the great era of Jewish immigration to the United States at the turn of the century. The 1st floor houses the American Jewish hall of fame, honoring such individuals as Golda Meir, Albert Einstein, Emma Lazarus, Jonas Salk and Irving Berlin.

191. BETH SHOLOM SYNAGOGUE

8231 Old York Road, Elkins Park, Pennsylvania, 19027

Site Type: Synagogue
Dates: Completed in 1954
Designations: U.S. National Historic Landmark, National Register of Historic Places, Pennsylvania Historical Marker
Web: www.bethsholomcongregation.org (official website)

The Beth Sholom Synagogue in Elkins Park enjoys the distinction of being the only synagogue designed by famed American architect Frank Lloyd Wright. It is one of the relatively few projects of his located in Pennsylvania and one of the last that he personally worked on. In a portfolio of very unique designs, Beth Sholom is among the most distinctive.

Congregation Beth Sholom was founded in Philadelphia in 1919. In the years after World War II the number of congregants grew significantly, but many had moved out to the suburbs. It was decided that a new synagogue was needed, and Frank Lloyd Wright was commissioned to design the new building.

Lloyd, then in the last decade of his life, designed what would be hailed as one of his greatest masterpieces. The Beth Sholom Synagogue was completed in the Philadelphia suburb of Elkins Park in 1954, and it immediately garnered national attention as one of his most distinctive buildings. In 2007 it was designated a National Historic Landmark and added to the National Register of Historic Places. In 2008 the synagogue was given a state historical marker by the Pennsylvania Historical and Museum Commission.

Of Interest: The Beth Sholom Synagogue is a thoroughly modern building incorporating symbolic elements throughout the entire structure. The most notable feature is the immense, translucent pyramid-shaped roof which looks like a futuristic combination of Mesoamerican and traditional Asian architecture. During the day it allows the sanctuary to be fully sunlit, while at night it shines like an immense beacon in the darkness. The pyramid is meant to resemble both a tent and a mountain, symbolizing the Israelites' journey through the wilderness. This symbolism continues into the huge sanctuary which has, among other things, beige carpeting designed to evoke imagery of the desert.

---

192. ADAS ISRAEL SYNAGOGUE

701 Third Street NW, Washington, DC, 20001

Site Type: Synagogue, Museum
Dates: Synagogue completed in 1876; museum opened in 1975
Designations: U.S. National Register of Historic Places
Web: https://capitaljewishmuseum.org (official website)

The Adas Israel Synagogue is the oldest synagogue standing in Washington, D.C. Thanks to its location in the national capital, the synagogue witnessed several historic firsts, including being the first to be visited by a sitting president. No longer used for worship, the synagogue is now home to the Lillian & Albert Small Jewish Museum run by the Jewish Historical Society of Greater Washington.

The first Jewish congregation in Washington, DC was formed in 1852. An act of Congress in 1855 specifically conferred the same privileges to Jewish places of worship that were granted to Christian churches, formally sanctioning first amendment rights in the national capital. In 1869 some of the members broke off from the Washington Hebrew Congregation to form the Adas Israel Congregation.

Adas Israel constructed its first synagogue in 1876. Its dedication was attended by President Ulysses Grant. It is believed that this was the first time a sitting United States president attended a synagogue worship service. It was only in use for three decades before the congregation grew too large and decided to relocate.

In the 1960s the synagogue was threatened with demolition. Thanks to the efforts of the local Jewish community and supportive government officials, the synagogue was packed onto a giant dolly and moved to a new location in 1969. Under the sponsorship of philanthropists Lillian and Albert Small it was reopened a few years later as a Jewish Museum. The building was added to the National Register of Historic Places in 1969.

Of Interest: The Adas Israel Synagogue is an elegant red-brick building that looks essentially the same as it did before its first move nearly half a century ago. Although there is no longer regular worship here, the sanctuary does host programs of the Jewish Historical Society and special events. NOTE - The building was recently moved to a new location where it will be part of the Capital Jewish Museum. At the time of this writing the new museum was scheduled to be open in 2021.

---

193. NATIONAL MUSEUM OF AMERICAN JEWISH MILITARY HISTORY

1811 R Street NW, Washington, DC, 20009

Site Type: Museum
Dates: Opened in 1958
Web: https://nmajmh.org (official website)

The National Museum of American Jewish Military History is one of America's most unique military museums. Established by the Jewish

War Veterans of the USA in the 1950s, it is located in that organization's national headquarters in Washington, DC. The museum was created to honor and tell the story of the Jewish veterans of America's many wars. It is part of the Dupont-Kalorama Museums Consortium.

Jews have served in uniform in almost every major conflict in American history. Over a hundred Jews fought in the patriot militias and the Continental Army during the American Revolution. Financing for the Colonial forces was primarily arranged by Haym Solomon, a Jewish financier and friend of George Washington. His efforts were critical in holding the American forces together and helped to shorten the war.

Perhaps as many as ten thousand Jews fought in the American Civil War, mostly for the Union, but a few for the Confederacy. Over half a million Jews fought for the United States during World War II, more than ten percent of the entire American Jewish population at the time. The Jewish War Veterans of the United States of America has been active since the late 19th century.

Of Interest: The National Museum of American Jewish Military History was founded in 1958 and moved to its present location in 1984. The main exhibit tells the story of Jews in the American military from Colonial times to the 21st century. There is a focus on World War II, due in part to the huge contribution of Jews fighting in that war as well as the particularly vile and anti-Semitic nature of the enemy in Europe. Also on site is an exhibit honoring Jewish veterans whose service was so distinguished that they received the Congressional Medal of Honor.

---

194. UNITED STATES HOLOCAUST MEMORIAL MUSEUM

100 Raoul Wallenberg Pl SW, Washington, DC, 20024

Site Type: Museum, Holocaust Memorial
Dates: Opened in 1993
Web: www.ushmm.org (official website)

The United States Holocaust Memorial Museum is one of the largest such museums in the world. It houses one of the most comprehensive collections of artifacts and documents from the Holocaust in any museum outside of Israel. Although it is not part of the Smithsonian Institute, it is one of the major museums located along the National Mall.

During the years of terror when the Nazis ruled Germany and for a time most of Europe, the United States was the world's greatest refuge for the Jewish people. Already home to a large Jewish population, not only was America a safe haven for Jews during the war, but hundreds of thousands of young Jewish men served in the United States military.

Nevertheless the Holocaust touched countless Jewish families here, and interest in a national memorial in the United States emerged soon after the war. The idea for a national Holocaust museum began to gain traction in the 1970s, and was authorized by Congress in 1980. The museum was formally dedicated and opened in 1993. Since its opening it has been one of the most popular museums in Washington DC.

Of Interest: The United States Holocaust Memorial Museum is huge, with a collection of over ten thousand artifacts and millions of documents and photographs. There is also an enormous archive of recorded testimony and film footage. The main exhibit is divided into three sections: anti-Semitism and pogroms during the early years of the Third Reich, the Final Solution implemented during the war years, and the liberation of the concentration camps. There are also exhibits on how Americans responded to the Holocaust, both during and after the war, as well as eyewitness accounts.

195. KAHAL KODESH BETH ELOHIM SYNAGOGUE

90 Hasell Street, Charleston, South Carolina, 29401

Site Type: Synagogue
Dates: Completed in 1840
Designations: U.S. National Historic Landmark, National Register of Historic Places
Web: www.kkbe.org (official website)

The Kahal Kodesh Beth Elohim Synagogue in Charleston is the second oldest surviving synagogue in America. Its congregation was among the first established in what would later be the United States. Because Charleston was one of the busiest ports in the American colonies, many Jews settled here during the colonial period. The Kahal Kodesh Beth Elohim congregation was instrumental in helping Judaism to become established throughout the American South.

In the aftermath of the Portuguese conquest of northern Brazil in the mid-17th century, many Jews who fled made their way to the ports of Savannah and Charleston in the British colonies. In 1669 John Locke, the great philosopher and statesman, personally prepared the colonial charter for South Carolina which expressly permitted Jews to live and worship freely in the colony. The first Jews to permanently settle here probably arrived about a decade later.

Throughout the colonial period the Jewish community of Charleston grew and thrived. German Jewish immigrants began arriving in the mid-1700s, and soon the Jewish population was so large that it was home to two congregations. Charleston's was the largest Jewish community in the New World for the better part of a century and a half. Many firsts took place here. Charleston was home to the first Jews to serve in the military, as well as some of America's earliest Jewish public leaders. The Jews of Charleston strongly supported the cause of the patriots during the American Revolution, and furnished a small, all-Jewish unit to fight for the colonies.

The Jewish community of Charleston reached its peak in the 1820s, after which it was surpassed in size by that of New York. This process accelerated after the American Civil War. However, the Charleston community remained very influential. It is believed that the introduction of English into Jewish worship services first took place here. Kahal Kodesh Beth Elohim Synagogue is a U.S. National Historic Landmark and is listed on the National Register of Historic Places.

Of Interest: The Kahal Kadosh Beth Elohim Synagogue was built in 1840, though the congregation was founded almost a century earlier. Constructed in a neoclassical format that was popular in the American South at the time, the colonnaded facade of this edifice is strongly evocative of an ancient Greek temple. The synagogue interior layout and design is more in line with traditional religious architecture of the period. An 18th century Jewish cemetery is located nearby.

196. MICKVE ISRAEL SYNAGOGUE

20 East Gordon Street, Savannah, Georgia, 31401

Site Type: Synagogue
Dates: Completed in 1878
Designations: U.S. National Register of Historic Places
Web: http://mickveisrael.org (official website)

Mickve Israel Synagogue is home to one of America's most historic Jewish congregations. It was founded by the first Jews to travel directly to the American colonies from England, rather than Jews fleeing from either Spanish or Portuguese territory. The synagogue is among the most historic Jewish places of worship in the American South.

Congregation Mickve Israel was founded by Sephardic Jewish Immigrants from England in 1733, just after the founding of the Georgia colony. The congregation was an integral part of the Savannah community from the outset. The Jewish community of Savannah was interrupted during the 1740s when Spain threatened to annex Georgia and most of the city's Jews fled to Charleston to avoid religious persecution at the hands of the Inquisition.

The community largely recovered by the time of the American Revolution, and a correspondence between the congregation and George Washington reflected the first president's commitment to the American Jews. The congregation constructed its first synagogue in 1841, and a second larger building, the current synagogue, in 1878. The Mickve Israel Synagogue was added to the National Register of Historic Places in 1980.

Of Interest: The Mickve Israel Synagogue is a Gothic Revival building with Moorish elements. The latter is especially reflected in the bell tower, strongly reminiscent of a minaret. The sanctuary features soaring ceilings supported by breathtaking columns carved from veined marble. Among the synagogue's treasures is its original Torah scroll, which was brought from England in the 1730s.

---

197. HOLOCAUST MEMORIAL OF MIAMI BEACH

1933-1945 Meridian Avenue, Miami Beach, Florida, 33139

Site Type: Holocaust Memorial
Dates: Dedicated in 1990
Web: http://holocaustmemorialmiamibeach.org (official website)

The Holocaust Memorial of Miami Beach is a sprawling display that may be one of the most heartwrenching monuments anywhere. This is perhaps fitting, as Florida became home to a large community of Holocaust survivors after the war. The sculptures are among the most evocative depictions of man's inhumanity to man ever cast. It may not be possible to walk away from this memorial with dry eyes.

South Florida has long been a popular destination for Jewish retirees and snowbirds. Roughly half a million Jews live in the Greater Miami area, approximately one in twelve of the residents. Many of these are descendants of Holocaust survivors who arrived in the post-war years. It is believed that at one time the Jewish community here included over twenty thousand survivors of the camps.

During the 1980s there were growing calls of interst for the creation of a Holocaust memorial in the Miami area. After many years of discoussions and preparations the project was finally approved. The monument was completed and dedicated in 1990, in time for many survivors to see it.

Of Interest: The Holocaust Memorial of Miami Beach is one of the most moving monuments in the world. No one who sees it will ever forget it. The memorial site consists of a walled in circular island in a man-made circular pond. At the heart of the island is an immense bronze arm, reaching up as if in desperation. The arm itself is made up of people trying to escape an unseen, horrific fate. Surrounding the arm are dozens of smaller statues of people with facial expressions evincing an unspeakable fear and horror. The surrounding wall bears the names of hundreds of thousands of Holocaust victims.

---

198. BETH ISRAEL SYNAGOGUE

2454 Heritage Park Row, San Diego, California, 92110

Site Type: Synagogue
Dates: Completed in 1889
Web: www.sdparks.org/content/sdparks/en/park-pages/heritage.html
(San Diego parks website)

Beth Israel is the oldest intact synagogue in California and one of the oldest still standing west of the Mississippi. Once home to the oldest and largest Jewish congregation in San Diego, it was in use for worship only until the 1920s. The building is now maintained as part of San Diego's Heritage Park, which is home to a number of historic homes and buildings.

Jewish immigrants arrived in San Diego in the 1850s, just after the first Jewish communities were formed in northern California. The congregation was not formally established until 1887, and the original wooden synagogue was completed in 1889. Due to the large influx of Jews to California in the early 20th century the congregation quickly outgrew the old building and relocated to a new synagogue in 1926.

Over the next century the old synagogue was used for a variety of purposes, including serving as a house of worship for other religious groups. It was later included in the San Diego Heritage Park, an historic district that extends off of the Old Town San Diego State Historic Park. No longer in active use, it is maintained as an historic site and is still used for special occasions and ceremonies.

Of Interest: Temple Beth Israel is one of the oldest surviving wood-frame synagogues still standing in California. It is also one of the oldest Moorish-style buildings in the American west. The façade, painted tan and brown, has four distinctive round windows marked with the Star of David, with additional such windows to the sides.

---

199. WILSHIRE BOULEVARD TEMPLE

3663 Wilshire Boulevard, Los Angeles, California, 90010

Site Type: Synagogue
Dates: Completed in 1929
Designations: U.S. National Register of Historic Places, Los Angeles Historic-Cultural Monument
Web: www.wbtla.org (official website)

The Wilshire Boulevard Temple is home to the oldest Jewish congregation in Los Angeles. One of the most beautiful synagogues in America, it is most famous for its association with the Golden Age of Hollywood. Some of the most powerful people in the movie industry have been members of this synagogue, with many personally contributing funds to the construction of the building.

The Wilshire Boulevard Temple can trace its roots back to the first

Jews who arrived in the Los Angeles area in the mid-19th century. The congregation was formally established in 1862, and it occupied a series of synagogues for over sixty years. The congregation expanded greatly in the early 20th century when many Jewish transplants began arriving here to work in the fledgling movie industry.

By the 1920s the congregation had grown so large that a new synagogue was needed. Many Hollywood moguls contributed to its construction. These included Jack, Harry and Albert Warner of Warner Brothers and Louis Mayer and Irving Thalberg of MGM. Wilshire Boulevard Temple was named a Los Angeles Historic-Cultural Monument in 1973 and listed on the National Register of Historic Places in 1981.

Of Interest: The Wilshire Boulevard Temple is a stunning structure that, not surprisingly, looks as though it was constructed as a movie set. A Neo-Byzantine building with Moorish elements and a towering dome, the surrounding block is lined with palm trees that evoke images of the Holy Land. The synagogue interior is graced with some of the most magnificent art to be found in any synagogue anywhere, including a series of massive murals sponsored by the Warner Brothers and painted by Hugo Ballin.

---

200. SIMON WIESENTHAL CENTER AND MUSEUM OF TOLERANCE

1399 S. Roxbury Drive, Los Angeles, California, 90035

Site Type: Museum, Holocaust Memorial
Dates: Opened in 1993
Web: www.wiesenthal.com (official website)

The Simon Wiesenthal Center is an organization dedicated to Holocaust research and the advancement of human rights. In the aftermath of World War II, when the full extent of the Holocaust became known, an immense effort was made by the Allies to bring the perpetrators to justice. However, when war crimes prosecutions bogged down during the Cold War, one man, Simon Wiesenthal, took on the burden himself. A Holocaust survivor, Wiesenthal spent his life personally hunting down Nazi war criminals. In 1977 he founded the Simon Wiesenthal Center as a means to continue the fight against anti-Semitism.

Simon Wiesenthal was a Ukrainian Jew born in 1908. Growing up in Eastern Europe during World War I and the interwar years, Wiesenthal's family moved numerous times. Eventually he settled in Lvov in Poland where he worked as an engineer. In September 1939 Lvov was annexed by Russia, and Wiesenthal spent the next two years in forced labor at a Soviet factory. After the area was overrun by the Nazis almost all of the members of his family were killed. Wiesenthal was incarcerated in a number of concentration camps. After the war he was liberated and miraculously reunited with his wife.

After the war Wiesenthal worked with the American army and various agencies in gathering information for the prosecution of war crimes. He helped to set up the Jewish Documentation Center in Austria where he worked for a few years. When the center was closed, Wiesenthal decided that his mission was not yet done, and taking the file on Adolf Eichmann, one of the architects of the Holocaust who had managed to escape, hunted him down. After an incredible effort, Wiesenthal found Eichmann in Argentina and brought him back to Israel where he was tried and executed. This was the first of several hundred Nazi criminals that Wiesenthal and his associates eventually brought to justice.

Simon Wiesenthal dedicated the rest of his life to fighting anti-Semitism and tracking down every perpetrator of the Holocaust that he could find. He opened the Simon Wiesenthal Center in the 1970s to further these ends. Wiesenthal was still working on open cases at the time of his death in 2005. He is survived by the organization that bears his name, and which is considered one of the most important Jewish educational and justice organizations in the world.

Of Interest: The Simon Wiesenthal Center in Los Angeles the world headquarters of the organization. It is home to the head office, as well as to the Simon Wiesenthal Center's archives and library. For visitors the main destination is the center's Museum of Tolerance. This museum is dedicated to education about prejudice in all of its forms, but in anti-Semitism and the Holocaust in particular. The Holocaust section features a large selection of artifacts and testimonials that highlight the horrors of the genocide perpetrated by the Nazis during World War II.

OVERVIEW OF JEWISH ETHNIC AND RELIGIOUS DISTINCTIONS

As of the time of the writing of this book there were roughly fifteen million people in the world who identified as being Jewish. Adding in all of those people who are considered Jewish under the Israeli law of return, the number increases to roughly twenty-four million. The Jewish people can be divided into three major ethnic groups and, depending on how they are counted, over fifty subdivisions. Add to that the fact that there are a number of ways that Jews classify themselves religiously and you have a very broad spectrum of Jewish identity, faith and culture. Here is a brief overview of some of the major groups:

JEWISH ETHNIC DISTINCTIONS

Ashkenazi Jews

The largest Jewish ethnic group by far is the Ashkenazi Jews. Consisting of roughly 60-65 percent of the world's Jewish population, the Ashkenazis trace their roots back to the Jews who first settled in the German Rhineland area during the Middle Ages. These Jews, who migrated from southern and eastern France during the Roman era, went on to establish communities throughout Eastern Europe and Russia. Until the early 20th century the common language of Ashkenazi Jews was Yiddish, a hybrid of German and Hebrew. During the Enlightenment the Ashkenazis became reestablished in Western Europe. From there they spread around the world, becoming the dominant Jewish ethnic group in the United States, Canada, Australia, New Zealand and parts of South America.

Ashkenazi Subgroups	Regions
Yekkes	Germany, Switzerland, Denmark, Norway, Sweden
Oberlanders & Unterlanders	Hungary, Austria, Czechia, Slovakia
Litvaks	Lithuania, Latvia, Belarus; parts of Poland and Ukraine
Galicians	Parts of Poland and Ukraine

Sephardic Jews

The smallest group is the Sephardic Jews. Representing roughly 10-15 percent of the world's Jews, the Sephardim originated in what is now Spain and Portugal during the Roman era. These Jewish communities developed along very different lines than the Ashkenazis, thanks to centuries of exposure to Muslim culture in Iberia. At the end of the 15th century the Jews were driven out of Spain and Portugal by the Inquisition. Many of these relocated to other countries in Western Europe, notably the Netherlands. Others fled to the safety of the Ottoman Empire, settling in what is now Greece, Turkey, Syria, Palestine and North Africa. The oldest Jewish communities in the Americas were Sephardim who came through Brazil and later spread to the Caribbean islands and the United States.

Sephardic Subgroups	Regions
Eastern Sephardim	Italy; former Ottoman territories in Turkey, Greece and Balkans
Western Sephardim	France, Britain, Low Countries and Latin America
North African Sephardim	Morocco, Algeria, Tunisia, Libya, Egypt

Eastern Jews

The phrase "Eastern Jews" is a vague term that loosely covers all of the ancient Jewish communities that were settled in Roman times and earlier. These include Jews who who are descended from those who lived in the Eastern Mediterranean, Middle East and Asia prior the arrival of the European colonial powers. Representing roughly 20-25 percent of the world's Jewish population, this group is by far the most diverse. The core group is the Mizrahi Jews, some of which come from communities that were established more than twenty-five centuries ago. The vast majority of Eastern Jews relocated to Israel in the modern era.

Eastern Subgroups – Middle East	Regions
Palestinian Jews	Israel, Jordan
Lebanese Jews	Lebanon
Syrian Jews	Syria
Babylonian Jews	Iraq
Kurdish Jews	Parts of Iraq, Iran and Turkey
Persian Jews	Iran
Yemenite Jews	Yemen
Egyptian Jews	Egypt
Eastern Subgroups – Africa	**Regions**
Libyan Jews	Libya
Tunisian Jews	Tunisia
Algerian Jews	Algeria
Berber Jews	Parts of Algeria
Moroccan Jews	Morocco
Falashim Jews	Ethiopia
Eastern Subgroups – Europe	**Regions**
Italkim	Italy

Romaniotes	Greece
Juhurim	Azerbaijan; parts of Caucasian Russia
Gruzim	Georgia
Krymchaks	Parts of Ukraine
Eastern Subgroups – Asia	**Regions**
Bukharan Jews	Uzbekistan; parts of Central Asia
Afghan Jews	Afghanistan
Pakistani Jews	Pakistan
Baghdadi Jews	Parts of India
Cochin Jews	Parts of India
Kaifeng Jews	China

Samaritans

Samaritans are descendants of the Israelite Northern Kingdom which was destroyed in the 8th century BCE. While technically not Jews, they are closely related, practice very similar religious customs and use a very similar form of the Torah in worship. There are several important religious points of contention, including the fact that Samaritans once worshipped at a temple other than the one at Jerusalem. Nevertheless Samaritans are recognized under Israeli law as having the Right of Return.

JEWISH RELIGIOUS DISTINCTIONS

Reform Judaism

Reform Judasm is the least traditionally observant form of Judaism for Jews who nevertheless consider themselves religious. Practices among Reform Jews vary widely, but in general are characterized by a focus on moral behavior and a general practice of traditions rather than on strict obedience to a religious legal code. Religious services tend to be shorter than in Conservative or Orthodox synagogues, with worship conducted in the vernacular with only a minimal usage of Hebrew.

Conservative Judaism

Conservative Judaism is generally regarded as the religiously mid-level form of Judaism. The smallest of the three major practices of religious Judaism, it is in some ways splitting the difference between Reform and Orthodox practices. Conservative Jews generally observe the Torah more strictly than Reformists, but less so than Orthodox Jews. Religious services are longer, more thorough, with a greater though not necessarily exclusive use of Hebrew.

Orthodox Judaism

Orthodox Judaism is the strictest form of the Jewish faith. The largest segment of those who consider themselves religious Jews, the Orthodox movement is practiced by those who strive to obey every word of the Torah every moment of their lives. Study and memorization of the Torah is a paramount activity, and even the least important laws and practices are taken seriously. Worship in Orthodox Judaism is a daily activity, with long services entirely in Hebrew.

Orthodox Judaism – Haredim

Haredi Judaism is a movement that is followed by many of the world's Orthodox Jews. The Haredim are Jews who not only observe strict Orthodox Judaism but who live almost entirely in closed communities. There are many different Haredim communities, with Hasidic Jews being perhaps the most well known. They are famous for their traditional manners of dress, which make them easily distinguishable not only from other Jewish groups but also from each other.

Non-Religious Jews

Non-Religious Jews are just that. They identify ethnically and culturally as Jews but do not practice Judaism as a religion. Jewish law is not recognized except as an exercise in tradition. Synagogue attendance and worship is generally limited to holidays and special occasions such as weddings and bar mitzvahs.

Rabbinic Judaism

Rabbinic Judaism is the form of Judaism practiced by the vast majority of religious Jews regardless of whether they are Reform, Conservative or Orthodox. This form of Judaism, which first evolved during the Hasmonean period, relies primarily on the rabbinic teachings passed down from the ancient Pharisees. Among Rabbinic Judaism's founders and early practitioners were giants such as Hillel, Shammai, Gamaliel, Akiva ben Yosef and Shimon bar Yochai. In addition to the Torah and Tanakh, Rabbinic Judaism also recognizes such texts as the Talmud and the Mishnah as authoritative.

Non-Rabbinic Judaism (including Karaite Judaism)

Non-Rabbinic Judaism is a much less commonly practiced form of Judaism. There are believed to be fewer than a hundred thousand Jewish practitioners of Non-Rabbinic Judaism, and most of these are Karaite Jews. The main distinction is that these Jews reject the rabbinic traditions and do not accept the authority of any books other than the Torah and Tanakh. This form of Judaism may have originated with descendents of the Saducees in exile in Mesopotamia. It flourished for a while in the Middle Ages, but is now practiced in only a handful of scattered communities.

INDEX OF SITES BY CATEGORY

SYNAGOGUES		
1. Western Wall	Jerusalem, Israel	Special Designation Synagogue
4. Hurva Synagogue	Jerusalem, Israel	
4. Ramban Synagogue	Jerusalem, Israel	
4. Karaite Synagogue	Jerusalem, Israel	
12. Great Synagogue of Jerusalem	Jerusalem, Israel	
16. Belz Great Synagogue	Jerusalem, Israel	
19. Great Synagogue of Tel Aviv	Tel Aviv-Yafo, Israel	
44. Magdala Synagogue	Migdal, Israel	Ruins / Archaeological Site
44. Capernaum Synagogue	Capernaum, Israel	Ruins / Archaeological Site
44. Nabratein Synagogue	Nabratein, Israel	Ruins / Archaeological Site
45. Abuhav Synagogue	Tzfat, Israel	
45. Caro Synagogue	Tzfat, Israel	
45. Ari Ashkenazi Synagogue	Tzfat, Israel	
45. Ari Sephardic Synagogue	Tzfat, Israel	
45. Chernobyl Synagogue	Tzfat, Israel	
49. Cave of the Patriarchs	Hebron, West Bank	Special Designation Synagogue
54. Tomb of Samuel	Nabi Samwil, West Bank	
62. Sidon Synagogue	Sidon, Lebanon	Medieval Synagogue

64. Central Synagogue of Aleppo	Aleppo, Syria	Medieval Synagogue
65. Dura Europas Synagogue	Dura Europas, Syria	Ruins / Archaeological Site
77. Ben Ezra Synagogue	Cairo, Egypt	
79. El Ghriba Synagogue	Djerba, Tunisia	
82. Gardens Shul	Cape Town, South Africa	
83. Ahrida Synagogue	Istanbul, Turkey	
84. Zulfaris Synagogue	Istanbul, Turkey	
85. Sardis Synagogue	Manisa, Turkey	Ruins / Archaeological Site
87. Delos Synagogue	Delos, Greece	Ruins / Archaeological Site
88. Sofia Synagogue	Sofia, Bulgaria	
89. Stobi Synagogue	Stobi, Macedonia	Ruins / Archaeological Site
90. Subotica Synagogue	Subotica, Serbia	
91. Dubrovnik Synagogue	Dubrovnik, Croatia	Medieval Synagogue
92. Great Synagogue of Rome	Rome, Italy	
95. Ostia Synagogue	Rome, Italy	Ruins / Archaeological Site
96. Great Synagogue of Florence	Florence, Italy	
98. Scolanova Synagogue	Trani, Italy	Medieval Synagogue
100. Holocaust Memorial Synagogue	Moscow, Russia	
102. Grand Choral Synagogue	St. Petersburg, Russia	
105. Brodsky Synagogue	Odessa, Ukraine	
108. Kenesa of Yevpatoria	Yevpatoria, Ukraine	

109. Sataniv Synagogue	Sataniv, Ukraine	
112. Great Synagogue of Grodno	Hrodna, Belarus	
116. Izaak Synagogue	Krakow, Poland	
116. High Synagogue	Krakow, Poland	
116. Old Synagogue	Krakow, Poland	
116. Popper Synagogue	Krakow, Poland	
116. Remuh Synagogue	Krakow, Poland	
116. Kupa Synagogue	Krakow, Poland	
119. Chachmei Lublin Yeshiva	Lublin, Poland	
120. Dohany Street Synagogue	Budapest, Hungary	
122. New Synagogue	Berlin, Germany	
127. Old Synagogue	Erfurt, Germany	Medieval Synagogue
130. New Synagogue	Mainz, Germany	
131. Rashi Shul Synagogue	Worms, Germany	
135. Staranova Synagogue	Prague, Czechia	Medieval Synagogue
136. Jubilee Synagogue	Prague, Czechia	
141. Great Synagogue of Stockholm	Stockholm, Sweden	
143. Portuguese Synagogue	Amsterdam, Netherlands	
153. Greater Synagogue of Barcelona	Barcelona, Spain	Medieval Synagogue
154. Ibn Shushan Synagogue	Toledo, Spain	Medieval Synagogue
154. El Transito Synagogue	Toledo, Spain	Medieval Synagogue
156. Cordoba Synagogue	Cordoba, Spain	Medieval Synagogue

158. Stone Synagogue	Obidos, Portugal	Medieval Synagogue
159. Bevis Marks Synagogue	London, England	
163. Plymouth Synagogue	Plymouth, England	
166. Paradesi Synagogue	Kochi, India	
171. Great Synagogue of Sydney	Sydney, Australia	
171. Central Synagogue of Sydney	Sydney, Australia	
173. Hobart Synagogue	Hobart, Australia	
175. Sint Eustasius Synagogue	Sint Eustasius, Netherlands	Ruins / Archaeo-logical Site
176. Mickve Israel-Emanuel Synagogue	Willimstad, Curacao	
177. Nidhe Israel Synagogue	Bridgetown, Barbados	
178. Sierra Justo Synagogue	Mexico City, Mexico	
180. Congregtion Emanu-El Synagogue	Victoria, Canada	
181. Spanish and Portuguese Synagogue	New York, New York	
182. Temple Emanu-El	New York, New York	
187. Kane Street Synagogue	Brooklyn, New York	
188. Touro Synagogue	Newport, Rhode Island	
189. Rodeph Shalom Synagogue	Philadelphia, Pennsylvania	
191. Beth Sholom Syna-gogue	Elkins Park, Pennsylvania	`
192. Adas Israel Synagogue	Washington, DC	
195. Kahal Kodesh Beth Elohim Synagogue	Charleston, South Carolina	
196. Mickve Israel Syna-gogue	Savannah, Georgia	

198. Beth Israel Synagogue	San Diego, California	
199. Wilshire Boulevard Synagogue	Los Angeles, California	

SITES OF THE TANAKH / HEBREW BIBLE		
6. Tomb of King David	Jerusalem, Israel	
7. Hezekiah's Tunnel	Jerusalem, Israel	
8. Kidron Valley & Silwan Necropolis	Jerusalem, Israel	
9. Mount of Olives Cemetery	Jerusalem, Israel	
10. Zedekiah's Cave	Jerusalem, Israel	
26. Valley of Elah	Bet Shemesh, Israel	
27. Abraham's Well	Be'er Sheva, Israel	
29. Ein Gedi Nature Preserve	Ein Gedi, Israel	
33. Elijah's Cave	Haifa, Israel	
38. Jezreel Valley	Tel Megiddo, Israel	
43. Tomb of the Matriarchs	Tiberias, Israel	
48. Tel Dan Nature Reserve	Dan, Israel	
49. Cave of the Patriarchs	Hebron, West Bank	
51. Tomb of Rachel	Bethlehem, West Bank	
53. Ruins of Ancient Jericho	Jericho, West Bank	
54. Tomb of Samuel	Nabi Samwil, West Bank	
56. Ruins of Tel Shiloh	Shilo, West Bank	
57. Tomb of Joshua	Kifl Hares, West Bank	
58. Ruins of Ancient Samaria	Sebastia, West Bank	
59. Ruins of Ancient Shechem & Tomb of Joseph	Nablus, West Bank	

60. Mount Gerizim	Nablus, West Bank	
63. Shouf Biiosphere Reserve	Becharre, Lebanon	
66. Mount Nebo	Madaba, Jordan	
67. Mount Hor & Tombs of Aaron and Miriam	Petra, Jordan	
68. Ruins of Bab Edh-Dhra and Numeira	Bab Edh-Dhra, Jordan	
69. Ruins of Ancient Ur	Nasiriyah, Iraq	
70. Ruins of Ancient Nineveh	Mosul, Iraq	
72. Tombs of Esther and Mordecai	Hamedan, Iran	
73. Tomb of Daniel	Shush, Iran	
75. Mount Sinai	Feran, Egypt	
76. Ruins of Pi-Rameses	Qantir, Egypt	

CEMETERIES AND BURIAL SITES		
6. Tomb of David	Jerusalem, Israel	
8. Silwan Necropolis	Jerusalem, Israel	
9. Mount of Olives Cemetery	Jerusalem, Israel	Grave of Menachim Begin
17. Mount Herzl Cemetery	Jerusalem, Israel	Graves of Theodor Herzl, Golda Meir, Yitzhak Rabin & Jonathan Netanyahu
31. Grave of David Ben-Gurion	Sde Boker, Israel	
41. Tomb of Akiva ben Yosef	Tiberias, Israel	
42. Tomb of Moses Maimonides	Tiberias, Israel	
43. Tomb of the Matriarchs	Tiberias, Israel	

46. Tombs of Hillel and Shammai	Meron, Israel	
47. Tomb of Shimon bar Yochai	Meron, Israel	
49. Cave of the Patriarchs	Hebron, West Bank	
51. Tomb of Rachel	Bethlehem, West Bank	
54. Tomb of Samuel	Nabi Samwil, West Bank	
55. Tomb of the Maccabees	Horbat Ga-Gardi, West Bank	
57. Tomb of Joshua	Kifl Hares, West Bank	
59. Tomb of Joseph	Nablus, West Bank	
67. Tombs of Aaron and Miriam	Petra, Jordan	
71. Grave of Asenath Barzani	Amadiya, Iraq	
72. Tombs of Esther and Mordecai	Hamedan, Iran	
73. Tomb of Daniel	Shush, Iran	
78. National Museum of Egyptian Civilization	Cairo, Egypt	Mummy of Rameses II
110. Gravesite of Ba'al Shem Tov	Medzhybizh, Ukraine	
113. Old Jewish Cemetery & Grave of Vilna Gaon	Vilnius, Lithuania	
125. Mendelssohn Gravesites	Berlin, Germany	
134. Josefov Ghetto Cemetery	Prague, Czechia	
148. Montparnasse & Grave of Alfred Dreyfus	Paris, France	

HISTORIC NEIGHBORHOODS AND KIBBUTZES		
31. Sde Boker Kibbutz	Sde Boker, Israel	Kibbutz
36. Lohamei HaGeta'ot Kibbutz	Lohamei HaGeta'ot, Israel	Kibbutz
39. Yifat Kibbutz	Yifat, Israel	Kibbutz
40. Degania Alef Kibbutz	Degania Alef, Israel	Kibbutz
23. Old Jaffa	Tel Aviv-Yafo, Israel	Historic Neighborhood
45. Synagogues of Tzfat	Tzfat, Israel	Historic Neighborhood
92. Jewish Ghetto of Rome	Rome, Italy	Historic Neighborhood
97. Jewish Ghetto of Venice	Venice, Italy	Historic Neighborhood
116. Kazimierz	Krakow, Poland	Historic Neighborhood
128. Cologne Archaeological Site	Cologne, Germany	Historic Neighborhood
134. Josefov Ghetto	Prague, Czechia	Historic Neighborhood
138. Trebic Ghetto	Trebic, Czechia	Historic Neighborhood
139. Judenplatz	Vienna, Austria	Historic Neighborhood
147. La Marais	Paris, France	Historic Neighborhood
155. Plaza de Zocodover	Toledo, Spain	Historic Neighborhood
156. Cordoba Jewish Quarter	Cordoba, Spain	Historic Neighborhood
157. Seville Jewish Quarter	Seville, Spain	Historic Neighborhood
165. Jewish Quarter of Samarkhand	Samarkhand, Uzbekistan	Historic Neighborhood
167. Shanghai Jewish Refugees Museum	Shanghai, China	Historic Neighborhood

CONCENTRATION CAMPS AND HOLOCAUST MEMORIALS

118. Auschwitz-Birkenau Memorial and Museum	Oswiecim, Poland	Concentration Camp
132. Dachau Concentration Camp	Dachau, Germany	Concentration Camp
137. Theresienstadt Concentration Camp Museum	Terezin, Czechia	Concentration Camp
18. Yad Vashem	Jerusalem, Israel	Holocaust Memorial
18. Garden of the Righteous among the Nations	Jerusalem, Israel	Holocaust Memorial
25. Forest of the Martyrs	Beit Meir, ISrael	Holocaust Memorial
36. Ghetto Fighter's House	Lohamei HaGeta'ot, Israel	Holocaust Memorial
82. Gardens Shul	Cape Town, South Africa	Holocaust Memorial
100. Holocaust Memorial Synagogue	Moscow, Russia	Holocaust Memorial
111. The Pit	Minsk, Belarus	Holocaust Memorial
115. Ghetto Heroes Monument	Warsaw, Poland	Holocaust Memorial
117. Oskar Schindler Factory Museum	Krakow, Poland	Holocaust Memorial
121. Shoes on the Danube Bank	Budapest, Hungary	Holocaust Memorial
124. Memorial to the Murdered Jews of Europe	Berlin, Germany	Holocaust Memorial
126. House of the Wannsee Conference	Wannsee, Germany	Holocaust Memorial
139. Judenplatz	Vienna, Austria	Holocaust Memorial

140. Danish Jewish Museum	Copenhagen, Denmark	Holocaust Memorial
142. Kazerne Dossin Memorial	Mechelen, Belgium	Holocaust Memorial
144. Anne Frank House	Amsterdam, Netherlands	Holocaust Memorial
146. Corrie Ten Boom House	Haarlem, Netherlands	Holocaust Memorial
149. Memorial of the Deportation Martyrs	Paris, France	Holocaust Memorial
162. Hyde Park Holocaust Memorial	London, England	Holcoaust Memorial
169. Port of Humanity Tsuruga Museum	Fukui, Japan	Holocaust Memorial
179. Canadian Museum of Immigration at Pier 21	Halifax, Nova Scotia	Holocaust Memorial
184. Museum of Jewish Heritage	New York, New York	Holocaust Memorial
194. United States Holocaust Museum	Washington, DC	Holocaust Memorial
197. Holocaust Memorial of Miami Beach	Miami Beach, Florida	Holocaust Memorial
200. Simon Wiesenthal Center	Los Angeles, California	Holocaust Memorial

MUSEUMS AND LIBRARIES		
2. Tower of David Museum	Jerusalem, Israel	History of Jerusalem
5. Old Yishav Court Museum	Jerusalem, Israel	History of Jerusalem
5. Last Battle for the Old City Museum	Jerusalem, Israel	History of Jerusalem
5. Ariel Center for Jerusalem	Jerusalem, Israel	History of Jerusalem
5. Temple Institute	Jerusalem, Israel	Great Temple

11. Rockefeller Museum	Jerusalem, Israel	Archaeology
12. Heichal Shlomo Jewish Heritage Center	Jerusalem, Israel	Art
14. Israel Museum & Shrine of the Book	Jerusalem, Israel	General Judaica
15. Bible Lands Museum	Jerusalem, Israel	History of Ancient Peoples
17. Herzl Museum	Jerusalem, Israel	Bio - Theodore Herzl
18. Yad Vashem	Jerusalem, Israel	Holocaust
20. Independence Hall Museum	Tel Aviv, Yafo	History of Israel
21. Eretz Israel Museum	Tel Aviv-Yafo, Israel	Jewish History and Culture
22. ANU – Museum of the Jewish People	Tel Aviv-Yafo, Israel	Jewish Diaspora
24. Babylonian Jewry Heritage Center	Or Yehuda, Israel	History of the Babylonian Jews
28. Israeli Air Force Museum	Be'er Sheva, Israel	Military
31. Ben-Gurion Desert Home	Sde Boker, Israel	Bio – David Ben-Gurion
34. National Maritime Museum	Haifa, Israel	Maritime History of Israel
34. Clandestine Immigration and Naval Museum	Haifa, Israel	Military History
35. Underground Prisoners Museum	Akko, Israel	History of Israel
36. Ghetto Fighter's House	Lohamei HaGeta'ot, Israel	Holocaust
37. Atlit Detainee Camp Museum	Atlit, Israel	History of Israel
39. Museum of Pioneer Settlement	Yifat, Israel	History of Israel

74. Baazov Museum of History of the Jews of Georgia	Tblisi, Georgia	History of the Jews of Georgia
78. National Museum of Egyptian Civilization	Cairo, Egypt	History of Egypt
82. Gardens Shul	Cape Town, South Africa	History of the Jews of South Africa
84. Jewish Museum of Turkey	Istanbul, Turkey	History of the Jews of Turkey
86. Jewish Museum of Thessaloniki	Thessaloniki, Greece	History of the Jews of Thessaloniki
101. Jewish Museum and Tolerance Center	Moscow, Russia	Holocaust
103. National Library of Russia	St. Petersburg, Russia	Library
106. Jewish Museum of Odessa	Odessa, Ukraine	History of the Jews of Odessa
114. Museum of the History of the Polish Jews	Warsaw, Poland	History of the Jews of Poland
117. Oskar Schnidler Factory Museum	Krakow, Poland	Holocaust
118. Auschwitz-Birkenau Memorial and Museum	Oswiecim, Poland	Holocaust
123. Berlin Jewish Museum	Berlin, Germany	History of the Jews of Berlin
126. House of the Wannsee Conference	Wannsee, Germany	Holocaust
128. Cologne Jewish Museum	Cologne, Germany	History of the Jews of Cologne
129. Rothschild Palace & Jewish Museum	Frankfurt, Germany	History of the Jews of Frankfurt
132. Dachau Concentration Camp	Dachau, Germany	Holocaust

134. Jewish Museum	Prague, Germany	History of the Jews of Prague
137. Theresienstadt Concentration Camp Museum	Terezin, Czechia	Holocaust
139. Judenplatz	Vienna, Austria	History of the Jews of Vienna
140. Danish Jewish Museum	Copenhagen, Denmark	Holocaust
142. Kazerne Dossin Memorial and Museum	Mechelen, Belgium	Holocaust
143. Jewish History Museum	Amsterdam, Netherlands	General Judaica
144. Anne Frank House	Amsterdam, Netherlands	Holocaust
145. Spinoza House and Museum	Rjinsburg, Netherlands	Bio – Baruch Spinoza
146. Corrie Ten Boom House	Haarlem, Netherlands	Holocaust
147. Museum of Jewish Art and History	Paris, France	General Judaica and Art
150. Louvre Museum	Paris, France	Archaeology
151. March Chagall National Museum	Nice, France	Art
160. Jewish Museum of London	London, England	General Judaica
161. British Library	London, England	Library
167. Shanghai Jewish Refugees Museum	Shanghai, China	History of the Jews of Shanghai
168. Kaifeng Museum	Kaifeng, China	Archaeology
169. Port of Humanity Tsuruga Museum	Fukui, Japan	History of the Port of Tsuruga
172. Jewish Museum of Australia	St. Kilda, Australia	History of the Jews of Australia

174. Kahal Zur Israel Synagogue Museum	Recife, Brazil	History of the Jews of Recife
179. Canadian Museum of Immigration at Pier 21	Halifax, Nova Scotia	History of Canadian Immigration
183. Jewish Museum of New York	New York, New York	General Judaica
184. Museum of Jewish Heritage	New York, New York	Holocaust
185. Jewish Theological Seminary Library	New York, New York	Library
190. National Museum of American Jewish History	Philadelphia, Pennsylvania	History of Jews of America
193. Museum of American Jewish Military History	Washington, DC	Military
194. United States Holocaust Museum	Washington, DC	Holocaust
200. Simon Wiesenthal Center	Los Angeles, California	Holocaust

ARCHAEOLOGICAL SITES		
3. Ancient Ruins of the Jewish Quarter	Jerusalem, Israel	
7. City of David Archaeological Park	Jerusalem, Israel	
26. Khirbet Qeiyafa	Bet Shemesh, Israel	
30. Masada National Park	Masada, Israel	
32. Timna Park	Timna, Israel	
38. Tel Megiddo National Park	Tel Megiddo, Israel	
48. Tel Dan Nature Reserve	Dan, Israel	
50. Ruins of the Betar Fortress	Battir, West Bank	

52. Qumran National Park	Qumram, West Bank	
53. Ruins of Ancient Jericho	Jericho, West Bank	
54. Nabi Samuel National Park	Nebi Samwil, West Bank	
55. Tomb of the Maccabees Archaeological Site	Horbat Ga-Gardi, West Bank	
56. Ruins of Tel Shiloh	Shilo, West Bank	
58. Ruins of Ancient Samaria	Sebastia, West Bank	
59. Ruins of Ancient Shechem	Nablus, West Bank	
60. Mount Gerezim	Nablus, West Bank	
68. Ruins of Bab Edh-Dhra and Numeira	Bab Edh-Dhra, Jordan	
69. Ruins of Ancient Ur	Nasiriyah, Iraq	
70. Ruins of Ancient Nineveh	Mosul, Iraq	
76. Ruins of Pi-Rameses	Qantir, Egypt	
80. Ruins of Aksum	Aksum, Ethiopia	
104. Ruins of Atil	Samosdelka, Russia	
128. Cologne Jewish Museum & Archaeological Site	Cologne, Germany	

NATURE RESERVES		
25. Forest of the Martyrs	Beit Meir, Israel	
26. Valley of Elah	Bet Shemesh, Israel	
29. Ein Gedi Nature Reserve	Ein Gedi, Israel	
32. Timna Park	Timna, Israel	
38. Tel Megiddo National Park	Tel Megiddo, Israel	

48. Tel Dan Nature Reserve	Dan, Israel	
52. Qumran National Park	Qumran, West Bank	
63. Shouf Biosphere Reserve	Becharre, Lebanon	

FORTRESSES, CASTLES AND PRISONS		
2. Tower of David Museum	Jerusalem, Israel	Medieval Fortress
26. Khirbet Qeiyafa	Bet Shemesh, Israel	Ancient Fortress Ruins
30. Masada National Park	Masada, Israel	Ancient Fortress Ruins
35. Underground Prisoners Museum	Akko, Israel	Prison
37. Atlit Detainee Camp Museum	Atlit, Israel	Prison
50. Ruins of the Betar Fortress	Battir, West Bank	Ancient Fortress Ruins
142. Kazerne Dossin Memorial and Museum	Mechelen, Belgium	Prison
164. Clifford's Tower	York, England	Medieval Castle

ODDS AND ENDS		
31. Ben-Gurion Desert Home	Sde Boker, Israel	Historic Residence
107. Sholem Aleichem Birth House	Pereiaslav, Ukraine	Historic Residence
129. Rothschild Palace	Frankfurt, Germany	Historic Residence
144. Anne Frank House	Amsterdam, Netherlands	Historic Residence
145. Spinoza House and Museum	Rjinsburg, Netherlands	Historic Residence

146. Corrie Ten Boom House	Haarlem, Netherlands	Historic Residence
61. Garden of Peace	Xylotymbou, Cyprus	Monument
81. Entebbe Raid Memorial	Entebbe, Uganda	Monument

TRADITIONAL LOCATIONS OF TOMBS OF FIGURES FROM HEBREW BIBLE

FIGURES FROM THE PATRIARCHAL FAMILY		
Terah	Harran, Turkey	Genesis
Lot	Bani Na'im, West Bank	Genesis
Abraham – Cave of the Patriarchs	Hebron, West Bank	Genesis
Sarah – Cave of the Patriarchs	Hebron, West Bank	Genesis
Hagar	Mecca, Saudi Arabia	Genesis
Ishmael	Mecca, Saudi Arabia	Genesis
Isaac – Cave of the Patriarchs	Hebron, West Bank	Genesis
Rebecca – Cave of the Patriarchs	Hebron, West Bank	Genesis
Jacob – Cave of the Patriarchs	Hebron, West Bank	Genesis
Leah – Cave of the Patriarchs	Hebron, West Bank	Genesis
Rachel	Bethlehem, West Bank	Genesis
Zilpah – Tomb of the Matriarchs	Tiberias, Israel	Genesis
Bilhah – Tomb of the Matriarchs	Tiberias, Israel	Genesis

OTHER FIGURES FROM THE TORAH		
Reuben – 1st son of Jacob	Nabi Rubin, Israel	Genesis
Simeon – 2nd son of Jacob	Kibbutz Eyal, Israel	Genesis

Judah – 4th son of Jacob	Yehud, Israel	Genesis
Dan – 5th son of Jacob	Beit Shemash, Israel	Genesis
Naphtali – 6th son of Jacob	Tel Kedesh, Israel	Genesis
Gad – 7th son of Jacob	Rehovat, Israel	
Salt, Jordan (alternate)	Genesis	
Asher – 8th son of Jacob	Tel Kedesh, Israel	Genesis
Zebulun – 10th son of Jacob	Sidon, Lebanon	Genesis
Joseph – 11th son of Jacob	Nablus, West Bank	Genesis
Benjamin – 12th son of Jacob	Kfar Saba, Israel	Genesis
Ephraim	Nablus, West Bank	Genesis
Manasseh	Nablus, West Bank	Genesis
Jochebed – Tomb of the Matriarchs	Tiberias, Israel	Exodus
Moses	Nabi Musa, West Bank	Exodus
Zipporah – Tomb of the Matriarchs	Tiberias, Israel	Exodus
Aaron	Petra, Jordan	Exodus
Elisheva – Tomb of the Matriarchs	Tiberias, Israel	Exodus
Jethro	Hittin, West Bank	Exodus
Eleazar	Awarta, West Bank	Numbers, Joshua
Ithamar	Awarta, West Bank	Numbers, Joshua
Phinehas	Awarta, West Bank	Numbers, Joshua

FIGURES FROM THE FORMER PROPHETS (NEVI'IM)		
Joshua	Kifl Hares, West Bank	
As-Salt, Jordan (alternate)	Numbers, Joshua	
Caleb	Kifl Hares, West Bank	Numbers, Joshua
Nun	Kifl Hares, West Bank	Joshua
Othniel	Hebron, West Bank	Judges

Shamgar	Tebnine, Lebanon	Judges
Deborah	Tel Kaddesh, Israel	Judges
Barak	Tel Kaddesh, Israel	Judges
Samson	Beit Shemesh, Israel	Judges
Eli	Shiloh, West Bank	Samuel
Elkanah	Kedita, Israel	Samuel
Hannah	Nebi Samwil, West Bank	Samuel
Samuel	Nebi Samwil, West Bank	Samuel
Jesse	Hebron, West Bank	Samuel
David	Jerusalem, Israel	Samuel
Absalom	Jerusalem, Israel	Samuel
Abner	Jerusalem, Israel	Samuel
Hushai	Yirka, Israel	Samuel
Nathan	Halhil, West Bank	Samuel, Kings
Jehoshaphat	Jerusalem, Israel	Kings
Elisha	Mt. Carmel, Israel	Kings
Huldah	Jerusalem, Israel	Kings
Zedekiah	Jerusalem, Israel	Kings

FIGURES FROM THE LATTER PROPHETS AND MINOR PROPHETS (NEVI'IM)		
Isaiah	Nahal Dishon, Israel	
Esfahanm, Iran (alternate)	Isaiah	
Ezekiel	Kefil, Iraq	Ezekiel
Hosea	Safed, Israel	Hosea
Jonah	Mashhad, Israel	
Hebron, Israel (alternate)	Jonah	
Micah	Kabul, Israel	Micah
Nahum	Al Qush, Iraq	
Elkesi, Israel (alternate)	Nahum	
Habakkuk	Huqoq, Israel	

Kadarim, Israel (alternate)	Habakkuk	
Zephaniah	En-Nabi Safi, Lebanon	Zephaniah
Haggai	Jerusalem, Israel	Haggai
Zechariah	Jerusalem, Israel	Zechariah
Malachi	Jerusalem, Israel	Malachi

FIGURES FROM THE WRITINGS (KETUVIM)		
Job	Salalah, Oman	Job
Jesse	Hebron, West Bank	Ruth
Ruth	Hebron, West Bank	Ruth
Esther	Hamadan, Iran	Esther
Mordecai	Hamadan, Iran	Esther
Daniel	Shush, Iran	
Kirkuk, Iraq	Daniel	
Ezra	Al-Azair, Iraq	Ezra
Zechariah	Jerusalem, Israel	Chronicles

OLDEST SYNAGOGUES IN THE WORLD

ANCIENT SYNAGOGUE RUINS		
89. Stobi Synagogue	Stobi, Macedonia	c. 2nd century BCE
Modi'in Synagogue	Modi'in, Israel	c. 2nd century BCE
87. Delos Synagogue	Delos, Greece	c. 2nd century BCE
53. Jericho Synagogue	Jericho, West Bank	c. 60 BCE
30. Masada Synagogue	Masada, Israel	c. 1st century BCE
44. Magdala Synagogue	Migdal, Israel	c. 1st century BCE
Herodium Synagogue	Herodium, West Bank	c. 1st century BCE
Gamla Synagogue	Gamla, Israel	c. 1st century CE
95. Ostia Synagogue	Ostia, Italy	c. 1st century CE
Jerash Synagogue	Jerash, Jordan	c. 1st century CE
Jobar Synagogue	Damascus, Syria	c. 1st century CE
Priene Synagogue	Priene, Turkey	c. 2nd century CE
65. Dura-Europas Synagogue	Dura-Europas, Syia	c. 244 CE
Kfar Bar'am Synagogue	Kafr Bir'im, Israel	c. 3rd century CE
85. Sardis Synagogue	Sardis, Turkey	c. 3rd century CE
44. Capernaeum Synagogue	Capernaeum, Israel	c. 4th century CE
Bova Marina Synagogue	Bova Marina, Italy	c. 4th century CE
128. Cologne Synagogue	Cologne, Germany	c. 4th century CE
44. Nabratein Synagogue	Nabratein, Israel	c. 6th century CE

SYNAGOGUES STILL STANDING WITH ONLY MINIMAL ORIGINAL ELEMENTS		
79. El Ghriba Synagogue	Djerba, Tunisia	Unknown

153. Greater Synagogue of Barcelona	Barcelona, Spain	c. 300 CE
77. Ben Ezra Synagogue	Cairo, Egypt	c. 9th century CE
131. Rashi Shul Synagogue	Worms, Germany	1034 CE
Carpentras Synagogue	Carpentras, France	1367 CE

SYNAGOGUES STILL STANDING, LARGELY INTACT BUT NOT IN ACTIVE USE		
62. Sidon Synagogue	Sidon, Lebanon	833 CE
155. Ibn Shushan Synagogue	Toledo, Spain	1180 CE
157. Synagogue of Santa Maria la Blanca	Seville, Spain	1180 CE
127. Old Synagogue	Erfurt, Germany	c. 13th century CE
156. Cordoba Synagogue	Cordoba, Spain	1305 CE
154. Samuel Halevi Abulafia Synagogue	Toledo, Spain	1357 CE
Maribor Synagogue	Maribor, Slovenia	c. 14th century CE
158. Stone Synagogue	Obidos, Portugal	c. 1400 CE

SYNAGOGUES STILL STANDING, LARGELY INTACT AND IN ACTIVE USE		
4. Karaite Synagogue	Jerusalem, Israel	c. 12th century CE
98. Scolanova Synagogue	Scolanova, Italy	c. 1200 CE
135. Staranova Synagogue	Prague, Czechia	1270 CE
91. Dubrovnik Synagogue	Dubrovnik, Croatia	1352 CE
Tlemcen Synagogue	Tlemcen, Algeria	1392 CE
Ferrara Synagogue	Ferrara, Italy	1421 CE
Old Synagogue	Krakow, Poland	1407 CE

OLDEST SYNAGOGUES IN SELECT COUNTRIES		
4. Karaite Synagogue	Jerusalem, Israel	c. 12th century CE
62. Sidon Synagogue	Sidon, Lebanon	833 CE
64. Great Synagogue of Aleppo	Aleppo, Syria	c. 15th century CE
Stadttempel	Vienna, Austria	1826 CE
112. Great Synagogue of Grodno	Hrodna, Belarus	1580 CE
Arlon Synagogue	Arlon, Belgium	1865 CE
Old Synagogue	Sarajevo, Bosnia	1587 CE
91. Dubrovnik Synagogue	Dubrovnik, Croatia	1352 CE
135. Staranova Synagogue	Prague, Czechia	1270 CE
Great Synagogue	Copenhagen, Denmark	1833 CE
Luneville Synagogue	Luneville, France	1786 CE
127. Old Synagogue	Erfurt, Germany	c. 13th century CE
Kahal Shalom Synagogue	Rhodes, Greece	1577 CE
Obuda Synagogue	Budapest, Hungary	1820 CE
Dublin Synagogue	Dublin, Ireland	1892 CE
98. Scolanova Synagogue	Trani, Italy	c. 1200 CE
143. Portuguese Synagogue	Amsterdam, Netherlands	1675 CE
116. Old Synagogue	Krakow, Poland	c. 15th century CE
158. Stone Synagogue	Obidos, Portugal	c. 1400 CE
Great Synagogue	Iasi, Romania	1671 CE
102. Grand Choral Synagogue	St. Petersburg, Russia	1893 CE
Maribor Synagogue	Maribor, Slovenia	c. 14th century CE
153. Greater Synagogue of Barcelona	Barcelona, Spain	c. 300 CE
109. Sataniv Synagogue	Sataniv, Ukraine	c. 1514 CE

159. Bevis Marks Synagogue	London, United Kingdom	1701 CE
Tlemcen Synagogue	Tlemcen, Algeria	1392 CE
82. Gardens Shul	Cape Town, South Africa	1863 CE
79. El Ghriba Synagogue	Djerba, Tunisia	Unknown
166. Paradesi Synagogue	Kochi, India	1568 CE
Yeshua Synagogue	Yangon, Malaysia	1854
173. Hobart Synagogue	Hobart, Australia	1845 CE
Aldea San Gregorio Synagogue	Aldea San Gregorio, Argentina	1893 CE
177. Nidhe Israel Synagogue	Bridgetown, Barbados	1654 CE
174. Kahal Zur Israel Synagogue	Recife, Brazil	1636 CE
180. Congregation Emanu-El Synagogue	Victoria, Canada	1863 CE
176. Mikve Israel-Emanuel Synagogue	Willemstad, Curacao	1730 CE
Shaare Shamayim Synagogue	Kingston, Jamaica	1912 CE
178. Sierra Justo Synagogue	Mexico City, Mexico	1938 CE
Neveh Shalom Synagogue	Paramaribo, Suriname	1843 CE
188. Touro Synagogue	Newport, United States	1763 CE

SELECT JEWISH MUSEUMS

ISRAEL		
2. Tower of David Museum	Jerusalem, Israel	www.tod.org.il
5. Old Yishuv Court Museum	Jerusalem, Israel	www.oyc.co.il
5. Last Battle for the Old City Museum	Jerusalem, Israel	None Available
5. Ariel Center for Jerusalem	Jerusalem, Israel	None Available
5. Temple Institute	Jerusalem, Israel	https://templeinstitute.org
11. Rockefeller Museum	Jerusalem, Israel	www.imj.org.il/en/wings/archaeology
14. Israel Museum	Jerusalem, Israel	www.imj.org.il
15. Bible Lands Museum	Jerusalem, Israel	www.blmj.org/en
17. Herzl Museum	Jerusalem, Israel	www.herzl.org.il
18. Yad Vashem	Jerusalem, Israel	www.yadvashem.org
Friends of Zion Museum	Jerusalem, Israel	www.fozmuseum.com
Jerusalem Archaeological Park	Jerusalem, Israel	www.archpark.org.il
20. Independence Hall Museum	Tel Aviv, Israel	http://ihi.org.il
21. Eretz Israel Museum	Tel Aviv, Israel	www.eretzmuseum.org.il/e
22. ANU - Museum of the Jewish People	Tel Aviv, Israel	www.anumuseum.org.il
Tel Aviv Museum of Art	Tel Aviv, Israel	www.tamuseum.org.il/he

24. Babylonian Jewry Heritage Center	Yehuda, Israel	www.bjhcenglish.com
28. Israeli Air Force Museum	Beersheba, Israel	www.iaf.org.il/46-en/ IAF.aspx
39. Museum of Pioneer Settlement	Yifat, Israel	www.pioneers.co.il

SOUTHEASTERN EUROPE		
73. David Baazov Museum of History of the Jews of Georgia	Tblisi, Georgia	None Available
84. Jewish Museum of Turkey	Istanbul, Turkey	www.muze500.com
86. Jewish Museum of Thessaloniki	Thessaloniki, Greece	www.jmth.gr
Jewish Museum of Greece	Athens, Greece	www.jewishmuseum.gr
Jewish Museum of Bucharest	Bucharest, Romania	www.museum. jewishfed.ro
Jewish Historical Museum	Belgrade, Serbia	www.jimbeograd.org
Museum of the Jews of Bosnia	Sarajevo, Bosnia	www.muzejsarajeva.ba
Jewish Museum of Rome	Rome, Italy	www.museoebraico. roma.it
96. Jewish Museum of Florence	Florence, Italy	www.firenzebraica.it
Jewish Museum of Venice	Venice, Italy	www.museoebraico.it/ en/museum
Jewish Museum of Bologna	Bologna, Italy	www.museoebraicobo.it
Jewish Museum of Ferrara	Ferrara, Italy	https://meis.museum
Jewish Museum of Livorno	Livorno, Italy	www.moked.it/ livornoebraica

EASTERN EUROPE		
101. Jewish Museum and Tolerance Center	Moscow, Russia	www.jewish-museum.ru
Center for East European Jewry	Kiev, Ukraine	http://ua.judaicacenter.kiev.ua
Sholem Aleichem Museum	Kiev, Ukraine	www.asholomaleichem-museum.com
106. Jewish Museum of Odessa	Odessa, Ukraine	https://english.migdal.org.ua/museum
Vina Gaon Jewish State Museum	Vilnius, Lithuania	www.jmuseum.lt
Jewish Museum of Riga	Riga, Latvia	www.jewishmuseum.lv
114. Museum of the History of the Polish Jews	Warsaw, Poland	www.polin.pl
Jewish Historical Institute	Warsaw, Poland	www.jhi.pl
Galicia Jewish Museum	Krakow, Poland	http://galiciajewishmuseum.org
117. Oskar Schindler Factory Museum	Krakow, Poland	https://muzeumkrakowa.pl/oddzialy/fabryka-schindlera
119. Cachmei Lublin Yeshiva	Lublin, Poland	www.hotelilan.pl
Hungarian Jewish Museum	Budapest, Hungary	www.milev.hu

CENTRAL EUROPE		
123. Berlin Jewish Museum	Berlin, Germany	www.jmberlin.de
128. Cologne Jewish Museum	Coloogne, Germany	www.museenkoeln.de/archaeologische-zone
129. Jewish Museum of Frankfurt	Frankfurt, Germany	www.juedischesmuseum.de

Jewish Museum of Munich	Munich, Germany	www.juedisches-museum-muenchen.de
Jewish Museum and Raschi House	Worms, Germany	www.worms.de/de/tourismus/museen/juedisches_museum
Jewish Culture Museum	Augsburg, Germany	www.jkmas.de
Jewish Museum of Westphalia	Dorsten, Germany	www.jmw-dorsten.de
Jewish Museum of Franconia	Furth, Germany	www.juedisches-museum.org
Jewish Museum of Switzerland	Basel, Switzerland	www.juedisches-museum.ch
139. Museum Judenplatz	Vienna, Asutria	www.jmw.at/exhibitions/museum-ju-denplatz
Jewish Museum of Vienna	Vienna, Austria	www.jmw.at
Austrian Jewish Museum	Eisenstadt, Austria	www.ojm.at
134. Jewish Museum of Prague	Prague, Czechia	www.jewishmuseum.cz
Museum of Jewish Culture	Bratislava, Slovakia	www.muzeum.sk/muzeum-zidovskej-kul-tury-snm-bratislava.html
140. Danish Jewish Museum	Copenhagen, Denmark	www.jewmus.dk
Jewish Museum of Stockholm	Stockholm, Swedem	www.judiskamuseet.se
Jewish Museum of Oslo	Oslo, Norway	www.jodiskmuseumoslo.no
Jewish Museum of Trondheim	Trondheim, Norway	www.aejm.org/members/jewish-museum-in-trondheim

WESTERN EUROPE		
143. Jewish History Museum	Amsterdam, Netherlands	www.jck.nl/nl/locatie/joods-historisch-museum
Jewish Museum of Belgium	Brussels, Belgium	www.mjb-jmb.org
147. Museum of Jewish Art and History	Paris, France	www.mahj.org
Jewish Museum of Alsace	Bouxwiller, France	http://judaisme.sdv.fr/today/musee
151. Marc Chagall National Museum	Nice, France	https://musees-nationaux-alpesmaritimes.fr/Chagall
Sephardic Museum	Toledo, Spain	www.culturaydeporte.gob.es/msefardi
Sephardic House	Cordoba, Spain	www.casadesefarad.es
Museum of Jewish History	Girona, Spain	www.girona.cat/call/esp/museu
160. Jewish Museum of London	London, England	www.jewishmuseum.org.uk
Jewish Military Museum	London, England	www.thejmm.org.uk
Manchester Jewish Museum	Manchester, England	www.manchesterjewishmuseum.com
Scottish Jewish Archives Centre	Glasgow, Scotland	www.sjac.org.uk
Irish Jewish Museum	Dublin, Ireland	https://jewishmuseum.ie

UNITED STATES		
Klutznick National Jewish Museum	Washington, DC	www.bnaibrith.org/museum-and-archives.html
193. Museum of American Jewish Military History	Washington, DC	https://nmajmh.org
Maine Jewish Museum	Portland, Maine	https://mainejewishmuseum.org
183. Jewish Museum of New York	New York, New York	https://thejewishmuseum.org
Jewish Children's Museum	New York, New York	www.jcm.museum
Yeshiva University Museum	New York, New York	www.yumuseum.org
YIVO Institute for Jewish Research	New York, New York	www.yivo.org
Jewish Museum of New Jersey	Newark, New Jersey	www.jewishmuseumnj.org
190. National Museum of American Jewish History	Philadelphia, Pennsylvania	www.nmajh.org
American Jewish Museum	Pittsburg, Pennsylvania	https://jccpgh.org
Jewish Museum of Maryland	Baltimore, Maryland	http://jewishmuseum-md.org
Maltz Museum of Jewish Heritage	Beachwood, Ohio	www.maltzmuseum.org
Spertus Museum	Chicago, Illinois	www.spertus.edu
Jewish Museum of Milwaukee	Milwaukee, Wisconsin	https://jewishmuseummilwaukee.org
Jewish Heritage Foundation of North Carolina	Durham, North Carolina	https://jewishnc.org
Breman Museum	Atlanta, Georgia	www.thebreman.org

Jewish Museum of Florida	Miami Beach, Florida	http://jmof.fiu.edu
Museum of the Southern Jewish Experience	Jackson, Mississippi	https://msje.org
Mizel Museum of Judaica	Denver, Colorado	https://mizelmuseum.org
Jewish History Museum	Tucson, Arizona	www.jewishhistorymuseum.org
Contemporary Jewish Museum	San Francicso, California	www.thecjm.org
Magnes Museum of Jewish Art and Life	Berkeley, California	https://magnes.berkeley.edu
Rhodes Jewish Museum	Los Angeles, California	www.rhodesjewishmuseum.org
Center for Iranian Jewish Oral History	Beverly Hills, California	None Available
Oregon Jewish Museum	Portland, Oregon	www.ojmche.org
Alaska Jewish Museum	Anchorage, Alaska	www.alaskajewishmuseum.com

AMERICAS		
St. John Jewish Historical Museum	New Brunswick, Canada	www.jewishmuseumsj.com
Jewish Museum of Montreal	Montreal, Canada	www.mimj.ca
Jewish Canadian Military Museum	Toronto, Canada	www.jcmm.ca
Jewish Museum of Western Canada	Winnipeg, Canada	www.jhcwc.org
Jewish Museum of British Columbia	Vancouver, Canada	www.jewishmuseum.ca
Museum of Jewish History and the Holocaust	Mexico City, Mexico	None Available

Sefardic Museum of Caracas	Caracas, Venezuela	http://museosefardi.com.ve
Jewish Museum of Rio de Janeiro	Rio de Janeiro, Brazil	www.museumjudaico.org.br
Jewish Museum of Sao Paulo	Sao Paulo, Brazil	http://novo.museujudaicosp.org.br
174. Kahal Zur Israel Synagogue Museum	Recife, Brazil	None Available
Jewish Museum of Paraguay	Asuncion, Paraguay	None Available
Jewish Museum of Buenos Aires	Buenos Aires, Argentina	www.museojudio.org.ar
Jewish Historical Community and Colonization Museum	Santa Fe, Argentina	www.museomoisesville.com.ar
Jewish Museum of Chile	Santiago, Chile	www.mij.cl

AFRICA, FAR EAST		
Museum of Moroccan Judaism	Casablanca, Morocco	www.jewishmuseumcasa.com
South African Jewish Museum	Cape Town, South Africa	www.sajewoshmuseum.co.za
167. Shanghai Jewish Refugees Museum	Shanghai, China	www.shhkjrm.com/node2/n4/n6/index.html
Sydney Jewish Museum	Darlinghurst, Australia	https://sydneyjewishmuseum.com.au
172 Jewish Museum of Australia	Kilda, Australia	www.jewishmuseum.com.au
Adelaide Jewish Museum	Adelaide, Australia	www.adelaidejmuseum.org

SELECT HOLOCAUST MUSEUMS, MEMORIALS AND CONCENTRATION CAMPS

ISRAEL		
18. Yad Vashem & Garden of the Righteous among the Nations	Jerusalem, Israel	www.yadvashem.org
25. Forest of the Martyrs	Beit Meir, Israel	www.kkl-jnf.org/tour-ism-and-recreation/forests-and-parks/martyrs-forest.aspx
36. Ghetto Fighter's House	Nahariya, Israel	www.gfh.org.il

CENTRAL EUROPE		
124. Memorial to the Murdered Jews of Europe	Berlin, Germany	www.visitberlin.de/en/memorial-murdered-jews-europe
Holocaust Tower	Berlin, Germany	www.jmberlin.de/en/libeskind-building-holo-caust-tower
Memorial in Memory of the Burning of Books	Berlin, Germany	www.visitberlin.de/en/book-burning-memorial-be-belplatz
126. House of the Wannsee Conference	Wannsee, Germany	None Available
Memorial at the Frankfurt Gross-markthalle	Frankfurt, Germany	www.juedischesmuseum.de/en/visit/grossmarkthal-le-frankfurt

Bergen-Belsen (transit camp)	Lonheide, Germany	https://bergen-belsen.stiftung-ng.de
Buchenwald (labor camp)	Weimar, Germany	www.buchenwald.de
132. Dachau (labor camp)	Dachau, Germany	www.kz-gedenks-taette-dachau.de
Dora-Mittelbau & Nordhausen (labor camp)	Nordhausen, Germany	None Available
Flossenburg (labor camp)	Flossenburg, Germany	www.gedenkstaette-flossen-buerg.de
Hadamar (eutha-nasia center)	Hadamar, Germany	www.gedenkstaette-hadamar.de
Neuengamme (labor camp)	Hamburg, Germany	www.kz-gedenks-taette-neuengamme.de
Oranienburg (transit camp)	Oranienburg, Germany	www.sachsenhausen-sbg.de
Ravensbruck (labor camp)	Furstenberg, Germany	www.ravensbrueck-sbg.de/en
Sachsenhausen (labor camp)	Oranienburg, Germany	www.sachsenhausen-sbg.de/en
139. Judenplatz Holocaust Memorial	Vienna, Austria	www.jmw.at/en/exhibitions/museum-judenplatz
House of Names	Graz, Austria	www.hausdernamen.at/english/exhibitions/house-of-names
Ebensee (labor camp)	Ebensee, Austria	https://memorial-ebensee.at
Mauthausen-Gusen (labor camp)	Mauthausen, Austria	www.mauthausen-memorial.org
Pinkas Synagogue	Prague, Czechia	www.jewishmuseum.cz/en/explore/sites/pinkas-syna-gogue
Holocaust Memorial	Valasske Mezirici, Czechia	www.zchor.org/valasske.htm

137. Theresiendtadt (transit camp)	Terezin, Czechia	www.terezin.org
Monument to the Memory of the Holocaust Victims	Stockholm, Sweden	None Available
Center for the Holocaust and Religious Minorities	Oslo, Norway	www.hlsenteret.no

EASTERN EUROPE		
114. Museum of the History of Polish Jews	Warsaw, Poland	www.polin.pl/en/about-museum
115. Ghetto Heroes Monument	Warsaw, Poland	None Available
Monument to the Memory of Children	Warsaw, Poland	None Available
Umschlagplatz Monument	Warsaw, Poland	None Available
Survivor's Park	Lodz, Poland	None Available
Radegast Train Station	Lodz, Poland	www.lodz-ghetto.com/the_radegast_station
Holocaust Memorial	Palmiry, Poland	None Available
117. Oskar Schindler Factory Museum	Krakow, Poland	None Available
118. Auschwitz-Birkenau (extermination camp)	Oswiecim, Poland	http://auschwitz.org
Belzec (extermination camp)	Tomaszow Lubelski, Poland	www.belzec.eu
Chelmo (extermination camp)	Chelmo, Poland	None Available

Gross-Rosen (labor camp)	Goczalkow Woj. Walbrzyskie, Poland	None Available
Majdanek (extermination camp)	Lublin, Poland	www.majdanek.eu
Plaszow (labor camp)	Krakow, Poland	None Available
Sobibor (extermination camp)	Sobibor, Poland	None Available
Stutthof (labor camp)	Sztutowo, Poland	None Available
Treblinka (extermination camp)	Malkinia, Poland	None Available
Holocaust Memorial Center	Budapest, Hungary	www.hdke.hu
121. Shoes on the Danube Bank	Budapest, Hungary	None Available
Vilna Gaon Jewish State Museum	Vilnius, Lithuania	www.jmuseum.lt
Ponary Massacre Memorial	Paneriai, Lithuania	www.jmuseum.lt/en/exposition/i/198/memorial-museum-of-paneriai
Holocaust Memorial	Seduva, Lithuania	None Available
Riga Ghetto and Holocaust in Latvia Museum	Riga, Latvia	www.spikeri.lv/en/iemitnieki/riga-ghetto-and-latvian-holocaust-museum
Kaiserwald (labor camp)	Riga, Latvia	None Available
Holocaust Memorial	Kalevi-Lilva, Estonia	None Available
111. The Pit	Minsk, Belarus	None Available
Janowska (extermination camp)	Lviv, Ukraine	None Available
100. Holocaust Memorial Synagogue	Moscow, Russia	None Available

SOUTHERN EUROPE		
Jasenovac Memorial Area	Jasenovac, Serbia	None Available
Dimitar Peshev Museum	Kyustendil, Bulgaria	None Available
Holocaust Memorial Center of Macedonia	Skopje, North Macedonia	None Available
Athens Holocaust Memorial	Athens, Greece	None Available
Jewish Museum of Greece	Athens, Greece	www.jewishmuseum.gr/en
Monument to Young Jews	Athens, Greece	None Available
86. Jewish Museum of Thessaloniki	Thessaloniki, Greece	www.jmth.gr
Monument of the Victims of the Holocaust	Rhodes, Greece	www.rhodesjewishmuseum.org/history/holocaust
Fondazione Museum of the Holocaust	Rome, Italy	None Available
Holocaust Memorial	Milan, Italy	www.memorialeshoah.it/milan-shoah-memorial
Museum of Italian Judaism and the Holocaust	Ferrara, Italy	www.meisweb.it/en
Museum of the Deportation	Prato, Italy	www.cittadiprato.it/EN/Sezioni/200/Deportation-Museum

WESTERN EUROPE		
Jewish Historical Museum	Amsterdam, Netherlands	https://jck.nl/en/location/jewish-historical-museum
144. Anne Frank House	Amsterdam, Netherlands	www.annefrank.org

146. Corrie Ten Boom Bouse	Haarlem, Netherlands	None Available
Amersfoort (transit camp)	Amersfoort, Netherlands	www.kampamersfoort.nl/en
Vught (transit camp)	Vught, Netherlands	None Available
Westerbork (transit camp)	Hooghalen, Netherlands	None Available
National Monument to the Jewish Martyrs	Brussels, Belgium	None Available
142. Kazerne Dossin Holocaust Memorial	Mechelen, Belgium	www.kazernedossin.eu
Memorial to the Victims of the Shoah	Luxembourg City, Luxembourg	None Available
Shoah Memorial	Paris, France	www.memorialdelashoah.org/en
149. Memorial to the Martyrs of the Deportation	Paris, France	None Available
Center of Contemporary Jewish Documentation	Paris, France	www.memorialdelashoah.org/en/archives-and-documentation
Memorial Center of Oradour	Oradour, France	None Available
Memorial House of the Murdered Jewish Children	Izieu, France	None Available
Memorial Museum to the Children of Vel d'Hiv	Orleans, France	www.cercil.fr
Natzweiler-Struthof (labor camp)	Natzwiller, France	www.struthof.fr/en/the-kl-natzweiler

162. Hyde Park Holocaust Memorial	London, England	None Available
Wiener Library for the Study of the Holocaust	London, England	www.wienerlibrary.co.uk
Beth Shalom Holocaust Centre	Laxton, England	www.holocaust.org.uk
UNITED STATES & CANADA		
194. United States Holocaust Memorial Museum	Washington, DC	www.ushmm.org
New England Holocaust Memorial	Boston, Massachusetts	www.nehm.org
184. Museum of Jewish Heritage	New York, New York	https://mjhnyc.org
Holocaust Memorial	Harrisburg, Pennsylvania	www.jewishharrisburg.org/community-directory/harrisburg-holocaust-monument
Holocaust Memorial Center	Farmington Hills, Michigan	www.holocaustcenter.org
Virginia Holocaust Museum	Richmond, Virginia	www.vaholocaust.org
Florida Holocaust Museum	St. Petersburg, Florida	www.flholocaustmuseum.org
197. Holocaust Memorial of Miami Beach	Miami Beach, Florida	http://holocaustmemorialmiamibeach.org
Dallas Holocaust Museum	Dallas, Texas	www.dhhrm.org
Holocaust Museum Houston	Houston, Texas	https://hmh.org
Holocaust History Project	San Antonio, Texas	https://learnandremember.org
Holocaust Center of Northern California	San Francisco, California	https://holocaustcenter.jfcs.org

200. Simon Wiesenthal Center	Los Angeles, California	www.wiesenthal.com
179. Canadian Museum of Immigration at Pier 21	Halifax, Canada	None Available
Montreal Holocaust Museum	Montreal, Canada	https://museeholocauste.ca/en
Sarah and Chaim Neuberger Holocaust Center	Toronto, Canada	www.holocaustcentre.com
Holocaust Memorial Sculpture	Edmonton, Canada	None Available
Vancouver Holocaust Education Center	Vancouver, Canada	www.vhec.org

ELSEWHERE IN THE WORLD		
Sephardic Center	Havana, Cuba	https://en.turismojudaico.com/contenido/59/Sephardic-hebrew-center---iehuda-halevi-synagogue
Tuvie Maizel Jewish and Holocaust Museum	Mexico City, Mexico	None Available
Memorial of Jewish Immigration and the Holocaust	Sao Paulo, Brazil	None Available
Holocaust Victims Memorial at Rio de Janeiro	Rio de Janeiro, Brazil	None Available
Holocaust Museum in Curitiba	Curitiba, Brazil	None Available
Holocaust Victims Memorial at Salvador	Salvador, Brazil	None Available

Holocaust Memorial Museum	Buenos Aires, Argentina	https://museodelholocausto.org.ar
82. Cape Town Holocaust Centre	Cape Town, South Africa	http://ctholocaust.co.za
167. Shanghai Jewish Refugees Museum	Shanghai, China	None Available
Hong Kong Holocaust and Tolerance Center	Hong Kong, China	www.hkhtc.org
Tokyo Holocaust Education Resource Center	Tokyo, Japan	None Available
Auschwitz Peace Museum	Shirakawa, Japan	http://am-j.or.jp
169. Port of Humanity Tsuruga Museum	Tsuruga, Japan	www.tmo-tsuruga.com/kk-museum
Sydney Jewish Museum	Sydney, Australia	https://sydneyjewishmuseum.com.au
Jewish Museum Holocaust and Research Center	Melbourne, Australia	www.jhc.org.au
Holocaust Center of New Zealand	Wellington, New Zealand	www.holocaustcentre.org.nz

About The Author

Howard Kramer is the creator and author of *The Complete Pilgrim*. He first took an interest in religious sites in his early twenties when traveling through Italy after college. In the three decades since he has traveled to nearly thirty countries and forty American states, visiting and photographing hundreds of the world's greatest places of religious interest. Howard has been writing about religious sites for the better part of the last decade, and *The Complete Pilgrim* is the culmination of years of his work and passion.